WEBSTER'S
Business Writing
Basics

WEBSTER'S
Business Writing
Basics

Created in Cooperation with
the Editors of
MERRIAM-WEBSTER

FEDERAL
STREET
PRESS

A Division of Merriam-Webster, Incorporated
Springfield, Massachusetts

This edition published by
Federal Street Press
A Division of Merriam-Webster, Incorporated
P.O. Box 281
Springfield, MA 01102

Federal Street Press books are available for bulk purchase for sales
promotion and premium use. For details write the manager of special
sales, Federal Street Press, P.O. Box 281, Springfield, MA 01102

ISBN 1-892859-27-0
Library of Congress Catalog Card Number: 00-111506

Printed in the United States of America
01   02   03   04   05   5   4   3   2   1

Contents

Preface

Webster's Business Writing Basics is a practical guide to more effective business-letter writing. It is designed to be an aid not only to executives, secretaries, and other businesspeople but also to anyone else who writes business-related correspondence.

The book is divided into eight chapters, each of which discusses in detail one topic relating to business correspondence. Each chapter is introduced by its own table of contents, listing all of the major sections in the chapter and the number of the page on which each section begins. Cross-references are placed throughout the text to guide the reader from one subject to another related subject. When specific information is needed, the detailed Index will indicate quickly where the desired material is to be found.

The overall organization of the book is designed to take the reader from the simplest and most often asked about aspects of business-letter writing through to the more complex and specialized aspects of the subject. Chapter 1, "Business Letter Elements and Formats," introduces the reader to the individual parts of the business letter and takes up general questions having to do with the format and appearance of business letters. Chapter 2, "A Guide to Punctuation and Style," covers matters such as punctuation; capitalization; the formation of plurals, possessives, and compounds; and the treatment of abbreviations and numbers.

Chapter 3, "Composition and Word Usage," is concerned with the compositional aspects of letter-writing and good usage. Chapter 4, "Forms of Address," is mostly devoted to a chart that shows the forms of address that are conventionally used for individuals whose offices, ranks, or professions warrant special courtesy.

In Chapter 5, "Sample Letters, " the reader is given pointers specifically applicable to composing letters. It includes 50 sample letters designed to meet the needs of specific business-related occasions. For each sample letter, there is a facsimile of the finished letter, accompanied by a description of the elements that go into such a letter.

Chapter 6, "Memos, Reports, and Other Documents," focus on business writing outside the realm of normal letter correspondence, with details about memos, minutes of business meetings, press releases, and research and documentation of reports.

Chapter 7, "E-mail," is an up-to-the-minute discussion of the growing area of e-mail communications, with a discussion of the technical aspects such as e-mail options, Internet connections and security as well as information on e-mail basics and on style and etiquette in e-mail communications. Chapter 8, "Office Mail," offers information on understanding and using the postal service and commercial delivery services.

This book represents a unique attempt to provide a thorough instruction in virtually every aspect of business writing, and it if offered in the belief that it will serve the reader well in all areas of business communications.

WEBSTER'S
Business Writing
Basics

Business Letter Elements and Formats

All the elements of letter style come together to produce a reflection on paper not only of the writer's ability and knowledge and the typist's competence but also of an organization's total image. Well-prepared letters reflect a firm's pride and concern for quality, whereas poorly prepared correspondence can produce such a negative impression that its recipients may have second thoughts about pursuing business with the firm. This may be a special consideration for small companies. The business letter, then, is actually an indicator of an organization's style. Thus, the impression created by clearly written, logically ordered, and attractively and accurately keyboarded letters can be a crucial factor in the success of any business.

An executive may devote a large portion of each workday to correspondence, and secretaries and administrative assistants may devote even more. And all this time costs money. However, the time and money will have been well spent if they result in clear, complete, and elegantly prepared correspondence. Most importantly:

1. The stationery should be of good-quality paper.
2. The letter elements should conform in placement and style with one of the generally accepted business letter formats.
3. The language should be clear, concise, grammatically correct, and devoid of padding and clichés.
4. The content should be logically presented, and the tone should be appropriate to the reader.
5. The information should be accurate and complete.

In this chapter we will discuss the first two of these points; Chapters 2, 3, and 5 will take up the remaining items.

NOTE: Throughout this chapter, wherever lines of type are counted ("six lines from the top," "two lines below," etc.), the number refers to the number of times you must press the Enter (or Return) key. Thus, the number of *blank* lines will always be one less than the number specified. Wherever spaces are counted ("indented five spaces," "five spaces to the right of center," the number refers to letter spaces, not the half-letter spaces that computer-keyboard space bars produce.

Material and Design Considerations

PAPER

Paper size, quality, and basis weight vary according to application. The various paper sizes and their uses are shown below.

Stationery type	Size	Application
Standard	8½" x 11" (occasionally 8" x 10½")	general business correspondence
Executive *or* Monarch	7¼" x 10½" *or* 7½ x 10"	high-level officer's correspondence
Half-sheet *or* Baronial	5½" x 8½"	extremely brief notes

Good-quality paper is essential to producing attractive and effective letters. Though paper with rag content is considerably more expensive than sulfite bond papers, many offices use rag-content paper because it suggests the company's merit and stature. Since the cost of paper has been estimated at less than five percent of the total cost of the average business letter, it is easy to understand why many firms consider high-quality paper to be worth the added expense, at least for certain types of correspondence.

The paper grain, or fiber direction, should be parallel to the type. In addition, all high-quality stationery has a *felt* side, or top side, from which a watermark may be read, and the letterhead should be printed or engraved on this side.

The weight of the paper must also be considered when ordering stationery supplies. *Basis weight,* also called *substance number,* is the weight in pounds of a ream of paper cut to a basic size. Basis 24 is the heaviest for stationery and is used for important correspondence; basis 13 is the lightest and is often used for international letters.

In some offices, carbon copies are still made. The paper used for carbon copies is lighter in weight and is available as inexpensive *manifold* paper, a stronger and more expensive *onionskin,* or a lightweight letterhead with the word COPY printed on it.

Continuation sheets and envelopes must match the letterhead sheet in color, basis weight, texture, size, and quality. Therefore, they should be ordered along with the letterhead to ensure a good match.

Letterhead and continuation sheets as well as envelopes should be stored in their original boxes to prevent soiling. A small supply may be kept in your drawer or near your printer, arranged so as to protect it from wear and tear.

Printing processes   *Offset printing* is often used when results of higher quality than those produced by photocopying are needed; it can also be more economical when printing thousands of copies. The process involves using a printing plate to make an inked impression on a rubber-blanketed cylinder and then transferring the impression to the paper. (The same process is used in book and magazine printing.) Offset printing can be used to print announcements, business cards, stationery, and many other commonly used business documents, but many firms prefer to use higher-quality thermographic or engraving processes to print their best stationery. Offset printing should be available from your local retail copying shop (see your Yellow Pages under "Printing").

Thermography is similar to old-fashioned letterpress, only in this case a special ink containing a yeastlike powder is applied by the press and heated slightly to cause the printed lettering to rise—hence its more common name, *raised-letter printing*. Thermography is used to create a slightly more sophisticated look than that produced by offset, and it is slightly more expensive too. Check your Yellow Pages under "Thermographers" for services in your area.

Engraving is the highest-quality—and most costly—printing process. It is generally used to convey an image of the company as exceptionally prestigious. In engraving, an engraved metal die to which ink is applied is firmly pressed onto the paper being printed, leaving slightly raised lettering on the sheet's front and slightly indented lettering (in reverse) on the back. For the names of engravers in your area, check your local Yellow Pages under "Engraving—Stationery."

In an effort to control supply costs, some companies keep two grades of letterhead—for example, both thermographically printed and offset-printed letterhead—and reserve the more expensive grade exclusively for higher-level correspondence.

Software programs are now available that allow you to print letterhead using a laser printer in the office. Usually you must first send a copy of the firm's letterhead to the software manufacturer, who then writes a short program and sends it to you on a diskette. Once the program is installed, you simply tell the computer whether you are printing a letter, envelope, or some kind of standard form. A little training and experience are usually needed to master the use of the software, but offices using this technology have found the savings to be worth the small effort and expense.

LETTER BALANCE

It has often been said that an attractive letter should look like a symmetrically framed picture, with even margins framing the typed lines, which should be balanced under the letterhead. Word processors have standard (default) settings for text pages and options for print previewing that can help you prepare letters that are properly formatted and pleasing to the eye. However, regardless of the kind of equipment available to you, the following steps will help you create letters with the desired appearance:

1. Estimate the letter's length before beginning to type.
2. Note any long quotations, tables, long lists, or footnotes that should be set off by means of indentation, centering, or a different type size.
3. Consider setting the left and right margins according to the estimated letter length: approximately 1″ for long letters (300 words or more, or at least two pages), 1½″ for medium-length ones (about 100–300 words), and 2″ for short ones (100 words or less). However, many offices use a standard 6″ typing line (i.e., 1¼″ left and right margins) for all letters on full-size stationery, since it eliminates the need to reset margins; the default (automatic) setting in word-processing programs is usually 6″.
4. Remember that the closing parts of a letter take 10-12 lines and that at least three lines of the message should be carried over to any continuation sheet.
5. Single-space within paragraphs; double-space between paragraphs. Very short letters (up to three sentences) may be double-spaced throughout. (More precise line spacing may be specified by using the line-spacing option from the Format menu.)

Short letters may be typed or printed on half-sheets, on Executive-size stationery, or on full-size stationery with wide margins. When typing very short letters on full-size stationery, consider the following formatting possibilities:

1. Use the standard 1¼″ left and right margins but increase the space between the date and the inside address, between the complimentary close and the signature, and between the signature and the transcriber's initials or enclosure notations.
2. Use the standard left and right margins but double-space. Double-spacing should be used only in very short letters (about six lines or less, or up to three sentences). If a double-spaced letter contains more than one paragraph, indent the paragraph openings.
3. Use wider margins and/or a combination of points 1 and 2 above.

LETTERHEAD DESIGN

Some letterheads are confined to the center of the page, others extend across the top from the left to the right margin, and still others are positioned to the right or left of center. Sometimes a firm's name (or a corporate name and logo) appear at the top of the page and its address and other data at the bottom. Regardless of layout and design, a typical letterhead contains some or all of the following elements:

1. Full name of the organization (and logo, if a corporate entity)
2. Street address
3. Suite, room, or building number
4. Post-office box number
5. City, state, and zip code

6. Telephone, fax, and e-mail numbers
7. Other data such as branch offices, names of partners and associates, or services offered

The names of particular departments or divisions may be printed on the letterhead of large or diversified companies. An elaborate letterhead may require a particular letter format to keep the letter from looking unbalanced. For example, a letterhead with a long list of names on the left side might be best balanced by using the Modified Block format, in which the date, reference numbers, and signature appear on the right.

High corporate officers frequently use personalized or executive letterhead, in which the standard letterhead design is supplemented with the name of the office (such as "Office of the President") or with the full name and business title of the officer (such as "John M. Dennehy, Jr., Chief Counsel") printed in small letters one or two lines beneath the letterhead, usually at or near the left margin. The officer's title may appear on the same line as his or her name if space permits, or it may be blocked directly below the name. For executive stationery, the letterhead is often engraved (rather than printed) on a better grade of paper than the standard stationery. Executive stationery is also smaller than the standard (see above). Envelopes should match the paper and should be printed with the executive's name and return address.

Standard Letter Formats

The choice of letter format, like the choice of letterhead design, is usually determined by the company. However, it is important to be familiar with the various formats so that you can apply them when necessary to particular types of letters consistently and accurately. The three most common letter formats used today are the *Full Block* (also called *Block*), the *Modified Block,* and the *Semiblock* (also called *Modified Semiblock*) formats. The *Simplified* letter, the *Official* letter, and the *Half-sheet* are also used. All these formats are described and illustrated below.

The various elements (or parts) of a standard business letter are shown in Figure 1.1. Those elements shown (see labels) are common to most business letters. However, only those with an asterisk are essential elements of any business letter regardless of its format; the rest may or may not be included, depending on the format being used and the nature of the letter itself. For more on the individual elements, see the explanations below and the "Letter Elements and Styling" section later in this chapter.

Figure 1.1   The Parts of a Business Letter

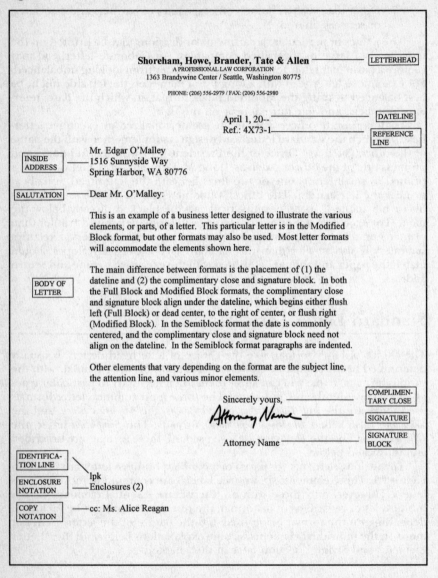

Word-processing programs offer various letter templates that can be used to format standard business letters. However, before using such programs make sure that their style is appropriate to your office and that using them will actually save you time; otherwise it may be better to either format your own letters individually or create your own template.

THE FULL BLOCK LETTER

Letters using the Full Block format (see Fig. 1.2) exhibit the following characteristics:

1. All elements aligned flush left.
2. No indentations (with the exception of tables and displayed quotations).

THE MODIFIED BLOCK LETTER

Letters using the Modified Block format (see Fig. 1.3) exhibit the following characteristics:

1. Dateline, complimentary close, and signature block aligned ("blocked") either (a) at dead center, (b) to the right of center, or (c) with the longest line flush right. All other elements (with the exceptions noted below) positioned flush left.
2. No paragraph indentations.
3. Attention line (if used) usually flush left, but sometimes centered.
4. Subject line (if used) usually flush left, but sometimes centered.

THE SEMIBLOCK LETTER

Letters using the Semiblock format (see Fig. 1.4) exhibit the following characteristics:

1. Dateline commonly (a) centered, less commonly (b) beginning dead center, (c) beginning to the right of center, or (d) flush right. Complimentary close and signature block need not be aligned with the date, but are themselves usually blocked and begin at or to the right of center or with the longest line flush right.
2. Paragraphs indented five to ten spaces.
3. Attention line (if used) usually flush left, but sometimes centered.
4. Subject line (if used) usually centered, but sometimes indented to match paragraph indentations.

THE SIMPLIFIED LETTER

Letters using the Simplified format (see Fig. 1.5) exhibit the following characteristics:

Figure 1.2   The Full Block Letter

January 1, 20--
X-123-4

Consumer Relations Department
LKJ Corporation
1234 Thomas Boulevard
Warwick, RI 10655

Attention Mr. James Green

Ladies and Gentlemen:

SUBJECT: FULL BLOCK LETTER

This is a facsimile of the Full Block letter, all of whose elements begin flush left.

The dateline may be typed two to six lines below the last letterhead line; here it is placed
three lines below the letterhead. The reference line, if any, is typed immediately below
the dateline.

Placement of the inside address varies according to letter length; here it is typed two lines
below the reference line. An attention line, if required, is typed two lines below the last
inside-address line.

The salutation is typed two lines below the attention line, or two to four lines below the
last inside-address line. An optional subject line may be typed two lines below the
salutation.

The message begins two lines below the salutation, or two lines below the subject line if
there is one. The message is single-spaced with a blank line between paragraphs. At least
three message lines must be carried over to a continuation sheet; the complimentary close
and signature block should never stand alone on such a sheet. The last word on a sheet
should not be divided. The continuation-sheet heading is typed about one inch from
the top edge of the page. Any reference line from the first sheet must be repeated in the
continuation-sheet headings. The message continues four lines below the last line of the
heading.

Merriam-Webster Inc.

47 Federal Street • P.O. Box 281 • Springfield, MA 01102 • Telephone (413) 734-3134 • Facsimile (413) 731-5979

Figure 1.2 *(continued)*

Consumer Relations Department
LKJ Corporation
January 1, 20--
X-123-4
Page 2

The complimentary close is typed two lines below the last message line and may be
followed by the optional company name in all-capitals. At least four blank lines are
allowed for the written signature, followed by the writer's typed name. The writer's title
and/or department may be included in the typed signature block if they do not appear in
the printed letterhead.

Initials identifying the typist are typed two lines below the last signature-block line. (The
author's initials usually do not appear in the Full Block letter.) Any enclosure notation is
typed immediately below the identification initials. The courtesy-copy notation, if
needed, is placed one or two lines below any other notation, depending on available
space.

Sincerely yours,

MERRIAM-WEBSTER INC.

Executive Name

Executive Name

gbb
Enclosures (2)

cc: Marlene T. Hansen, Esq.

Figure 1.3   The Modified Block Letter

January 1, 20--

REGISTERED MAIL
PERSONAL

Mr. William B. Gerard, III
Treasurer
XYZ Corporation
1234 Langley Boulevard
Boyleston, CA 97735

Dear Mr. Gerard:

RE Modified Block Letter

This is a facsimile of the Modified Block letter. It differs from the Full Block letter chiefly in the placement of its dateline, complimentary close, and signature block, all of which are aligned and positioned either (1) at center, (2) toward the right margin, or (3) at the right margin.

While the dateline may be positioned from two to six lines below the last line of the letterhead, its standard position is three lines below the letterhead. In this facsimile, the dateline begins at dead center. If a reference line is required, it is blocked on the line above or below the date.

Special mailing notations and on-arrival notations such as the two shown above are all-capitalized and aligned flush left about two lines below the dateline.

The inside address begins about four lines below the dateline except where there are special notations, in which case it begins two lines below the last notation. This spacing can be expanded or contracted according to the letter length. The inside address, the salutation, and all paragraphs of the message are aligned flush left. The salutation is typed two to four lines below the last line of the inside address. A subject line, if used, is typed two lines below the salutation in capital letters and is either blocked flush left or, as shown here, centered on the page.

Merriam-Webster Inc.

47 Federal Street • P.O. Box 281 • Springfield, MA 01102 • Telephone (413) 734-3134 • Facsimile (413) 731-5979

Figure 1.3 *(continued)*

Mr. Gerard   -2-   January 1, 20--

The message begins two lines below the salutation or the subject line. The message is single-spaced within each paragraph and double-spaced between paragraphs; however, in very short letters, the paragraphs may be double-spaced within each paragraph and triple-spaced between paragraphs. Continuation sheets should contain at least three message lines. The last word on a sheet should not be divided. The continuation-sheet heading may be blocked flush left as in the Full Block letter or laid out across the top of the page as shown here. It is positioned about one inch from the top edge of the sheet, and the message is continued four lines beneath it.

The complimentary close is typed two lines below the last line of the message and is aligned vertically with the dateline--in this case, beginning dead center.

The signature line is typed at least four lines below the complimentary close. The writer's title and department name may be included if they do not already appear in the printed letterhead. All elements of the signature block align with each other and with the complimentary close and dateline.

Identification initials are usually only those of the secretary, providing that the writer and the signer are the same person. These initials appear two lines below the signature block. Any enclosure notation is typed on the line below the initials, and any courtesy-copy notation appears one or two lines below any other notations, depending on space available.

Sincerely yours,

Executive Name

Executive Name
Executive Title

gbb
Enclosures (5)

cc Ms. Santucci
     Dr. Franklin

Figure 1.4   The Semiblock Letter

January 1, 20--

Ms. Carol D. Felkins
Sales Manager
Radin Company
234 Sundry Boulevard
Millborough, GA 33215

Dear Ms. Felkins:

SEMIBLOCK LETTER

This is a facsimile of the Semiblock letter. In this style, the dateline is commonly centered or begins at dead center, slightly to the right of center, or flush right. The inside address and salutation are aligned flush left, while the paragraph openings are indented. The complimentary close and signature block need not be aligned under the date. Identification initials, enclosure notations, and courtesy-copy notations are aligned flush left.

A reference line would be blocked on the line above or below the date. Any special mailing notation or on-arrival notation would be typed flush left about two lines below the dateline and two lines above the inside address. An attention line, if required, is usually aligned flush left, two lines below the inside address; it may also be centered. The subject line, if any, is typed two lines below the salutation and usually centered on the page but may also be indented to match paragraph indentations, as shown here.

The text is single-spaced within paragraphs and double-spaced between paragraphs unless the letter is extremely short, in which case it may be double-spaced throughout.

Continuation sheets should contain at least three message lines, and the last word on a sheet should never be divided. The heading for a continuation sheet begins at least one inch from the top edge of the page and follows the format shown in this letter.
The complimentary close is typed two lines below the last line of the message. The

Merriam-Webster Inc.
47 Federal Street • P.O. Box 281 • Springfield, MA 01102 • Telephone (413) 734-3134 • Facsimile (413) 731-5979

Figure 1.4 *(continued)*

Ms. Felkins   -2-   January 1, 20--

signature line, four lines below the complimentary close, is aligned with it if possible. If the name or title will be long, the complimentary close should begin at dead center or about five spaces to the right of center to ensure enough room for the signature block.

Yours,

Executive Name

Executive Name

gbb

Enclosures: 2

cc: Dr. Edgar Dinnerston
    Crane Engineering Associates
    91011 Jones Street
    Savannah, GA 33289

A postscript, if needed, is typically positioned two to four lines below the last notation. In the Semiblock letter, the first line is indented like the message paragraphs. It is not necessary to head the postscript with the abbreviation *P.S.* The postscript should be initialed by the writer.

EN

Figure 1.5   The Simplified Letter

January 1, 20--

Mr. George I. Needham
Director of Marketing
TLC Corporation
1234 Exeter Boulevard
Kansas City, MO 44371

SIMPLIFIED LETTER

Mr. Needham, this is the Simplified letter, which is used mostly for general business applications such as mass mailings and relatively impersonal form letters. Its main features-- block format, fewer internal parts, and the absence of punctuation in the heading and closing-- reduce the number of keystrokes and formatting adjustments you must make, thus saving time and decreasing the possibility of error.

The dateline is typed four to six lines below the last letterhead line, so that the inside address, also flush left, about three lines below the dateline, can be seen through a window envelope when the letter is folded. The official Postal Service state abbreviation should be used, followed by one space and the zip code.

The traditional salutation has been replaced by an all-capitalized subject line (without the heading SUBJECT) typed flush left, three lines beneath the inside address.

The message begins three lines below the subject line. The first sentence includes a greeting to the reader by name, as shown above. The last paragraph should repeat the reader's name. All paragraphs are blocked flush left, single-spaced internally, with a blank line between paragraphs. Tables and numbered lists are also blocked flush left and set off from the rest of the message by blank lines at top and bottom. Long quotations and unnumbered lists should be indented five to ten spaces from the left and right margins and similarly set off from the rest of the message by blank lines at top and bottom.

Merriam-Webster Inc.

47 Federal Street • P.O. Box 281 • Springfield, MA 01102 • Telephone (413) 734-3134 • Facsimile (413) 731-5979

Figure 1.5 *(continued)*

Mr. Needham
Page 2
January 1, 20--

If a continuation sheet is required, at least three message lines must be carried over. Continuation-sheet format and margins must match those of the first sheet. At least six blank lines are left from the top edge of the page to the first line of the heading, which is blocked flush left, single-spaced internally, and typically composed of the addressee's courtesy title and last name, the page number, and the date. The rest of the message begins four lines beneath the last heading line.

There is no complimentary close in the Simplified letter, although a warm closing sentence may end the message. The writer's name (and title if needed) is typed flush left all in capitals at least five lines below the last message line. Some companies use a spaced hyphen between the writer's surname and professional title; others prefer a comma instead. The writer's department name may be typed flush left all in capitals one line below the signature line.

The identification initials, flush left and two lines below the signature block, are the typist's initials only. An enclosure notation may be typed on the next line below. Courtesy-copy notation may be typed one or two lines below the last notation, depending on available space. If there is no enclosure line, the courtesy-copy notation is typed two lines below the last line above.

Executive Name

NAME - BUSINESS TITLE

gbb
Enclosures (2)

cc: Alice L. Barnes

1. All elements aligned flush left; no indentations (with the exception of displayed quotations and unnumbered lists).
2. Salutation replaced by the subject line, all-capitalized and unpunctuated.
3. Addressee's name in the first sentence of the message.
4. No complimentary close.
5. Typed signature all-capitalized and followed on the same line by the writer's title (if used).

THE OFFICIAL LETTER

Letters using the Official format (see Fig. 1.6) exhibit the following characteristics:

1. Written on personalized Executive ($7\frac{1}{2}'' \times 10\frac{1}{2}''$) letterhead.
2. Inside address below the signature.

THE HALF-SHEET

Letters written on half-sheet ($5\frac{1}{2}'' \times 8\frac{1}{2}''$) stationery exhibit the following characteristics (see Fig. 1.7):

1. Written on half-sheet paper.
2. Full Block, Modified Block, or Semiblock formats.

Letter Elements and Styling

The various elements of a business letter are listed below in order and described in the sections that follow.

Dateline	Salutation	Identification initials
Reference line	Subject line	Enclosure notation
Special mailing notations	Message	Copy notation
On-arrival notations	Continuation sheets	Postscript
Inside address	Complimentary close	Path name
Attention line	Signature block	

Many firms establish standard letter formats and stylings in order to save time, and these standards should always be followed. However, certain applications of common letter elements will still require individual decisions.

Figure 1.6   The Official Letter

Officer's Name
Officer's Title

January 1, 20--

Dear Ms. Washington:

This is a facsimile of the Official letter format, often used by an officer of the firm or corporate executive for personal correspondence written on his or her own personalized company stationery. The paper size is Executive or Monarch.

The Official letter is characterized by the page placement of the inside address: It is typed flush left, two to five lines below the signature block or the written signature. Paragraphs may be either indented or blocked.

A typed signature block is not needed on personalized Executive or Monarch stationery. However, if the writer's signature either is difficult to decipher or might be unfamiliar to the addressee, it may be typed four lines below the complimentary close.

The secretary's initials, if included, are typed two lines below the inside address. Any enclosure notation appears two lines below the initials, or two lines below the inside address, also flush left.

Sincerely,

Executive Name

Ms. Mary Washington
490 Jay Street
Abbeyville, WI 64921

Figure 1.7   The Half-sheet

January 1, 20--

Mr. Theodore R. Manfred
235 Plimsoul Place
Sheldrake, AL 55321

Dear Ted:

This is a facsimile of the half-sheet, which is used for the briefest of notes--those containing one or two sentences or two very short paragraphs.

The Full Block, Modified Block, or Semiblock format may be used.

Sincerely yours,

Executive Name

gbb

DATELINE

The dateline may be typed two to six lines below the printed letterhead; three lines below is recommended for most letters.

The dateline consists of the month, the day, and the year ("January 1, 20—"). Ordinals ("1st," "2d," "24th," etc.) should not be used, and the months should not be represented with abbreviations or numerals.

The dateline is commonly placed in one of five positions, depending on the letter format or the letterhead layout. It is typed flush *left* in Full Block and Simplified formats. It may be typed flush *right,* or may begin either at dead center or about five spaces to the right of center, in the Modified Block or Semiblock formats. In the Semiblock format it may also be centered.

REFERENCE LINE

A numerical reference line—showing the number of a file, correspondence, order, invoice, or policy—is included when the addressee has specifically requested that correspondence contain such a line, or when it is needed for your own filing. Most offices require that it be vertically aligned with (i.e., blocked on) the date and typed on the line directly above or below the dateline. Some firms use the abbreviation *Ref* (or *Ref.*) and a colon preceding the reference number. (See also "Subject Line," page 24.)

Reference line blocked left:	*Reference line blocked right:*
January 1, 20—	January 1, 20—
X-123-4	Ref: X-123-4
or	*or*
X-123-4	Ref: X-123-4
January 1, 20—	January 1, 20—

A reference line on the first sheet must be carried over to the continuation sheets. The style should match the style used on the first page. For example, if the reference line appears on a line below the date on the first sheet, it should be typed there on the continuation sheet. The following example illustrates the style of a continuation-sheet reference line in the Simplified or Full Block format:

Mr. Carlton B. Jones
January 1, 20—
X-123-4
Page 2

The next example illustrates the positioning of a reference line on the continuation sheet of a Modified Block or Semiblock letter. (See also "Continuation Sheets" below.)

Mr. Carlton B. Jones   -2-   January 1, 20—
      Ref: X-123-4

SPECIAL MAILING NOTATIONS

If a letter is to be sent by any method other than regular mail, that fact may be indicated on the letter itself as well as on the envelope (see pages 32–41 for details on envelope style). The all-capitalized special mailing notation, such as CERTIFIED MAIL, SPECIAL DELIVERY, or AIRMAIL (for foreign mail only), is always aligned flush left about four lines below the dateline, and about two lines above the inside address. Some organizations prefer that these notations appear on all copies, others prefer that they be typed only on the originals, and many omit them altogether.

Vertical spacing (such as between the dateline and the special mailing notation) may vary with letter length, more space being left for short or medium-length letters.

ON-ARRIVAL NOTATIONS

The on-arrival notations that may appear on the letter itself are PERSONAL and CONFIDENTIAL. The first indicates that the letter may be opened and read only by its addressee; the second indicates that the letter may also be opened and read by any other persons authorized to view such material. These all-capitalized notations are usually positioned four lines below the dateline and usually two but not more than four lines above the inside address. They are always blocked flush left. If there is a special mailing notation, the on-arrival notation is blocked on the line beneath it.

If either PERSONAL or CONFIDENTIAL appears on the letter, it must also appear on the envelope (see pages 32–41 for envelope style).

INSIDE ADDRESS

An inside address typically includes the following elements:

1. Addressee's courtesy title and full name
2. Addressee's business title, if required
3. Full name of addressee's business affiliation
4. Full address

If the letter is addressed to an organization in general but to the attention of a particular individual, the inside address typically includes the following elements:

1. Full name of the organization
2. Department name, if required
3. Full address

(See also "Attention Line" below.)

The inside address is usually placed two to six lines below the date; three lines is probably the most standard. (The inside address in the Simplified letter is typed three lines below the date.) The placement of the inside address in relation to the date may vary according to letter length or organization policy. The inside address is blocked flush left and single-spaced.

A courtesy title (such as *Mr., Ms., Dr.,* or *The Honorable*) precedes the addressee's full name, even if a business or professional title (such as *Treasurer* or *Chief of Staff*) follows the surname. No courtesy title, however, should ever precede the name when *Esquire* or an abbreviation for a degree follows the name. (See also Chapter 4, "Forms of Address.")

Before typing the addressee's name, refer to the signature block of previous correspondence from that person to confirm its exact spelling and style. This may also be obtained from printed executive letterhead. A business or professional title, if included, should also match the title used in previous correspondence or in official literature (such as an annual report or a business directory). If an individual holds more than one office (for example, "Vice President and General Manager"), the title shown in the signature block of previous correspondence should be copied, or the title of the higher office (in this case, Vice President) may be selected. Business and professional titles should not be abbreviated. If a title is so long that it might overrun the center of the page, it may be typed on two lines with the second line indented two spaces:

Mr. John P. Hemphill, Jr.
Vice President and Director
    of Research and Development

Be particularly careful with the spelling, punctuation, and official abbreviations of company names. Note, for example, whether an ampersand (&) is used for the word *and,* whether series of names are separated by commas, and whether the word *Company* is spelled out or abbreviated.

The addressee's title may be placed on the same line as the name. Alternatively, it may be put on the second line, either by itself or followed by the name of the organization. The following are acceptable inside-address styles for business and professional titles:

Mr. Arthur O. Brown
General Counsel
XYZ Corporation
1234 Peters Street
Jonesville, ZZ 56789

Dr. Joyce A. Cavitt, Dean
School of Business and Finance
Stateville University
Stateville, ST 98765

Anna B. Kim, Esquire
Powell, Smith & Klem, P.C.
67 Green Street
North Bend, XX 12345

Mrs. Juanita Casares
President, C & A Realty
Johnson Beach, ZZ 56789

Street addresses should be spelled out and not abbreviated unless window envelopes are being used. Numerals are used for all building, house, apartment, room, and suite numbers except for *One,* which is written out.

One Bayside Drive
6 Link Road
1436 Fremont Avenue

Numbered street names from *First* through *Twelfth* are usually written out; numerals are usually used for all numbered street names above *Twelfth.*

167 West Second Avenue
One East Ninth Street
19 South 22nd Street

An apartment, building, room, or suite number, if required, follows the street address on the same line.

62 Park Towers, Suite 9
Rosemont Plaza Apartments, Apt. 117

Note that neither *No.* nor # is used after the words *Suite, Apartment,* or *Building.*

Names of cities (except those including the word *Saint,* such as *St. Louis* or *St. Paul*) should be typed out in full (e.g., *Fort Wayne, Mount Prospect*). The name of the city is followed by a comma, the name of the state, and the zip code. The state name may or may not be abbreviated (though "District of Columbia" is always written *DC* or *D.C.*); however, most firms now use the official Postal Service abbreviations on all inside addresses. If the letter will be sent in a window envelope, the official abbreviation must be used. See page 34 for a list of these abbreviations.

An inside address should consist of no more than six lines. No line should overrun the center of the page; lengthy organization names, like lengthy business titles, may be carried over to a second line and indented two spaces.

Sometimes a single letter must be sent to two persons at different addresses, both of whom should receive an original. In these cases, the inside address should consist of two complete names and addresses separated by a line space. The names should be in alphabetical order unless one person is obviously more important than the other. An alternative method is to place the inside addresses side by side, beginning on the same line. For salutations used in letters to multiple addressees, see page 199.

ATTENTION LINE

If the writer wishes to address a letter to an organization in general but bring it to the attention of a particular individual, an attention line may be typed two lines below the last line of the inside address and two lines above the salutation, if any. The attention line is usually blocked flush left. Some companies prefer that it be centered on the page instead, which is acceptable in all letters except the Simplified and the Full Block, where the attention line must be typed flush left. It should be neither underlined nor entirely capitalized. The word *Attention* is not abbreviated, and may be followed by a colon (in the Simplified format, the colon is always omitted):

Attention Mr. James Chang
Attention: Mr. James Chang

Even though the attention line routes the letter to a particular person, such a letter is still considered to be written to the organization, so a collective-noun salutation (e.g., "Ladies and Gentlemen") should be used.

SALUTATION

The salutation—used with all letter styles except the Simplified—is typed flush left two lines beneath the inside address or the attention line, if any. Additional space may be added after the inside address of a short letter that is to be enclosed in a window envelope. The salutation is followed by a colon; only in informal personal correspondence is it followed by a comma.

When addressing an organization, or when addressing a person whose name and gender are unknown to the letter-writer, the traditional "Dear Sir" (when addressing a particular individual) and "Gentlemen" (when addressing a group or organization) have been replaced by "Dear Sir or Madam" and "Ladies and Gentlemen," respectively.

When addressing an entire company, or a company officer whose name and sex are unknown, it is now also common to simply address the company by name ("Dear XYZ Company") or the title or department of the intended recipient ("Dear Personnel Supervisor," "Dear Personnel Department," "Dear XYZ Engineers"). Use of this type of salutation has increased markedly in recent years.

Occasionally a letter-writer is faced with an addressee's name that gives no clue as to the addressee's sex. Traditionally in these uncertain cases, convention has required the writer to use the masculine courtesy title in the salutation; for example, "Dear Mr. Lee Schmidtke," "Dear Mr. T. A. Gagnon." However, most writers now prefer such forms as "Dear Mr. or Ms. Schmidtke" or "Dear T. A. Gagnon." (One way to avoid the problem of gender is to use the Simplified letter, which eliminates the salutation altogether.)

"To whom it may concern" is very impersonal and is usually used only when the writer is unfamiliar with both the person and the organization being addressed—for example, when addressing a letter of recommendation.

The salutation for a married couple may be written in one of the following ways:

Dear Mr. and Mrs. Hathaway
Dear Dr. and Mrs. Simpson
Dear Dr. and Mr. Singh

For more information about choosing appropriate salutations, including salutations for two or more persons and for people with specialized titles, see pages 199–205.

SUBJECT LINE

The subject line serves as an immediate point of reference for the reader as well as a convenient filing aid at both ends of the correspondence. It gives only the gist of a letter, and should not require more than one line.

In the Simplified letter, which does not include a salutation, the subject line (an essential element) is positioned flush left, three lines below the last line of the inside address. It may be entirely capitalized and not underlined, or the main words may begin with capital letters and the entire heading be underlined.

If a subject line is included in a letter with a salutation, it is frequently positioned flush left, two lines beneath the salutation, and may be entirely capitalized. In the Modified Block and Semiblock formats, the subject line may be centered or even indented to match the indention of the paragraphs. Many offices today prefer to position the subject line two lines above the salutation rather than below it.

The subject line may be entirely capitalized, or capitalized headline-style (that is, with the initial letter of all words except coordinating conjunctions, articles, and short prepositions capitalized). The word *Subject, Reference,* or *Re* is often used to introduce the line.

> SUBJECT: PROPOSED SALE OF ROE PROPERTY
> Subject: Proposed Sale of Roe Property
> Reference: Proposed Sale of Roe Property
> Re: Proposed Sale of Roe Property

The subject line should not be confused with the reference line (see above), even though the subject line often begins with the word *Reference.* They differ not only in position but also in appearance and purpose: the reference line indicates a numerical classification, whereas the subject line identifies the content of the letter.

MESSAGE

The body of the letter—the message—should begin two lines below either the salutation or the subject line, if the latter follows the salutation. In the Simplified letter, however, the message is typed three lines below the subject line.

Paragraphs are single-spaced internally. Double-spacing is used to separate paragraphs. If a letter is extremely brief, it may be double-spaced throughout with indented paragraphs, or triple-spaced between paragraphs.

The first lines of indented paragraphs (as in the Semiblock letter) should begin five or 10 spaces ($\frac{1}{2}''$–$1''$) from the left margin; five spaces ($\frac{1}{2}''$) is most common. (On a word processor, the automatic tab stop may be set to whichever measure is desired.)

Long quotations should be centered five to 10 spaces ($\frac{1}{2}''$–$1''$) from the left and right margins, single-spaced, with a blank line above and below. Long enumerations should be indented and similarly set off with a blank line above and below. Enumerations with items requiring more than one line apiece may require single-spacing within each item and double-spacing between items. Tables should be centered. See Figure 1.8.

Figure 1.8   Page Placement of Items Inset within the Message

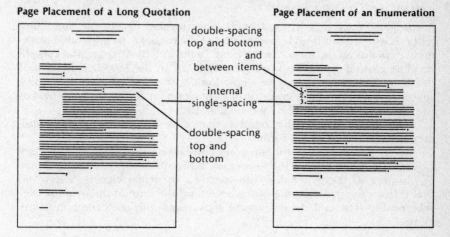

Page Placement of a Long Quotation   **Page Placement of an Enumeration**

double-spacing top and bottom and between items

internal single-spacing

double-spacing top and bottom

End-of-line word division should be avoided in the following instances:

1. Do not divide a word at the end of the first line.
2. Do not divide a word if it will leave part of the word by itself as the last line of a paragraph.
3. Do not separate a person's name from his or her courtesy title.

CONTINUATION SHEETS

If a letter is long enough to require a continuation sheet or sheets, at least three message lines must be carried over to the next page. The complimentary close and/or typed signature block should never stand alone on a continuation sheet. The last word on a page should not be divided.

Leave at least a 1″ margin at the top of the continuation sheet. The two most common types of continuation-sheet heading are illustrated in Figs. 1.2 and 1.3. The format shown in Fig. 1.2 is used with Simplified and Full Block letters. The flush-left heading begins with the addressee's courtesy title and full name, continues on the next line with the date, repeats the reference number (if used) on the third line, and ends with the page number. Some companies prefer that the page number appear as the first line of the continuation-sheet heading, especially if a reference number is not used.

Another style is illustrated in Fig. 1.3. Here the heading extends across the page, 1″ from the top edge of the sheet. The addressee's full name is typed flush left, the page number is centered and enclosed with spaced hyphens, and the date is aligned flush right—all on the same line. If a reference line is used, it is typed flush right one line below the date. This format is often used with the Modified Block and the Semiblock letters.

COMPLIMENTARY CLOSE

A complimentary close is used in all letter formats except the Simplified letter. It is typed two lines below the end of the message. Its horizontal placement depends on the format being used. In the Full Block letter, the complimentary close is typed flush left (see Fig. 1.2). In the Modified Block and the Semiblock letters, it may be aligned under the dateline (e.g., about five spaces to the right of center, or flush right or under some particular part of the printed letterhead). See Figs. 1.3 and 1.4.

Only the first word of the complimentary close is capitalized. The complimentary close ends with a comma.

When typing a letter for someone else, always use the complimentary close that is dictated, since the writer may have a special reason for the choice of phrasing. If the writer does not specify a particular closing, select one that reflects the general tone of the letter and the state of the writer-reader relationship. The table below lists the most commonly used complimentary closes.

Complimentary Closes for Business Correspondence

General Tone and Degree of Formality	Complimentary Close
Highly formal (used in diplomatic, governmental, or ecclesiastical correspondence)	Respectfully yours Respectfully Very respectfully
Polite, formal (used in general correspondence)	Very truly yours Yours very truly Yours truly
Less formal (used in general correspondence)	Very sincerely yours Sincerely yours Yours sincerely Sincerely Yours Cordially Cordially yours Very sincerely
Informal, friendly (used when writer and reader are on a first-name basis)	As ever Best wishes Best regards Kindest regards Warmest personal regards Regards

Complimentary closes on letters written over a period of time to a particular person may become gradually more informal and friendly. Once an informal pattern has been established, they should not revert to a more formal style.

SIGNATURE BLOCK

The first line of the signature block indicates responsibility for the letter. Either the name of the writer or the name of the firm may appear there. In the former case, the writer's name is typed at least four lines below the complimentary close; in the latter, the firm's name is typed all in capital letters two lines below the complimentary close and the writer's name at least four lines below the firm's name (see Fig. 1.9).

Figure 1.9   Common Signature-Block Styles

Sincerely yours,

Martin Lindeman

Martin K. Lindeman
Director of Sales

Very truly yours,

CASTLETON WARBURG

Elise Wong

Elise T. Wong
Account Representative

Very truly yours,

Martin Lindeman

MARTIN K. LINDEMAN
Director of Sales

In the Simplified letter, the name of the writer is typed entirely in capitals, flush left, at least five lines below the last line of the message. If the writer's professional title is not included in the printed letterhead, it may be typed on the same line as the name entirely in capitals and separated from the last element of the name by a spaced hyphen. Some organizations prefer a comma in place of the hyphen. A combination of the two may be used if the title is complex.

JOHN P. HEWETT - CHIEF ADMINISTRATOR
JOHN P. HEWETT, CHIEF ADMINISTRATOR
JOHN P. HEWETT - CHIEF ADMINISTRATOR, FINANCIAL
  DIVISION
   or
JOHN P. HEWETT - CHIEF ADMINISTRATOR
FINANCIAL DIVISION

In the Full Block letter, the signature block is aligned flush left. Each important word of the writer's title and department name (if included) is capitalized. The title and department name may be omitted if they appear in the letterhead:

If title and dept. needed for identification:	John D. Russell, Director
If dept. appears on letterhead:	Research and Development John D. Russell Director
If both title and dept. appear on letterhead:	John D. Russell

In the Modified Block and the Semiblock letters, the signature block begins with the name of the writer typed at least four lines below the complimentary close. The signature block is normally aligned (blocked) directly below the complimentary close; in the Semiblock letter, however, it may be centered under the complimentary close, particularly if it would otherwise overrun the right margin.

The name of the firm may be typed in capitals on the second line beneath the complimentary close and blocked with the close. The writer's name is typed in capitals and lowercase at least four lines below the firm's name. The writer's title, if needed, is typed in capitals and lowercase on the line below the name. If the company name is long enough to overrun the right margin, it may be centered beneath the complimentary close in the Semiblock letter.

When a letter is written and signed by two individuals, it is generally best to place the names side by side, with the first name either flush left (in block formats) or beginning left of center (in other formats) in order to leave enough room for two horizontally aligned signatures. See Figure 1.10.

If horizontal positioning is not feasible, the names may be placed one under the other.

If you sign a letter for the writer, your initials should appear either immediately below and to the right of the writer's name or centered under the name. (See Figure 1.11.)

If you sign a letter in your own name for someone else, your own title appears below your name; in your title, your employer's name appears in the form of his or her courtesy title and surname only. (See Figure 1.12.)

Figure 1.10 Signature Block When Two People Sign a Letter

Very truly yours,

Gretchen Talbott   *Lisa Smith Carter*

Gretchen Talbott   Lisa Smith Carter
Senior Vice President   Treasurer

Figure 1.11 Signature When Secretary Signs the Writer's Name

Barton K. Wheeler /an   *Barton K. Wheeler*
                                              an

Figure 1.12 Signature Block When Secretary Signs as a Representative

Yours sincerely,   Yours sincerely,

Paula Seymour   *Peter Kirchoff*

Paula Seymour   Peter Kirchoff
Secretary to Ms. Talbott   Assistant to Senator Silver

A letter may be invalid without a signature in ink. Therefore, make sure all letters intended to be signed are actually signed before they are mailed.

IDENTIFICATION INITIALS

The initials of the typist and sometimes those of the writer are placed two lines below the signature block and aligned flush left in all letter formats. Most offices formerly preferred that three capitalized initials be used for the writer's name, and two lowercase initials for the typist's. Today the writer's initials are usually omitted if the name is already typed in the signature block or if it appears in the letterhead. In many offices, the typist's initials appear only on office copies for record-keeping purposes. The following are the most common styles:

> hol
> hl
> /hol
> FCM/hol
> FCM:hl
> FCM:hol

ENCLOSURE NOTATION

If a letter is to be accompanied by an enclosure or enclosures, a notation such as one of the following should be typed flush left one or two lines below either the identification initials (if any) or the signature block. The unabbreviated form *Enclosure* is usually preferred.

> Enclosure
> enc. *or* encl.
> Enclosures (3)
> 3 encs. *or* Enc. 3

If the enclosures are of special importance, they should be numerically listed and briefly described, with no line spacing between the items.

> Enclosures: Lease for signature (2 copies)
> Itemization of May 24 bill

The following type of notation may then be typed in the top right corner of each page of each of the enclosures:

> Enclosure (1) to Johnson Associates letter No. 1-234-X, dated January 1, 20—, page 2 of 8

If the enclosure is bound, a single notation attached to its cover sheet will suffice.

When additional material is being mailed separately, a notation such as the following may be used:

> Separate mailing: ZYX Corp. Annual

Some letter writers (or their secretaries) type visual reminders, such as three hyphens or periods, in the left margin by each line in which an item to be enclosed is mentioned.

COPY NOTATION

Copies of letters and memos, traditionally called *carbon copies,* are now often called *courtesy copies* or simply *office copies.* In some offices, *c* for *copy* or *pc* for *photocopy* is used instead of the traditional *cc* for *carbon copy* or *courtesy copy.*

A copy notation showing the distribution of courtesy copies to other individuals should be aligned flush left and typed two lines below the signature block if there are no other notations or initials, or two lines below any other notations. If space is very tight, the courtesy-copy notation may appear on the line below any notations or initials.

> cc
> cc:
> c
> Copy to

Multiple recipients of copies should be listed alphabetically. Sometimes only their initials are shown.

> WPB
> TLC
> CNR

More often, the individual's names are shown and sometimes also their addresses, especially if the writer feels that such information can be useful to the addressee.

> cc: William L. Ehrenkreutz, Esq. cc Ms. Lee Jameson
> 45 Park Towers, Suite 1 Copy to Mr. Javier Linares
> Smithville, ST 56789 Copies to Mr. Houghton
> Mr. Rhys
> Dr. Daniel I. Maginnis Mr. Smythe
> 1300 Dover Drive
> Jonesville, ZZ 12345

If the recipient of the copy is to receive an enclosure or enclosures as well, that individual's full name and address as well as a description of each enclosure and the total number of enclosed items should be shown in the courtesy-copy notation.

> cc: Ms. Barbara S. Lee (2 copies, Signed Agreement)
> 123 Jones Street
> Smithville, ST 56789
> Mrs. Sara T. Torchinsky
> Mrs. Laura E. Yowell

If the first names or initials are given along with the last names, courtesy titles (*Mr., Ms.,* etc.) may be omitted.

> cc: William L. Ehrenkreutz cc: W. L. Ehrenkreutz
> Daniel Maginnis D. Maginnis

Typists usually leave either one or two spaces between the *cc:* and the names that follow. If only one name follows the *cc:* and it is given in all initials, the space or spaces may be omitted.

> cc:JBH

If the writer wishes that copies of the letter be distributed without the list of recipients being shown on the original, the blind-courtesy-copy notation *bcc* or *bcc:*, followed by an alphabetical list of the recipients' initials or names, may be typed on the copies only, either in the same page position as a regular copy notation or in the upper left corner.

Carbon or courtesy copies are not usually signed. The secretary may type the signature, preceded by the symbol /S/ or /s/, to indicate that the writer signed the original copy.

POSTSCRIPT

A postscript is aligned flush left two to four lines below the last notation (depending on space available). If the paragraphs are blocked flush left, the postscript should also begin flush left; if the paragraphs are indented, the first line of the postscript should also be indented. All postscripts are single-spaced. The writer should initial a postscript. While it is not incorrect to head a postscript with the initials *P.S.* (for an initial postscript) or *P.P.S.* (for subsequent ones), these headings are unnecessary and can be omitted.

PATH NAME

Some firms include as the last element in business letters the *path name*, indicating the location of a letter on the typist's computer or the firm's computer network. The path name is usually entered as a word-processing footer (end-of-document note) and appears in small lowercase type below the copy notation, postscript, or identification initials (whichever is last), usually positioned flush left.

Envelope Addresses

The following information may appear on any envelope regardless of its size. The first two items are essential.

1. The addressee's full name and address, typed approximately in the vertical and horizontal center
2. The sender's name and address, printed or typed in the upper left corner
3. Special mailing notation or notations, typed below the stamp
4. On-arrival notation or notations, typed about nine lines below the top edge on the left side

The address block on a regular envelope should be no larger than $1\frac{1}{2}''$ x $3\frac{3}{4}''$. There should be $5/8''$ from the bottom of the address block to the bottom edge of the envelope, which should be free of print. On regular envelopes, the address block usually begins about five spaces to the left of center. It should be single-spaced. Block style should be used. Unusual or italic typefaces should be avoided.

If a window envelope is being used, all address data must appear within the window space, with ¼" margins between the address and the edges of the window.

POSITION OF ELEMENTS

The elements of the address block should be styled and positioned as in the following examples. Though the initial examples below are shown in traditional capital-and-lowercase style, the U.S. Postal Service recommends an all-capitals style for any letters intended for automated processing (such as mass mailings); see "Addressing for Automation," page 37.

First line   The addressee's courtesy title and full name are typed on the first line. If his or her business title is included in the inside address, it may be typed either on the first line of the address block or alone on the next line, depending on the length of title and name.

> Mr. Lee O. Idlewild, President

> Mr. Lee O. Idlewild
> President

If the addressee is an organization, its full name is typed on the first line. If a particular department is specified, its name is typed under the name of the organization.

> XYZ Corporation
> Sales Department

Next line(s)   The full street address should be typed out, although such words as *Street, Avenue,* and *Boulevard* may be abbreviated. Type the room, suite, or apartment number immediately after the last element of the street address on the same line with it. A building name, if used, goes on a separate line above the street address.

Both the street address and a post-office box number may be included in the address, but the letter will be delivered to the location specified on the next-to-last line. Thus, a post-office box number must be typed on the line immediately above the last line in order to assure delivery to the box itself. (When a station name is included, the box number precedes the station name.)

Last line   The last line contains the city, state, and zip code. One space separates the state abbreviation and the zip code, which should never be on a line by itself. The zip code is mandatory, as are the official Postal Service state abbreviations; see the following table.

Two-letter Abbreviations for States and U.S. Dependencies

Alabama	AL	Kentucky	KY	Ohio	OH
Alaska	AK	Louisiana	LA	Oklahoma	OK
Arizona	AZ	Maine	ME	Oregon	OR
Arkansas	AR	Maryland	MD	Pennsylvania	PA
California	CA	Massachusetts	MA	Puerto Rico	PR
Colorado	CO	Michigan	MI	Rhode Island	RI
Connecticut	CT	Minnesota	MN	South Carolina	SC
Delaware	DE	Mississippi	MS	South Dakota	SD
District of Columbia	DC	Missouri	MO	Tennessee	TN
Florida	FL	Montana	MT	Texas	TX
Georgia	GA	Nebraska	NE	Utah	UT
Guam	GU	Nevada	NV	Vermont	VT
Hawaii	HI	New Hampshire	NH	Virginia	VA
Idaho	ID	New Jersey	NJ	Virgin Islands	VI
Illinois	IL	New Mexico	NM	Washington	WA
Indiana	IN	New York	NY	West Virginia	WV
Iowa	IA	North Carolina	NC	Wisconsin	WI
Kansas	KS	North Dakota	ND	Wyoming	WY

When a post-office box number is part of an address, you can usually create the full zip + 4 code by simply adding the box number (preceded by zeros if necessary) to the regular zip code:

> XYZ Corporation
> P. O. Box 600
> Smithville, ST 56788-0600

Other elements   The on-arrival notations PERSONAL and CONFIDENTIAL must be typed entirely in capital letters, about nine lines below the top left edge of the envelope. Any other on-arrival instructions, such as *Hold for Arrival* or *Please Forward*, may be typed in capitals and lowercase, underlined, about nine lines below the top left edge.

If an attention line is used in the letter itself, it too must appear on the envelope, usually following the company name in the address block. (But see "Addressing for Automation," page 37.)

> XYZ Corporation
> Sales Department
> Attention Mr. E. R. Bailey
> 1234 Smith Boulevard
> Smithville, ST 56789

Any special mailing notation such as CERTIFIED, REGISTERED MAIL, or SPECIAL DELIVERY is typed entirely in capitals just below the stamp or about nine lines below the top right edge. It should not overrun a ½″ margin.

The name of the writer may be typed in above or below a printed return address. On a plain envelope, the return address should be typed at least two lines below the top edge of the envelope and ½″ from the left edge.

Figure 1.13 Commercial Envelope Showing On-Arrival and Special Mailing Notations

```
♦ ♦ ♦ ♦ ♦ ♦ ♦ ♦ ♦ ♦ ♦ ♦ ♦ ♦
Avalon Farms, Inc.
400 Dry Creek Road
Avalon, Iowa 50707




                         Mr. Louis Raines, Ass't Sales Director
CONFIDENTIAL             Lammermoor Products                        CERTIFIED
                         4 North Forest Way
                         East Lansing, MI 48340
```

See Chapter 7 for a detailed treatment of mailing procedures.

FOREIGN ADDRESSES

When typing a foreign address, refer to the return address on the envelope of previous correspondence for the correct ordering of the elements. If an envelope is not available, check the letterhead on previous correspondence. If neither is available, the address should be typed as it appears in the inside address of the dictated letter. The following guidelines may be of assistance:

1. All foreign addresses should be typed in English or in English characters. If an address must be in foreign characters (such as Russian), an English translation should be inserted between the lines in the address block.

2. Foreign courtesy titles may be substituted for the English but are not necessary.

3. The name of the country should be spelled out in capital letters by itself on the last line. Canadian addresses always carry the name CANADA after the name of the province.

4. When applicable, foreign postal-district numbers should be included. These are positioned either before or after the name of the city, never after the name of the country.

Canadian addresses should adhere to the form requested by the Canada Post for quickest delivery through its automated handling system. As shown in the following examples, the name of the city, all-capitalized, is followed by the name of the province, in initial capitals and lowercase letters, on the same line. The postcode follows on a separate line. For mail originating in the United States, CANADA is added on a final line. Note that capitalization and punctuation differ slightly in French-language addresses.

Mr. F. F. MacManus	Les Entreprises Optima Ltée
Fitzgibbons and Brown	6789, rue Principale
5678 Main Street	OTTAWA (Ontario)
HALIFAX, Nova Scotia	K1A 0B3
B3J 2N9	CANADA
CANADA	

The Canadian postcode always consists of *letter-digit-letter (space) digit-letter-digit.* Failure to include the correct code may result in considerable delay in delivery. When space is limited, the code may be typed on the same line with the province, separated from it by at least two spaces.

OTTAWA, Ontario K1A 0B3
> *or*
OTTAWA, ON K1A 0B3

The following two-letter provincial and territorial abbreviations may also be used when space is limited:

Two-letter Abbreviations for Canadian Provinces, Territories, and Islands

Alberta	AB	Newfoundland	NF	Quebec	PQ
British Columbia	BC	Northwest Territories	NT	Saskatchewan	SK
Labrador	LB	Nova Scotia	NS	Yukon Territory	YT
Manitoba	MB	Ontario	ON		
New Brunswick	NB	Prince Edward Island	PE		

CHECKING CONTENTS OF OUTGOING LETTERS

Before sending out your letters, recheck the following five essential elements:

1. *Signature* Check that all outgoing letters have been signed, since a letter may be invalid without a signature.

2. *Enclosures* Check that all enclosures cited in the enclosure notation at the bottom of the letter have been included.

3. *Reference and copy notations* When answering a letter identified by a reference number, be sure the number is repeated in the reference line of your reply letter. Be sure envelopes have been addressed to any individuals outside the firm who are listed in carbon-copy *(cc)* and blind-carbon-copy *(bcc)* notations and that copies have been routed to any in-house recipients. An extra copy should always be kept for filing.

4. *Addresses* The inside address and the envelope address should generally be identical. (When addressing for automated handling, the address styles may be different; see "Addressing for Automation" below.) If the letter is being mailed to a post-office box, be sure the zip code of the box number, rather than that of the street address, is being used. Check that the literal destination of the mail appears on the line immediately above the city and state.

5. *Envelope notations* In addition to a return address, which should always be printed in the upper left corner, check that any attention line, on-arrival notice (such as CONFIDENTIAL, PERSONAL, or Please Forward), or mailing-service direction (such as CERTIFIED MAIL or SPECIAL DELIVERY) that appears on the letter has been typed on the envelope.

FOLDING, INSERTING, AND SEALING

The diagrams in Fig. 1.14 depict the correct ways to fold and insert letters.

When sealing and stamping envelopes by hand, use a moist sponge or moistening device, since licking envelopes or stamps can result in cuts. A large number of envelope flaps can be moistened quickly by placing them one behind the other with only the gummed edge showing. A blotter will absorb any spilled water.

ADDRESSING FOR AUTOMATION

To take full advantage of the post office's computerized sorting equipment and thus speed mail delivery and significantly reduce the cost of large mailings, the Postal Service recommends that all envelopes be addressed properly for automation. Two basic methods are available to businesses: (1) producing printed addresses that are "readable" or "scannable" by the post office's optical character readers (OCRs), and (2) applying barcodes to the address area to facilitate even faster and more economical scanning and sorting.

OCR-compatible addresses   The use of OCR-compatible addresses allows the post office to automatically scan and verify an address and then apply a Postal Service barcode to the lower right corner of the mailpiece. The basic procedures for addressing envelopes under this method are as follows:

1. The address must be typed or computer-printed, single-spaced, and blocked (aligned on a straight left margin). It must be at least ½″ from either side of the envelope (or about 1″ in the case of large envelopes) and at least 5/8″ but no more than 2¾″ up from the bottom. It should be typed entirely in capital letters without punctuation. The type must not use script, italic, light, bold, or other nonstandard fonts. There should be no print to the right of or below the address, in order to allow for the post-office barcode.

Figure 1.14   Folding and Inserting Stationery

Small Envelope

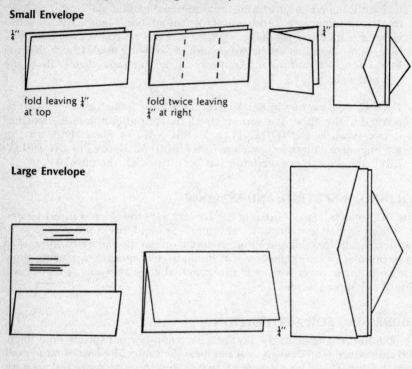

fold leaving ¼"
at top

fold twice leaving
¼" at right

Large Envelope

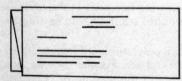

Window Envelope

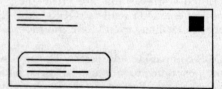

Some stationery has a fold line
indicating where to fold for
insertion in window envelopes.

Insert so that at least ¼" is left between the
side and bottom edges of the address
and the window.

2. Nonaddress data (such as account numbers, subscription order codes, presort codes, and advertising) should appear first.

3. Any attention line or other information that facilitates delivery within a company is considered nonaddress data and should appear *above* the recipient line.

The recipient line includes the name of the intended recipient (business or individual) and should appear immediately above the actual delivery address and below any nonaddress data. If the address contains both the name of a business and the name of an individual or department within that business, place the name of the business on the recipient line and the name of the individual above it (as nonaddress data).

```
CLYDE REEVES
PO BOX 319


C REEVES CORP
186 PARK ST
CLYDE REEVES PRES
C REEVES CORP


ATTN MR R C SMITH
C REEVES CORP
```

5. The delivery-address line can be a street address, post-office box number, rural-route number and box number, or highway contract route number and box number. For mail addressed to occupants of multi-unit buildings, place the apartment, suite, or room number at the end of the delivery-address line. For dual addresses—addresses that include both a street address and a post-office box number—place the address to which you want the mailpiece to go (generally the post-office box) directly above the last line.

```
ATTN MR R C SMITH
C REEVES CORP
186 PARK ST ROOM 14
HARTFORD CT 06106


ATTN MR R C SMITH
C REEVES CORP
186 PARK ST ROOM 14
PO BOX 33
HARTFORD CT 06106-0033
```

6. The last line of the address should contain the city, state abbreviation (see list on page 34), and zip (or zip + 4) code.

The Postal Service asks that the following abbreviations be used when addressing for automation:

North	N	West	W	Northwest	NW
East	E	Northeast	NE	Southwest	SW
South	S	Southeast	SE		

Apartment	APT	Floor	FL	Room	RM
Building	BLDG	Suite	STE	Department	DEPT

Alley	ALY	Flats	FLT	Parkway	PKY
Annex	ANX	Ford	FRD	Pines	PNES
Arcade	ARC	Forest	FRST	Place	PL
Avenue	AVE	Forge	FRG	Plain	PLN
Bayou	BYU	Fork	FRK	Plains	PLNS
Beach	BCH	Forks	FRKS	Plaza	PLZ
Bend	BND	Fort	FT	Point	PT
Bluff	BLF	Freeway	FWY	Port	PRT
Bottom	BTM	Gardens	GDNS	Prairie	PR
Boulevard	BLVD	Gateway	GTWY	Radial	RADL
Branch	BR	Glen	GLN	Ranch	RNCH
Bridge	BRG	Green	GRN	Rapids	RPDS
Brook	BRK	Grove	GRV	Rest	RST
Burg	BG	Harbor	HBR	Ridge	RDG
Bypass	BYP	Haven	HVN	River	RIV
Camp	CP	Heights	HTS	Road	RD
Canyon	CYN	Highway	HWY	Shoal	SHL
Cape	CPE	Hill	HL	Shoals	SHLS
Causeway	CSWY	Hills	HLS	Shore	SHR
Center	CTR	Hollow	HOLW	Shores	SHRS
Circle	CIR	Inlet	INLT	Spring	SPG
Cliffs	CLFS	Island	IS	Springs	SPGS
Club	CLB	Islands	ISS	Square	SQ
Corner	COR	Junction	JCT	Station	STA
Corners	CORS	Key	KY	Stravenue	STRA
Course	CRSE	Knolls	KNLS	Stream	STRM
Court	CT	Lake	LK	Street	ST
Courts	CTS	Lakes	LKS	Summit	SMT
Cove	CV	Landing	LNDG	Terrace	TER
Creek	CRK	Lane	LN	Trace	TRCE
Crescent	CRES	Light	LGT	Track	TRAK
Crossing	XING	Loaf	LF	Trail	TRL
Dale	DL	Locks	LCKS	Trailer	TRLR
Dam	DM	Lodge	LDG	Tunnel	TUNL
Divide	DV	Manor	MNR	Turnpike	TPKE
Drive	DR	Meadows	MDWS	Union	UN
Estates	EST	Mill	ML	Valley	VLY
Expressway	EXPY	Mills	MLS	Viaduct	VIA
Extension	EXT	Mission	MSN	View	VW
Falls	FLS	Mount	MT	Village	VLG
Ferry	FRY	Mountain	MTN	Ville	VL
Field	FLD	Neck	NCK	Vista	VIS
Fields	FLDS	Orchard	ORCH	Wells	WLS

See the sections on "Mail Merge" and "Envelopes and Labels," page 45, and Chapter 8, "Office Mail," for more on envelopes and addressing.

Word-Processing Techniques

Word-processing programs are designed to make the creation, formatting, editing, and printing of text easier. The subject of word processing is a large one, and no brief treatment can attempt to describe more than a very few of the extraordinary capacities that have been developed. Since the reader is probably familiar with the essentials of word processing, the following is merely a list of important features sometimes overlooked by inexperienced users. (The most widely used programs today, including Corel WordPerfect, Microsoft Word, and Lotus WordPro, are so similar in their capacities that virtually every useful feature is available on all of them.) Spending five or ten minutes at the beginning of every day learning one or two new features of your word-processing program will make you thoroughly expert in just a few months.

Your most valuable resource will likely be the program's Help function. By clicking on the word "Help" at the top of your screen, you can gain quick access to much of the contents of the user's manual and solve many (though not all) of the problems you will encounter.

One other feature essential to acquiring self-confidence with your computer is the Undo option. By means of the Undo button (or an Undo menu choice), you can automatically erase almost any keyboarding mistake you make, including major blunders, as long as the file you are working on remains open. Clicking the Undo button lets you reverse your last action; by clicking it repeatedly, you can undo a series of previous actions. If you decide you like your change after all, you can click on Redo to reinstate it. Among other things, the Undo feature permits you to experiment with formatting changes, since it lets you review a series of possible formats while leaving you free to return to the original formatting.

Automatic file backup   Just as you should always back up your files—that is, keep them in two separate places, such as on the hard drive and a diskette—to protect against accidental damage or loss (easily done using the Save As feature), you should also have a system for saving the previous version of any file you have revised, in case it becomes necessary to consult the earlier version. Some programs offer a system for automatically saving the previous version.

Automatic formatting   This feature lets the user format, or design, an entire document at once. After you type a document with minimal formatting, the software reviews its structure and suggests appropriate format-ting—choosing, for example, particular typefaces and sizes for headings and a particular paragraphing style. You can review the appearance of the formatted document and choose to accept or reject any or all of the suggested changes.

Columns   This capability, especially useful when formatting lists, permits you to divide your page into a desired number of columns and specify the amount of space between them.

Comments/Annotations   By positioning the cursor at a point in your docu-ment and selecting a menu item called Comment or Annotation, you may add a comment about the sentence or paragraph without interrupting the flow of the document. A symbol will appear on-screen where the cursor was, and a box will open in which you may write your comment. The next person who reads the electronic document can click on the symbol to open the box and read the comment.

Copy   Within a file, the Copy feature (from the Edit menu) allows you to select any block of text and duplicate it, then paste it into another file or into an e-mail message. At the directory or menu level, a Copy feature lets you duplicate an entire file so that an alternative version can be cre-ated without losing the original.

Drag and drop   You can move text by highlighting it, positioning the pointer on it, and holding down the mouse button while moving the pointer to the desired location. This can be very helpful for moving table entries, for example, and even for moving text between two different documents that can be called up on the screen at the same time. Complete files can be moved between folders by dragging and dropping the file name within the File Manager program.

File searching   Users with many saved files often forget where a file dealing with a particular subject is stored or what name it was given. A Find option permits the user to search for a string of characters, either in the index of file names or in the body of every file. Thus, if you need to find any file where you used the language "new conference table," you can type the phrase into a search box and quickly locate all the files that contain it. If you want to find a file whose name you think includes the word "logo," you can locate all files with that string of letters in their names.

Find and replace   If you type a word or phrase into the Find box (on the Edit menu), the software will find every occurrence of the word or phrase in the document you have open. The Replace feature lets you specify another word or phrase to substitute for the original; you can choose to review each replacement as the software finds each occurrence of the original word, or (if you are sure that the proposed change needs no review—for example, when correcting a misspelled company name) you can make a "global" change instantly. Various special search options are available, including "Match case," which will find (and replace, if desired) only those instances of the text in which the words are capitalized or lowercased in exactly the way you typed them in.

Graphics You may add, or *import,* graphics created through a separate graphics program into your word-processing document, a capability that has further blurred the line between word processing and desktop publishing.

Headers and footers You may need to display repetitive identification at the top or bottom of each page: the name of the file, the document's formal title, section numbers, and so on. These lines may appear as *headers* (lines running across the top of the page, as on the page you are reading) or as *footers* (lines running across the bottom of the page), both of which can be generated automatically by means of the Header and Footer option.

Line spacing The space between lines on a page, called *leading* or *line spacing,* is determined by the software. The Line Spacing feature lets you increase or decrease the standard leading.

Opening recent documents The files you have worked on most recently appear at the bottom of the File menu, or at Documents on the Start menu, and a given file can be opened by clicking on its name. If the file is on a diskette, the diskette must naturally be in the drive when you ask for the document.

Page breaks You can begin a new page within a document (for example, to set off a list or table) by using the Page Break option. Page breaks are normally displayed as dotted lines on-screen; those inserted manually are distinctively marked.

Password protection You may establish your own access code so that no one else can get into any sensitive file. Look for "Passwords" in the Help function.

Print preview   This essential feature (also called Page View) saves paper and time by letting you see exactly how a printed document will look before you print it, so that you can then make any necessary adjustments to its layout.

Redlining   Redlining is a way of showing revisions within a document. By using the Track Changes or Document Review option, you can choose to display all your deletions struck through with a line, and your additions as colored or underlined text. This can be useful when more than one person is working on a document, since each can easily see what the other has done.

Show nonprinting symbols   You may choose the option of viewing nonprinting symbols such as paragraph markers, tab markers, and the small dots representing spaces. Careful keyboarders choose to view these symbols at all times, since the visible symbols clarify precisely what has been entered.

Sorting   The valuable Sort feature allows you to take an unordered list (name-and-address files or index entries, for example) and instantly alphabetize it.

Spell checking   A very popular option is to have your computer check the spelling of all the words in your text. Depending on which option you choose, you may either run the spell checker after finishing your document or you may specify that it run as you are typing the document, in which case all questionably spelled word will be highlighted in some way the moment they are typed.

Symbols and special characters   All kinds of special characters and symbols—accents and other diacritics, foreign alphabets, a great variety of decorative symbols, and alternative fonts—can be inserted into documents from a menu option. If you will be using a particular character frequently, it may be available via a keyboard shortcut, or you can record a special macro (see below) for rapid insertion.

Templates   A template consists of a number of predefined settings and elements that provide the layout and design for a particular type of document. A template for business letters, for example, might include the company logo and letterhead at the top, a particular paragraph style and typeface for the body of the letter, and preset margins. A data-entry template might appear as a printed form on-screen. Word processors come with a selection of predefined templates, and you can also create your own.

MAIL MERGE

The Mail Merge (or simply Merge) function merges a document (usually a form letter) with an address list to produce a series of personalized documents, thereby making mass mailings much easier to accomplish. Merging requires that the relevant database (the company's customer list, for example) be entered into the mail-merge function. Each *data record* (that is, each customer's name and address, plus whatever other information is included with each name) must be divided into its individual elements, which are entered into the fields provided. When a form letter is sent out, you need only type the field labels (Title, First Name, etc.) into the appropriate spots in the letter; the mail merge then goes through the database, filling in the appropriate information for each letter.

Merging's other uses include the sorting of data records not only alphabetically and numerically but by various geographical criteria, the extraction of lists of customers (those who have ordered recently, for example, or those who are behind on payments), and the printing of mailing labels and envelopes. Your Help function can instruct you on such sophisticated uses.

ENVELOPES AND LABELS

Addressing individual envelopes is as simple on a computer as on a typewriter, and typing multiple labels or envelopes is far quicker on a computer. The "Envelopes and Labels" function is available as a menu choice.

To address an envelope, use the Envelope option to call up the envelope box on the screen, and type the envelope's delivery address in the appropriate box. (You may also type a return address.) Your program and printer can also provide U.S. Postal Service POSTNET barcodes (encoding the five- or nine-digit zip code for handling by automation) immediately above the envelope address; you need only select that option in the envelope box for the computer to "translate" the zip code into a barcode.

Sheets of various standard-size labels can be printed rapidly by choosing the Labels (or Envelopes and Labels) option. To ensure that the labels print properly, you must first specify the label manufacturer's product number in a box provided on the screen.

Using mail merge to address envelopes or labels for a mass mailing is just as easy as creating personalized form letters. Since envelopes are bulkier than letter sheets, however, you will probably have to print only a few at a time, using an envelope cassette to feed them into the printer.

BOILERPLATE

Boilerplate is the informal term for language that tends to be reused word-for-word from document to document. Boilerplate of various kinds is common in letters and contracts; many of the sample letters in Chapter 5 contain language that the imaginary companies would probably regard as boilerplate.

Creating your own boilerplate is usually as simple as choosing the boilerplate function (called AutoText in Microsoft Word), highlighting the text you want to store, and giving it an identifying name. When you want to add it to a document, you can go to the boilerplate function, choose it, and drop it into place.

A somewhat similar feature automatically replaces an abbreviated or easily typed version of a sentence, phrase, symbol, or other brief and frequently repeated text element with its full version. Thus, you could specify that "ABC" typed in a letter would always automatically translate into "Amalgamated Ball Bearing Corp." (your company name), or that "compclose" would translate as "Yours very truly, / Janice R. Jerome / Fulfillment Manager" formatted as a complimentary close.

TABLES

Whenever you have to type material that must align both vertically and horizontally, you should probably create a table. Though you can achieve a similar alignment by using the tab key, tabbing can result in text being moved around in very confusing ways when text automatically wraps at the end of a line. Text typed in a table grid, by contrast, always stays within the proper row and column.

From the Table menu at the top of the screen, choose Create or Insert Table, specify the number of columns and rows you think you will need (you can always add or subtract from these later), and begin typing in the grid boxes that appear on the screen. You can move from box to box using either the tab key or the arrow keys on the right side of the keyboard. To add or delete columns or rows, place the cursor at the appropriate location and choose the Insert (Rows or Columns) or Delete (Rows or Columns) option from the Table menu. To change the width of a row or column, align the mouse pointer with the horizontal or vertical gridline and drag the gridline to the desired point. Text placed in a wrong box can be moved using the "drag and drop" method.

Though tables do not offer all the computational capacities of spreadsheets, they do permit various automatic calculations, including calculation of sums at the bottom of number columns (look for "Sums" in the Help function).

MACROS

A *macro* (short for *macroinstruction*) is a series of commands that you can specify to be accomplished by a single command. If you must use a standard table format for a weekly sales report, for example, a macro allows you to create the format just once (for example, an eight-column table with twenty rows, with a shaded background for the eight standard headings, all of which use a particular typeface, etc.). Then, every time you need the table, you type the macro command, and the standard table will appear. Similarly, if you must routinely type an unusual symbol or a six-character label, it can be turned into a macro and be accomplished by a single command.

Recording (that is, creating) a macro is a simple task. When you have found the appropriate menu and menu option, you click on the Record option, choose a name for your macro, and perform all the steps you want the macro to perform. You then signal that the macro is finished and it immediately becomes available—from a new toolbar button, a menu item, or even a function key on the keyboard itself, whichever you choose—for handy use.

Chapter 2

A Guide to Punctuation and Style

Punctuation

Punctuation marks are used to help clarify the structure and meaning of sentences. They separate groups of words for meaning and emphasis; they convey an idea of the variations in pitch, volume, pauses, and intonation of the spoken language; and they help avoid ambiguity. The choice of what punctuation to use, if any, will often be clear and unambiguous. In other cases, a sentence may allow for several punctuation patterns. In cases like these, varying notions of correctness have developed, and two writers might, with equal correctness, punctuate the same sentence quite differently, relying on their individual judgment and taste.

APOSTROPHE

The apostrophe is used to form most possessives and contractions as well as some plurals and inflections.

1. The apostrophe is used to indicate the possessive of nouns and indefinite pronouns. (For details, see the section beginning on page 108.)

the girl's shoe	anyone's guess
children's laughter	the Browns' house
Dr. Collins's office	the AMA's convention

48

2. Apostrophes are sometimes used to form plurals of letters, numerals, abbreviations, symbols, and words referred to as words. (For details, see the section beginning on page 103.)

> cross your *t*'s
> three 8's   *or*   three 8s
> two L.H.D.'s   *or*   two L.H.D.s
> used &'s instead of *and*'s

3. Apostrophes mark omissions in contractions made of two or more words and in contractions of single words.

> wasn't   she'd rather not   ass'n
> they're   Jake's had it   dep't

4. The apostrophe is used to indicate that letters have been intentionally omitted from a word in order to imitate informal speech.

> "Singin' in the Rain," the popular song and movie
> "Snap 'em up" was his response.

Sometimes such words are so consistently spelled with an apostrophe that the spelling becomes an accepted variant.

> rock 'n' roll [*for* rock and roll]
> ma'am [for madam]
> sou'wester [*for* southwester]

5. Apostrophes mark the omission of digits in numerals.

> class of '98
> fashion in the '90s

If the apostrophe is used when writing the plurals of numerals, either the apostrophe that stands for the missing figures is omitted or the word is spelled out.

> 90's   *or*   nineties   *but not*   '90's

6. In informal writing, apostrophes are used to produce forms of verbs that are made of individually pronounced letters. An apostrophe or a hyphen is also sometimes used to add an *-er* ending to an abbreviation; if no confusion would result, the apostrophe is usually omitted.

> OK'd the budget   4-H'er
> X'ing out the mistakes   49er

BRACKETS

Outside of mathematics and chemistry texts, brackets are primarily used for insertions into carefully handled quoted matter. They are rarely seen in general writing but are common in historical and scholarly contexts.

1. Brackets enclose editorial comments, corrections, and clarifications inserted into quoted matter.

Surely that should have peaked [sic] the curiosity of a serious researcher.

Here they much favour the tiorba [theorbo], the arclute [archlute], and the cittarone [chitarrone], while we at home must content ourselves with the lute alone.

In Blaine's words, "All the vocal aristocracy showed up—Nat [Cole], Billy [Eckstine], Ella [Fitzgerald], Mabel Mercer—'cause nobody wanted to miss that date."

2. Brackets enclose insertions that take the place of words or phrases.

And on the next page: "Their assumption is plainly that [Durocher] would be the agent in any such negotiation."

3. Brackets enclose insertions that supply missing letters.

A postscript to a December 17 letter to Waugh notes, "If D[eutsch] won't take the manuscript, perhaps someone at Faber will."

4. Brackets enclose insertions that alter the form of a word used in an original text.

He dryly observes (p. 78) that the Gravely investors had bought stocks because "they want[ed] to see themselves getting richer."

5. Brackets are used to indicate that capitalization has been altered. This is generally optional; it is standard practice only where meticulous handling of original source material is crucial (particularly legal and scholarly contexts).

As Chief Justice Warren held for the Court, "[T]he Attorney General may bring an injunctive action . . ."
or in general contexts
"The Attorney General may bring . . . "

Brackets also enclose editorial notes when text has been italicized for emphasis.

But tucked away on page 11 we find this fascinating note: "In addition, we anticipate that *siting these new plants in marginal neighborhoods will decrease the risk of organized community opposition*" [italics added].

6. Brackets function as parentheses within parentheses, especially where two sets of parentheses could be confusing.

Posner's recent essays (including the earlier *Law and Literature* [1988]) bear this out.

7. In mathematical copy, brackets are used with parentheses to indicate units contained within larger units. They are also used with various meanings in chemical names and formulas.

$x + 5[(x + y)(2x-y)]$
$Ag[Pt(NO_2)_4]$

With Other Punctuation

8. Punctuation that marks the end of a phrase, clause, item in a series, or sentence follows any bracketed material appended to that passage.

> The report stated, "if we fail to find additional sources of supply [of oil and gas], our long-term growth will be limited."

When brackets enclose a complete sentence, closing punctuation is placed within the brackets.

> [Since this article was written, new archival evidence of document falsification has come to light.]

COLON

The colon is usually a mark of introduction, indicating that what follows it—generally a clause, a phrase, or a list—has been pointed to or described in what precedes it. (For the use of capitals following a colon, see paragraphs 7–8 on page 84.)

With Phrases and Clauses

1. A colon introduces a clause or phrase that explains, illustrates, amplifies, or restates what has gone before.

> An umbrella is a foolish extravagance: if you don't leave it in the first restaurant, a gust of wind will destroy it on the way home.
> Dawn was breaking: the distant peaks were already glowing with the sun's first rays.

2. A colon introduces an appositive.

> The issue comes down to this: Will we offer a reduced curriculum, or will we simply cancel the program?
> That year Handley's old obsession was replaced with a new one: jazz.

3. A colon introduces a list or series, often following a phrase such as *the following* or *as follows*.

> She has trial experience on three judicial levels: county, state, and federal.
> Anyone planning to participate should be prepared to do the following: hike five miles with a backpack, sleep on the ground without a tent, and paddle a canoe through rough water.

It is occasionally used like a dash to introduce a summary statement following a series.

> Baseball, soccer, skiing, track: he excelled in every sport he took up.

4. Although the colon usually follows a full independent clause, it also often interrupts a sentence before the clause is complete.

> The nine proposed program topics are: offshore supply, vessel traffic, ferry services, ship repair, . . .

Information on each participant includes: name, date of birth, mailing address, . . .

For example: 58 percent of union members voted, but only 44 percent of blue-collar workers as a whole.

The association will:

Act with trust, integrity, and professionalism.

Operate in an open and effective manner.

Take the initiative in seeking diversity.

With Quotations

5. A colon usually introduces lengthy quoted material that is set off from the rest of a text by indentation but not by quotation marks.

> The *Rumpole* series has been nicely encapsulated as follows:
>
> Rumpled, disreputable, curmudgeonly barrister Horace Rumpole often wins cases despite the disdain of his more aristocratic colleagues. Fond of cheap wine ("Château Thames Embankment") and Keats's poetry, he refers to his wife as "She Who Must Be Obeyed" (an allusion to the title character of H. Rider Haggard's *She*).

6. A colon is often used before a quotation in running text, especially when (1) the quotation is lengthy, (2) the quotation is a formal statement or is being given special emphasis, or (3) a full independent clause precedes the colon.

> Said Murdoch: "The key to the success of this project is good planning. We need to know precisely what steps we will need to take, what kind of staff we will require, what the project will cost, and when we can expect completion."
>
> The inscription reads: "Here lies one whose name was writ in water."
>
> This was his verbatim response: "At this time Mr. Wilentz is still in the company's employ, and no change in his status is anticipated imminently.

Other Uses

7. A colon separates elements in bibliographic publication data and page references, in biblical citations, and in formulas used to express time and ratios. No space precedes or follows a colon between numerals.

> Stendhal, *Love* (New York: Penguin, 1975)
> *Paleobiology* 3:121
> John 4:10
> 8:30 a.m.
> a winning time of 3:43:02
> a ratio of 3:5

8. A colon separates titles and subtitles.

> *Southwest Stories: Tales from the Desert*

9. A colon follows the salutation in formal correspondence.

> Dear Judge Wright: Dear Product Manager:
> Dear Laurence: Ladies and Gentlemen:

10. A colon follows headings in memorandums, government correspondence, and general business letters.

TO: VIA:
SUBJECT: REFERENCE:

11. An unspaced colon separates the writer's and typist's initials in the identification lines of business letters.

WAL:jml

A colon also separates copy abbreviations from the initials of copy recipients. (The abbreviation *cc* stands for *carbon* or *courtesy copy; bcc* stands for *blind carbon* or *courtesy copy.*) A space follows a colon used with the fuller name of a recipient.

cc:RSP   bcc:MWK
  JES   bcc: Mr. Jones

With Other Punctuation

12. A colon is placed outside quotation marks and parentheses that punctuate the larger sentence.

> The problem becomes most acute in "Black Rose and Destroying Angel": plot simply ceases to exist.
> Wilson and Hölldobler remark on the same phenomenon in *The Ants* (1990):

COMMA

The comma is the most frequently used punctuation mark in English and the one that provides the most difficulties to writers. Its most common uses are to separate items in a series and to set off or distinguish grammatical elements within sentences.

Between Main Clauses

1. A comma separates main clauses joined by a coordinating conjunction, such as *and, but, or, nor,* or *so.*

> She knew very little about the new system, and he volunteered nothing.
> The trial lasted for nine months, but the jury took only four hours to reach its verdict.
> We will not respond to any more questions on that topic this afternoon, nor will we respond to similar questions in the future.
> All the first-floor windows were barred, so he had clambered up onto the fire escape.

2. When one or both of the clauses are short or closely related in meaning, the comma is often omitted.

> They said good-bye and everyone hugged.

If commas set off another phrase that modifies the whole sentence, the comma between main clauses is often omitted.

> Six thousand years ago, the top of the volcano blew off in a series of powerful eruptions and the sides collapsed into the middle.

3. Commas are sometimes used to separate short and obviously parallel main clauses that are not joined by conjunctions.

> One day you're a successful corporate lawyer, the next day you're out of work.

Use of a comma to join clauses that are neither short nor obviously parallel, called *comma fault* or *comma splice*, is avoided. Clauses not joined by conjunctions are normally separated by semicolons. For details, see paragraph 1 on page 80.

4. If a sentence is composed of three or more clauses that are short and free of commas, the clauses are occasionally all separated by commas even if the last two are not joined by a conjunction. If the clauses are long or punctuated, they are separated with semicolons; the last two clauses are sometimes separated by a comma if they are joined by a conjunction. (For more details, see paragraph 5 on page 81.)

> Small fish fed among the marsh weed, ducks paddled along the surface, an occasional muskrat ate greens along the bank.
> The kids were tired and whiny; Napoleon, usually so calm, was edgy; Tabitha seemed to be going into heat, and even the guinea pigs were agitated.

With Compound Predicates

5. Commas are not normally used to separate the parts of a compound predicate.

> The firefighter tried to enter the burning building but was turned back by the thick smoke.

However, they are often used if the predicate is long and complicated, if one part is being stressed, or if the absence of a comma could cause a momentary misreading.

> The board helps to develop the financing and marketing strategies for new corporate divisions, and issues periodic reports on expenditures, revenues, and personnel appointments.
> This is an unworkable plan, and has been from the start.
> I try to explain to him what I want him to do, and get nowhere.

With Subordinate Clauses and Phrases

6. Adverbial clauses and phrases that begin a sentence are usually set off with commas.

> Having made that decision, we turned our attention to other matters.
> In order to receive a high school diploma, a student must earn 16 credits from public or private secondary schools.
> In addition, staff members respond to queries, take new orders, and initiate billing.

If the sentence can be easily read without a comma, the comma may be omitted. The phrase will usually be short—four words or less—but even after a longer phrase the comma is often omitted.

> As cars age, they depreciate. *or* As cars age they depreciate.
> In January the firm will introduce a new line of investigative services.
> On the map the town appeared as a small dot in the midst of vast emptiness.
> If nobody comes forward by Friday I will have to take further steps.

7. Adverbial clauses and phrases that introduce a main clause other than the first main clause are usually set off with commas. If the clause or phrase follows a conjunction, one comma often precedes the conjunction and one follows the clause or phrase. Alternatively, one comma precedes the conjunction and two more enclose the clause or phrase, or a single comma precedes the conjunction. Short phrases, and phrases in short sentences, tend not to be enclosed in commas.

> They have redecorated the entire store, but[,] to the delight of their customers, it retains much of its original flavor.
> We haven't left Springfield yet, but when we get to Boston we'll call you.

8. A comma is not used after an introductory phrase if the phrase immediately precedes the main verb.

> From the next room came a loud expletive.

9. A subordinate clause or phrase that modifies a noun is not set off by commas if it is *restrictive* (or *essential*)—that is, if its removal would alter the noun's meaning.

> The man who wrote this obviously had no firsthand knowledge of the situation.
> They entered through the first door that wasn't locked.

If the meaning would not be altered by its removal, the clause or phrase is considered *nonrestrictive* (or *nonessential*) and usually is set off by commas.

> The new approach, which was based on team teaching, was well received.
> Wechsler, who has done solid reporting from other battlefronts, is simply out of his depth here.
> They tried the first door, which led nowhere.

10. Commas set off an adverbial clause or phrase that falls between the subject and the verb.

> The Clapsaddle sisters, to keep up appearances, rode to the park every Sunday in their rented carriage.

11. Commas set off modifying phrases that do not immediately precede the word or phrase they modify.

> Scarbo, intent as usual on his next meal, was snuffling around the butcher's bins.
> The negotiators, tired and discouraged, headed back to the hotel.
> We could see the importance, both long-term and short-term, of her proposal.

12. An absolute phrase (a participial phrase with its own subject that is grammatically independent of the rest of the sentence) is set off with commas.

> Our business being concluded, we adjourned for refreshments.
> We headed southward, the wind freshening behind us, to meet the rest of the fleet in the morning.
> I'm afraid of his reaction, his temper being what it is.

With Appositives

13. Commas set off a word, phrase, or clause that is in apposition to (that is, equivalent to) a preceding or following noun and that is nonrestrictive.

> It sat nursing its front paw, the injured one.
> Aleister Crowley, Britain's most infamous satanist, is the subject of a remarkable new biography.
> A cherished landmark in the city, the Hotel Sandburg has managed once again to escape the wrecking ball.
> The committee cochairs were a lawyer, John Larson, and an educator, Mary Conway.

14. Restrictive appositives are not set off by commas.

> He next had a walk-on role in the movie *The Firm*.
> Longfellow's poem *Evangeline* was a favorite of my grandmother's.
> The committee cochairs were the lawyer John Larson and the educator Mary Conway.
> Lord Castlereagh was that strange anomaly[,] a Labor-voting peer.

With Introductory and Interrupting Elements

15. Commas set off transitional words and phrases.

> Indeed, close coordination will be essential.
> Defeat may be inevitable; however, disgrace is not.
> The second report, on the other hand, shows a strong bias.

When such words and phrases fall in the middle of a clause, commas are sometimes unnecessary.

> They thus have no chips left to bargain with.
> The materials had indeed arrived.
> She would in fact see them that afternoon.

16. Commas set off parenthetical elements, such as authorial asides.

> All of us, to tell the truth, were completely amazed.
> It was, I should add, not the first time I'd seen him in this condition.

17. Commas are often used to set off words or phrases that introduce examples or explanations, such as *namely, for example,* and *that is.*

> He expects to visit three countries, namely, France, Spain, and Germany.
> I would like to develop a good, workable plan, that is, one that would outline our goals and set a timetable for accomplishing them.

Such introductory words and phrases may also often be preceded by a dash, parenthesis, or semicolon. Regardless of the punctuation that precedes the word or phrase, a comma usually follows it.

> Sports develop two valuable traits—namely, self-control and the ability to make quick decisions.
> In writing to the manufacturer, be as specific as possible (i.e., list the missing or defective parts, describe the malfunction, and identify the store where the unit was purchased).
> Most had traveled great distances to participate; for example, three had come from Australia, one from Japan, and two from China.

18. Commas set off words in direct address.

> This is our third and final notice, Mr. Sutton.
> The facts, my fellow Americans, are very different.

19. Commas set off mild interjections or exclamations.

> Ah, the mosaics in Ravenna are matchless.
> Uh-oh, His Eminence seems to be on the warpath this morning.

With Contrasting Expressions

20. A comma is sometimes used to set off contrasting expressions within a sentence.

> This project will take six months, not six weeks.

21. When two or more contrasting modifiers or prepositions, one of which is introduced by a conjunction or adverb, apply to a noun that follows immediately, the second is set off by two commas or a single comma, or not set off at all.

> A solid, if overly wordy, assessment
> *or* a solid, if overly wordy assessment
> *or* a solid if overly wordy assessment
> This street takes you away from, not toward, the capitol.
> *or* This street takes you away from, not toward the capitol.
> grounds for a civil, and maybe a criminal, case
> *or* grounds for a civil, and maybe a criminal case
> *or* grounds for a civil and maybe a criminal case

Dashes or parentheses are often used instead of commas in such sentences.

> grounds for a civil (and maybe a criminal) case

22. A comma does not usually separate elements that are contrasted through the use of a pair of correlative conjunctions such as *either . . . or, neither . . . nor,* and *not only . . . but also.*

> Neither my brother nor I noticed the error.
> He was given the post not only because of his diplomatic connections but also because of his great tact and charm.

When correlative conjunctions join main clauses, a comma usually separates the clauses unless they are short.

> Not only did she have to see three salesmen and a visiting reporter, but she also had to prepare for next day's meeting.
>
> Either you do it my way or we don't do it at all.

23. Long parallel contrasting and comparing clauses are separated by commas; short parallel phrases are not.

> The more that comes to light about him, the less savory he seems.
>
> The less said the better.

With Items in a Series

24. Words, phrases, and clauses joined in a series are separated by commas.

> Men, women, and children crowded aboard the train.
>
> Her job required her to pack quickly, to travel often, and to have no personal life.
>
> He responded patiently while reporters shouted questions, flashbulbs popped, and the crowd pushed closer.

When the last two items in a series are joined by a conjunction, the final comma is often omitted, especially where this would not result in ambiguity. In individual publications, the final comma is usually consistently used, consistently omitted, or used only where a given sentence would otherwise be ambiguous or hard to read. It is consistently used in most nonfiction books; elsewhere it tends to be used or generally omitted equally often.

> We are looking for a house with a big yard, a view of the harbor[,] and beach and docking privileges.

25. A comma is not generally used to separate items in a series all of which are joined with conjunctions.

> I don't understand what this policy covers or doesn't cover or only partially covers.
>
> They left behind the fogs and the wood storks and the lonesome soughing of the wind.

26. When the elements in a series are long or complex or consist of clauses that themselves contain commas, the elements are usually separated by semicolons, not commas. See paragraph 7 on page 81.

With Coordinate Modifiers

27. A comma is generally used to separate two or more adjectives, adverbs, or phrases that modify the same word or phrase.

> She spoke in a calm, reflective manner.
>
> They set to their work again grimly, intently.

The comma is often omitted when the adjectives are short.

one long thin strand	skinny young waiters
a small white stone	in this harsh new light
little nervous giggles	

The comma is generally omitted where it is ambiguous whether the last modifier and the noun—or two of the modifiers—constitute a unit.

the story's stark dramatic power
a pink stucco nightclub

In some writing, especially works of fiction, commas may be omitted from most series of coordinate modifiers as a matter of style.

28. A comma is not used between two adjectives when the first modifies the combination of the second plus the noun it modifies.

the last good man	the only fresh water
a good used car	the only freshwater lake
his protruding lower lip	their black pickup truck

A comma is also not used to separate an adverb from the adjective or adverb that it modifies.

this formidably difficult task

In Quotations

29. A comma usually separates a direct quotation from a phrase identifying its source or speaker. If the quotation is a question or an exclamation and the identifying phrase follows the quotation, the comma is replaced by a question mark or an exclamation point.

She answered, "I'm afraid it's all we've got."
"The comedy is over," he muttered.
"How about another round?" Elaine piped up.
"I suspect," said Mrs. Horowitz, "we haven't seen the last of her."
"You can sink the lousy thing for all I care!" Trumbull shouted back.
"And yet . . . ," she mused.
"We can't get the door op—" Captain Hunt is heard shouting before the tape goes dead.

In some cases, a colon can replace a comma preceding a quotation; see paragraph 6 on page 52.

30. When short or fragmentary quotations are used in a sentence that is not primarily dialogue, they are usually not set off by commas.

He glad-handed his way through the small crowd with a "Looking good, Joe" or "How's the wife" for every beaming face.
Just because he said he was "about to leave this minute" doesn't mean he actually left.

Sentences that fall within sentences and do not constitute actual dialogue are not usually set off with commas. These may be mottoes or maxims, unspoken or imaginary dialogue, or sentences referred to as sentences; and they may or may not be enclosed in quotation marks. Where quotation marks are not used, a comma is often inserted to mark the beginning of the shorter sentence clearly. (For the use of quotation marks with such sentences, see paragraph 6 on page 76.)

> "The computer is down" was the response she dreaded.
> He spoke with a candor that seemed to insist, This actually happened to me and in just this way.
> The first rule is, When in doubt, spell it out.

When the shorter sentence functions as an appositive (the equivalent to an adjacent noun), it is set off with commas when nonrestrictive and not when restrictive.

> We had the association's motto, "We make waves," printed on our T-shirts.
> He was fond of the slogan "Every man a king, but no man wears a crown."

31. A comma introduces a directly stated question, regardless of whether it is enclosed in quotation marks or if its first word is capitalized. It is not used to set off indirect discourse or indirect questions introduced by a conjunction (such as *that* or *what*).

> I wondered, what is going on here?
> The question is, How do we get out of this situation?
> *but*
> Margot replied quietly that she'd never been happier.
> I wondered what was going on here.
> The question is how do we get out of this situation.

32. The comma is usually omitted before quotations that are very short exclamations or representations of sounds.

> He jumped up suddenly and cried "I've got it!"

Replacing Omitted Words

33. A comma may indicate the omission of a word or phrase in parallel constructions where the omitted word or phrase appears earlier in the sentence. In short sentences, the comma is usually omitted.

> The larger towns were peopled primarily by shopkeepers, artisans, and traders; the small villages, by peasant farmers.
> Seven voted for the proposal, three against.
> He critiqued my presentation and I his.

34. A comma sometimes replaces the conjunction *that*.

> The smoke was so thick, they were forced to crawl.
> Chances are, there are still some tickets left.

With Addresses, Dates, and Numbers

35. Commas set off the elements of an address except for zip codes.

> Write to Bureau of the Census, Washington, DC 20233.
> In Needles, California, their luck ran out.

When a city name and state (province, country, etc.) name are used together to modify a noun that follows, the second comma may be omitted but is more often retained.

> We visited their Enid, Oklahoma plant.
> *but more commonly*
> We visited their Enid, Oklahoma, plant.

36. Commas set off the year in a full date.

> On July 26, 1992, the court issued its opinion.
> Construction for the project began on April 30, 1995.

When only the month and year are given, the first comma is usually omitted.

> In December 1903, the Wright brothers finally succeeded in keeping an airplane aloft for a few seconds.
> October 1929 brought an end to all that.

37. A comma groups numerals into units of three to separate thousands, millions, and so on.

> 2,000 case histories   a population of 3,450,000
> 15,000 units   a fee of $12,500

Certain types of numbers do not contain commas, including decimal fractions, street addresses, and page numbers. (For more on the use of the comma with numbers, see paragraphs 1–3 on page 138.)

> 2.5544
> 12537 Wilshire Blvd.
> page 1415

With Names, Degrees, and Titles

38. A comma separates a surname from a following professional, academic, honorary, or religious degree or title, or an abbreviation for a branch of the armed forces.

> Amelia P. Artandi, M.D.
> Robert Hynes Menard, Ph.D., L.H.D.
> John L. Farber, Esq.
> Sister Mary Catherine, S.C.
> Admiral Herman Washington, USN

39. A comma is often used between a surname and the abbreviations *Jr.* and *Sr.*

> Douglas Fairbanks, Sr.   *or*   Douglas Fairbanks Sr.
> Dr. Martin Luther King, Jr.   *or*   Dr. Martin Luther King Jr.

40. A comma is often used to set off corporate identifiers such as *Incorporated, Inc., Ltd., P.C.,* and *L.P.* However, many company names omit this comma.

> StarStage Productions, Incorporated
> Hart International Inc.
> Walsh, Brandon & Kaiser, P.C.
> The sales manager from Doyle Southern, Inc., spoke at Tuesday's meeting.

Other Uses

41. A comma follows the salutation in informal correspondence and usually follows the complimentary close in both informal and formal correspondence.

> Dear Rachel,
> Affectionately,
> Very truly yours,

42. The comma is used to avoid ambiguity when the juxtaposition of two words or expressions could cause confusion.

> Under Mr. Thomas, Jefferson High School has flourished.
> He scanned the landscape that opened out before him, and guided the horse gently down.

43. When normal sentence order is inverted, a comma often precedes the subject and verb. If the structure is clear without it, it is often omitted.

> That we would succeed, no one doubted.
> And a splendid occasion it was.

With Other Punctuation

44. Commas are used next to brackets, ellipsis points, parentheses, and quotation marks. Commas are not used next to colons, dashes, exclamation points, question marks, or semicolons. If one of the latter falls at the same point where a comma would fall, the comma is dropped. (For more on the use of commas with other punctuation, see the sections for each individual mark).

> "If they find new sources [of oil and gas], their earnings will obviously rebound. . . . "
> "This book takes its place among the most serious, . . . comprehensive, and enlightened treatments of its great subject."
> There are only six small files (at least in this format), which take up very little disk space.
> According to Hartmann, the people are "savage," their dwellings are "squalid," and the landscape is "a pestilential swamp."

DASH

The dash can function like a comma, a colon, or a parenthesis. Like commas and parentheses, dashes set off parenthetical material such as examples, supplemental facts, and explanatory or descriptive phrases. Like a colon, a dash introduces clauses that explain or expand upon something that precedes them. Though sometimes considered a less formal equivalent of the colon and parenthesis, the dash may be found in all kinds of writing, including the most formal, and the choice of which mark to use is often a matter of personal preference.

The common dash (also called the *em dash,* since it is approximately the width of a capital M in typeset material) is usually represented by two hyphens in typed and keyboarded material. (Word-processing programs make it available as a special character.)

Spacing around the dash varies. Most newspapers insert a space before and after the dash; many popular magazines do the same; but most books and journals omit spacing.

The *en dash* and the *two-* and *three-em dashes* have more limited uses, which are explained in paragraphs 13–15 on pages 65–66.

Abrupt Change or Suspension

1. The dash marks an abrupt change or break in the structure of a sentence.

> The students seemed happy enough with the new plan, but the alumni—there was the problem.

2. A dash is used to indicate interrupted speech or a speaker's confusion or hesitation.

> "The next point I'd like to bring up—" the speaker started to say.
> "Yes," he went on, "yes—that is—I guess I agree."

Parenthetical and Amplifying Elements

3. Dashes are used in place of commas or parentheses to emphasize or draw attention to parenthetical or amplifying material.

> With three expert witnesses in agreement, the defense can be expected to modify its strategy—somewhat.
> This amendment will finally prevent corporations—large and small—from buying influence through exorbitant campaign contributions.

When dashes are used to set off parenthetical elements, they often indicate that the material is more digressive than elements set off with commas but less digressive than elements set off by parentheses. For examples, see paragraph 16 on page 56 and paragraph 1 on page 70.

4. Dashes set off or introduce defining phrases and lists.

> The fund sought to acquire controlling positions—a minimum of 25% of outstanding voting securities—in other companies.
> Davis was a leading innovator in at least three styles—bebop, cool jazz, and jazz-rock fusion.

5. A dash is often used in place of a colon or semicolon to link clauses, especially when the clause that follows the dash explains, summarizes, or expands upon the preceding clause in a somewhat dramatic way.

> The results were in—it had been a triumphant success.

6. A dash or a pair of dashes often sets off illustrative or amplifying material introduced by such phrases as *for example, namely,* and *that is,* when the break in continuity is greater than that shown by a comma, or when the dash would clarify the sentence structure better than a comma. (For more details, see paragraph 17 on pages 56–57.)

> After some discussion the motion was tabled—that is, it was removed indefinitely from the board's consideration.
>
> Lawyers should generally—in pleadings, for example—attempt to be as specific as possible.

7. A dash may introduce a summary statement that follows a series of words or phrases.

> Crafts, food booths, children's activities, cider-making demonstrations—there was something for everyone.
>
> Once into bankruptcy, the company would have to pay cash for its supplies, defer maintenance, and lay off workers—moves that could threaten its future.

8. A dash often precedes the name of an author or source at the end of a quoted passage—such as an epigraph, extract, or book or film blurb—that is not part of the main text. The attribution may appear immediately after the quotation or on the next line.

> Only the sign is for sale.
> —Søren Kierkegaard
>
> "I return to her stories with more pleasure, and await them with more anticipation, than those of any of her contemporaries."—William Logan, *Chicago Tribune*

With Other Punctuation

9. If a dash appears at a point where a comma could also appear, the comma is omitted.

> Our lawyer has read the transcript—all 1,200 pages of it—and he has decided that an appeal would not be useful.
>
> If we don't succeed—and the critics say we won't—then the whole project is in jeopardy.

In a series, dashes that would force a comma to be dropped are often replaced by parentheses.

> The holiday movie crowds were being entertained by street performers: break dancers, a juggler (who doubled as a sword swallower), a steel-drummer, even a three-card-monte dealer.

10. If the second of a pair of dashes would fall where a period should also appear, the dash is omitted.

> Instead, he hired his mother—an odd choice by any standard.

Much less frequently, the second dash will be dropped in favor of a colon or semicolon.

> Valley Health announced general improvements to its practice—two to start this week: evening office hours and a voice-mail message system.
>
> His conduct has always been exemplary—near-perfect attendance, excellent productivity, a good attitude; nevertheless, his termination cannot be avoided.

11. When a pair of dashes sets off material ending with an exclamation point or a question mark, the mark is placed inside the dashes.

> His hobby was getting on people's nerves—especially mine!—and he was extremely good at it.
>
> There would be a "distinguished guest speaker"—was there ever any other kind?—and plenty of wine afterwards.

12. Dashes are used inside parentheses, and vice versa, to indicate parenthetical material within parenthetical material. The second dash is omitted if it would immediately precede the closing parenthesis; a closing parenthesis is never omitted.

> We were looking for a narrator (or narrators—sometimes a script calls for more than one) who could handle a variety of assignments.
>
> The wall of the Old City contains several gates—particularly Herod's Gate, the Golden Gate, and Zion Gate (or "David's Gate")—with rich histories.

En Dash and Long Dashes

13. The *en dash* generally appears only in typeset material; in typed or keyboarded material the simple hyphen is usually used instead. (Word-processing programs provide the en dash as a special character.) Newspapers similarly use the hyphen in place of the en dash. The en dash is shorter than the em dash but longer than the hyphen. It is most frequently used between numbers, dates, or other notations to signify "(up) to and including."

> pages 128–34   September 24–October 5
> 1995–97   8:30 a.m.–4:30 p.m.

The en dash replaces a hyphen in compound adjectives when at least one of the elements is a two-word compound. It replaces the word *to* between capitalized names, and is used to indicate linkages such as boundaries, treaties, and oppositions.

> post–Cold War era
> Boston–Washington train
> New Jersey–Pennsylvania border
> male–female differences   *or*   male-female differences

14. A *two-em dash* is used to indicate missing letters in a word and, less frequently, to indicate a missing word.

   The nearly illegible letter is addressed to a Mr. P—— of Baltimore.

15. A *three-em dash* indicates that a word has been left out or that an unknown word or figure is to be supplied.

   The study was carried out in ——, a fast-growing Sunbelt city.

ELLIPSIS POINTS

Ellipsis points (also known as *ellipses, points of ellipsis,* and *suspension points*) are periods, usually in groups of three, that signal an omission from quoted material or indicate a pause or trailing off of speech. A space usually precedes and follows each ellipsis point. (In newspaper style, spaces are usually omitted.)

1. Ellipsis points indicate the omission of one or more words within a quoted sentence.

   We the People of the United States . . . do ordain and establish this Constitution for the United States of America.

2. Ellipsis points are usually not used to indicate the omission of words that precede the quoted portion. However, in some formal contexts, especially when the quotation is introduced by a colon, ellipsis points are used.

   He ends with a stirring call for national resolve that "government of the people, by the people, for the people shall not perish from the earth."
   Its final words define the war's purpose in democratic terms: " . . . that government of the people, by the people, for the people shall not perish from the earth."

Ellipsis points following quoted material are omitted when it forms an integral part of a larger sentence.

   She maintained that it was inconsistent with "government of the people, by the people, for the people."

3. Punctuation used in the original that falls on either side of the ellipsis points is often omitted; however, it may be retained, especially if this helps clarify the sentence.

   Now we are engaged in a great civil war testing whether that nation . . . can long endure.
   But, in a larger sense, we can not dedicate, . . . we can not hallow this ground.
   We the People of the United States, in Order to . . . promote the general Welfare, and secure the Blessings of Liberty . . . , do ordain and establish this Constitution for the United States of America.

4. If an omission includes an entire sentence within a passage, the last part of a sentence within a passage, or the first part of a sentence other than

the first quoted sentence, the period preceding or following the omission is retained (with no space preceding it) and is followed by three ellipsis points. When the first part of a sentence is omitted but the quoted portion acts as a sentence, the first quoted word is usually capitalized.

> We have come to dedicate a portion of that field, as a final resting place for those who here gave their lives that this nation might live. . . . But, in a larger sense, we can not dedicate—we can not consecrate—we can not hallow—this ground.
>
> Now we are engaged in a great civil war. . . . We are met on a great battlefield of that war.
>
> The brave men, living and dead, who struggled here, have consecrated it, far above our poor power to add or detract. . . . From these honored dead we take increased devotion to that cause for which they gave the last full measure of devotion. . . .

Alternatively, the period may be dropped and all omissions may be indicated simply by three ellipsis points.

5. If the last words of a quoted sentence are omitted and the original sentence ends with punctuation other than a period, the end punctuation often follows the ellipsis points, especially if it helps clarify the quotation.

> He always ends his harangues with some variation on the question, "What could you have been thinking when you . . . ?"

6. When ellipsis points are used to indicate that a quotation has been intentionally left unfinished, the terminal period is omitted.

> The paragraph beginning "Recent developments suggest . . . " should be deleted.

7. A line of ellipsis points indicates that one or more lines have been omitted from a poem. (For more on poetry and extracts, see the section on pages 77–78.)

> When I heard the learned astronomer,
> . . . .
> How soon unaccountable I became tired and sick,
> Til rising and gliding out I wandered off by myself,
> In the mystical moist night-air, and from time to time,
> Looked up in perfect silence at the stars.

8. Ellipsis points are used to indicate faltering speech, especially if the faltering involves a long pause or a sentence that trails off or is intentionally left unfinished. Generally no other terminal punctuation is used.

> The speaker seemed uncertain. "Well, that's true . . . but even so . . . I think we can do better."
>
> "Despite these uncertainties, we believe we can do it, but . . . "
>
> "I mean . . . " he said, "like . . . How?"

9. Ellipsis points are sometimes used informally as a stylistic device to catch a reader's attention, often replacing a dash or colon.

> They think that nothing can go wrong . . . but it does.

10. In newspaper and magazine columns consisting of social notes, local events listings, or short items of celebrity news, ellipsis points often take the place of paragraphing to separate the items. (Ellipsis points are also often used in informal personal correspondence in place of periods or paragraphing.)

> Congratulations to Debra Morricone, our up-and-coming singing star, for her full scholarship to the Juilliard School this fall! . . . And kudos to Paul Chartier for his winning All-State trumpet performance last Friday in Baltimore! . . . Look for wit and sparkling melody when the Lions mount their annual Gilbert & Sullivan show at Syms Auditorium. This year it's . . .

EXCLAMATION POINT

The exclamation point is used to mark a forceful comment or exclamation.

1. An exclamation point can punctuate a sentence, phrase, or interjection.

> There is no alternative!
> Without a trace!
> My God! It's monstrous!

2. The exclamation point may replace the question mark when an ironic, angry, or emphatic tone is more important than the actual question.

> Aren't you finished yet!
> Do you realize what you've done!
> Why me!

Occasionally it is used *with* the question mark to indicate a very forceful question.

> How much did you say?!
> You did what!?

3. The exclamation point falls within brackets, dashes, parentheses, and quotation marks when it punctuates only the enclosed material. It is placed outside them when it punctuates the entire sentence.

> All of this proves—at long last!—that we were right from the start.
> Somehow the dog got the gate open (for the third time!) and ran into the street.
> He sprang to his feet and shouted "Point of order!"
> At this rate the national anthem will soon be replaced by "You Are My Sunshine"!

4. If an exclamation point falls where a comma could also go, the comma is dropped.

> "Absolutely not!" he snapped.
> They wouldn't dare! she told herself over and over.

If the exclamation point is part of a title, it may be followed by a comma. If the title falls at the end of a sentence, no period follows it.

> *Hello Dolly!*, which opened in 1964, would become one of the ten longest-running shows in Broadway history.
> His favorite management book is still *Up the Organization!*

HYPHEN

Hyphens have a variety of uses, the most significant of which is to join the elements of compound nouns and modifiers.

1. Hyphens are used to link elements in compound words. (For more on compound words, see the section beginning on page 111.)

> secretary-treasurer fund-raiser
> cost-effective spin-off

2. In some words, a hyphen separates a prefix, suffix, or medial element from the rest of the word. Consult a dictionary in doubtful cases. (For details on using a hyphen with a prefix or a suffix, see the section beginning on page 120.)

> anti-inflation
> umbrella-like
> jack-o'-lantern

3. In typed and keyboarded material, a hyphen is generally used between numbers and dates with the meaning "(up) to and including." In typeset material it is replaced by an en dash. (For details on the en dash, see paragraph 13 on page 65.)

> pages 128–34
> the years 1995–97

4. A hyphen marks an end-of-line division of a word.

> In 1975 smallpox, formerly a great scourge, was declared totally eradicated by the World Health Organization.

5. A hyphen divides letters or syllables to give the effect of stuttering, sobbing, or halting speech.

> "S-s-sammy, it's my t-toy!"

6. Hyphens indicate a word spelled out letter by letter.

> l-i-a-i-s-o-n

7. Hyphens are sometimes used to produce inflected forms of verbs made of individually pronounced letters or to add an *-er* ending to an abbreviation. However, apostrophes are more commonly used for these purposes. (For details on these uses of the apostrophe, see paragraph 6 on page 49.)

> DH-ing for the White Sox   *or*   DH'ing for the White Sox
> a dedicated UFO-er   *or*   a dedicated UFO'er

PARENTHESES

Parentheses generally enclose material that is inserted into a main statement but is not intended to be an essential part of it. For some of the cases described below, commas or dashes are frequently used instead. (For examples, see paragraph 16 on page 56 and paragraph 3 on page 63.) Parentheses are particularly used when the inserted material is only incidental. Unlike commas and dashes, an opening parenthesis is always followed by a closing one. Because parentheses are almost always used in pairs, and their shapes indicate their relative functions, they often clarify a sentence's structure better than commas or dashes.

Parenthetical Elements

1. Parentheses enclose phrases and clauses that provide examples, explanations, or supplementary facts or numerical data.

> Nominations for principal officers (president, vice president, treasurer, and secretary) were heard and approved.
> Four computers (all outdated models) will be replaced.
> First-quarter sales figures were good (up 8%), but total revenues showed a slight decline (down 1%).

2. Parentheses sometimes enclose phrases and clauses introduced by expressions such as *namely, that is, e.g.,* and *i.e.,* particularly where parentheses would clarify the sentence's structure better than commas. (For more details, see paragraph 17 on pages 56–57.)

> In writing to the manufacturer, be as specific as possible (i.e., list the defective parts, describe the malfunction, and identify the store where the unit was purchased), but also as concise.

3. Parentheses enclose definitions or translations in the main part of a sentence.

> The company announced plans to sell off its housewares (small-appliances) business.
> The *grand monde* (literally, "great world") of prewar Parisian society consisted largely of titled aristocracy.

4. Parentheses enclose abbreviations that follow their spelled-out forms, or spelled-out forms that follow abbreviations.

> She cited a study by the Food and Drug Administration (FDA).
> They attended last year's convention of the ABA (American Booksellers Association).

5. Parentheses often enclose cross-references and bibliographic references.

> Specialized services are also available (see list of stores at end of brochure).
> The diagram (Fig. 3) illustrates the action of the pump.
> Subsequent studies (Braxton 1990; Roh and Weinglass 1993) have confirmed these findings.

6. Parentheses enclose numerals that confirm a spelled-out number in a business or legal context.

> Delivery will be made in thirty (30) days.
> The fee is Four Thousand Dollars ($4,000), payable to UNCO, Inc.

7. Parentheses enclose the name of a state that is inserted into a proper name for identification.

> the Kalispell (Mont.) Regional Hospital
> the *Sacramento* (Calif.) *Bee*

8. Parentheses may be used to enclose personal asides.

> Claims were made of its proven efficacy (some of us were skeptical).
> *or*
> Claims were made of its proven efficacy. (Some of us were skeptical.)

9. Parentheses are used to enclose quotations that illustrate or support a statement made in the main text.

> After he had a few brushes with the police, his stepfather had him sent to jail as an incorrigible ("It will do him good").

Other Uses

10. Parentheses enclose unpunctuated numbers or letters indicating individual elements or items in a series within a sentence.

> Sentences can be classified as (1) simple, (2) multiple or compound, and (3) complex.

11. Parentheses indicate alternative terms.

> Please sign and return the enclosed form(s).

12. Parentheses may be used to indicate losses in accounting.

Operating Profits
(in millions)

Cosmetics	26.2
Food products	47.7
Food services	54.3
Transportation	(17.7)
Sporting goods	(11.2)
Total	99.3

With Other Punctuation

13. When an independent sentence is enclosed in parentheses, its first word is capitalized and a period (or other closing punctuation) is placed inside the parentheses.

    The discussion was held in the boardroom. (The results are still confidential.)

A parenthetical expression that occurs within a sentence—even if it could stand alone as a separate sentence—does not end with a period but may end with an exclamation point, a question mark, or quotation marks.

    Although several trade organizations opposed the legislation (there were at least three paid lobbyists working on Capitol Hill), the bill passed easily.
    The conference was held in Portland (Me., not Ore.).
    After waiting in line for an hour (why do we do these things?), we finally left.

A parenthetical expression within a sentence does not require capitalization unless it is a quoted sentence.

    He was totally confused ("What can we do?") and refused to see anyone.

14. If a parenthetical expression within a sentence is composed of two independent clauses, a semicolon rather than a period usually separates them. Independent sentences enclosed together in parentheses employ normal sentence capitalization and punctuation.

    We visited several showrooms, looked at the prices (it wasn't a pleasant experience; prices in this area have not gone down), and asked all the questions we could think of.
    We visited several showrooms and looked at the prices. (It wasn't a pleasant experience. Prices in this area have not gone down.)

Entire paragraphs are rarely enclosed in parentheses; instead, paragraphs of incidental material often appear as footnotes or endnotes.

15. No punctuation (other than a period after an abbreviation) is placed immediately before an opening parenthesis within a sentence; if punctuation is required, it follows the final parenthesis.

    I'll get back to you tomorrow (Friday), when I have more details.
    Tickets cost $14 in advance ($12 for seniors); the price at the door is $18.
    The relevant figures are shown below (in millions of dollars):

16. Parentheses sometimes appear within parentheses when no confusion would result; alternatively, the inner parentheses are replaced with brackets.

> Checks must be drawn in U.S. dollars. (*Please note:* We cannot accept checks drawn on Canadian banks for amounts less than four U.S. dollars ($4.00). The same regulation applies to Canadian money orders.)

17. Dashes and parentheses may be used together to set off parenthetical material. (For details, see paragraph 12 on page 65.)

> The orchestra is spirited, and the cast—an expert and enthusiastic crew of Savoyards (some of them British imports)—comes through famously.

PERIOD

Periods almost always serve to mark the end of a sentence or abbreviation.

1. A period ends a sentence or a sentence fragment that is neither a question nor an exclamation.

> From the Format menu, choose Style.
> Robert decided to bring champagne.
> Unlikely. In fact, inconceivable.

Only one period ends a sentence.

> The jellied gasoline was traced to the Trenton-based Quality Products, Inc.
> Miss Toklas states categorically that "This is the best way to cook frogs' legs."

2. A period punctuates some abbreviations. No space follows an internal period within an abbreviation. (For details on punctuating abbreviations, see the section beginning on page 124.)

Assn.	Dr.	p.m.
Ph.D.	e.g.	etc.

3. Periods are used with a person's initials, each followed by a space. (Newspaper style omits the space.) If the initials replace the name, they are unspaced and may also be written without periods.

> J. B. S. Haldane
> L.B.J.   *or*   LBJ

4. A period follows numerals and letters when they are used without parentheses in outlines and vertical lists.

> I. Objectives
>   A. Economy
>   1. Low initial cost
>   2. Low maintenance cost
>   B. Ease of operation

Required skills are:
> 1. Shorthand
> 2. Typing
> 3. Transcription

5. A period is placed within quotation marks, even when it did not punctuate the original quoted material. (In British practice, the period goes outside the quotation marks whenever it does not belong to the original quoted material.)

> The founder was known to his employees as "the old man."
> "I said I wanted to fire him," Henry went on, "but she said, 'I don't think you have the contractual privilege to do that.'"

6. When brackets or parentheses enclose an independent sentence, the period is placed inside them. When brackets or parentheses enclose a sentence that is part of a larger sentence, the period for the enclosed sentence is omitted.

> Arturo finally arrived on the 23rd with the terrible news that Katrina had been detained by the police. [This later proved to be false; see letter 255.]
> I took a good look at her (she was standing quite close to me).

QUESTION MARK

The question mark always indicates a question or doubt.

1. A question mark ends a direct question.

> What went wrong?
> "When do they arrive?" she asked.

A question mark follows a period only when the period punctuates an abbreviation. No period follows a question mark.

> Is he even an M.D.?
> "Will you arrive by 10 p.m.?"
> A local professor would be giving a paper with the title "Economic Stagnation or Equilibrium?"

2. Polite requests that are worded as questions usually take periods, because they are not really questions. Conversely, a sentence that is intended as a question but whose word order is that of a statement is punctuated with a question mark.

> Could you please send the necessary forms.
> They flew in yesterday?

3. The question mark ends a question that forms part of a sentence. An indirect question is not followed by a question mark.

> What was her motive? you may be asking.
> I naturally wondered, Will it really work?
> I naturally wondered whether it would really work.
> He asked when the report was due.

4. The question mark punctuates each element of a series of questions that share a single beginning and are neither numbered nor lettered. When the series is numbered or lettered, only one question mark is generally used.

> Can you give us a reasonable forecast? Back up your predictions? Compare them with last year's earnings?
> Can you (1) give us a reasonable forecast, (2) back up your predictions, and (3) compare them with last year's earnings?

5. The question mark indicates uncertainty about a fact or the accuracy of a transcription.

> Homer, Greek epic poet (9th–8th? cent. B.C.)
> He would have it that Farjeon[?] is the onlie man for us.

6. The question mark is placed inside brackets, dashes, parentheses, or quotation marks when it punctuates only the material enclosed by them and not the sentence as a whole. It is placed outside them when it punctuates the entire sentence.

> I took a vacation in 1992 (was it really that long ago?), but I haven't had time for one since.
> What did Andrew mean when he called the project "a fiasco from the start"?
> Williams then asks, "Do you realize the extent of the problem [the housing shortage]?"

QUOTATION MARKS

The following paragraphs describe the use of quotation marks to enclose quoted matter in regular text, and for other, less frequent uses. For the use of quotation marks to enclose titles, see paragraph 70 on page 99.

Basic Uses

1. Quotation marks enclose direct quotations but not indirect quotations or paraphrases.

> Dr. Mee added, "We'd be grateful for anything you could do."
> "We just got the lab results," he crowed, "and the blood types match!"
> "I'm leaving," she whispered. "This meeting could go on forever."
> "Mom, we *tried* that already!" they whined in unison.
> "Ssshh!" she hissed.
> She said she was leaving.
> Algren once said something like, Don't ever play poker with anyone named Doc, and never eat at a diner called Mom's.

2. Quotation marks enclose fragments of quoted matter.

> The agreement makes it clear that he "will be paid only upon receipt of an acceptable manuscript."
> As late as 1754, documents refer to him as "yeoman" and "husbandman."

3. Quotation marks enclose words or phrases borrowed from others, and words of obvious informality introduced into formal writing. Words introduced as specialized terminology are sometimes enclosed in quotation marks but more often italicized.

> Be sure to send a copy of your résumé—or as some folks would say, your "biodata summary."
>
> They were afraid the patient had "stroked out"—had had a cerebrovascular accident.
>
> referred to as "closed" or "privately held" corporations
>> *but more frequently*
>
> referred to as *closed* or *privately held* corporations
>
> New Hampshire's only "green" B&B

4. Quotation marks are sometimes used to enclose words referred to as words. Italics are also frequently used for this purpose.

> changed every "he" to "she"
>> *or*
>
> changed every *he* to *she*

5. Quotation marks may enclose representations of sounds, though these are also frequently italicized.

> If it sounds like "quank, quank" [*or* like *quank, quank*], it may be the green treefrog.

6. Quotation marks often enclose short sentences that fall within longer sentences, especially when the shorter sentence is meant to suggest spoken dialogue. Mottoes and maxims, unspoken or imaginary dialogue, and sentences referred to as sentences may all be treated in this way.

> On the gate was the inscription "Arbeit macht frei" [*or Arbeit macht frei*]—"Work will make you free."
>
> The fact was, the poor kid didn't know "C'mere" from "Sic 'em."
>
> In effect, the voters were saying "You blew it, and you don't get another chance."
>
> Their reaction could only be described as "Kill the messenger."
>
> She never got used to their "That's the way it goes" attitude.
>> *or*
>
> She never got used to their that's-the-way-it-goes attitude.

Quotation marks are often omitted in sentences of this kind when the structure is clear without them. (For the use of commas in such sentences, see paragraphs 29–30 on pages 59–60.)

> The first rule is, When in doubt, spell it out.

7. Direct questions are enclosed in quotation marks when they represent quoted dialogue, but usually not otherwise.

> She asked, "What went wrong?"
> The question is, What went wrong?
> We couldn't help wondering, Where's the plan?
> *or*
> We couldn't help wondering, "Where's the plan?"

8. Quotation marks enclose translations of foreign or borrowed terms.

> This is followed by the Dies Irae ("Day of Wrath"), a climactic movement in many settings of the Requiem.
> The term comes from the Latin *sesquipedalis,* meaning "a foot and a half long."

They also frequently enclose definitions.

> *Concupiscent* simply means "lustful."
> *or*
> *Concupiscent* simply means lustful.

9. Quotation marks sometimes enclose letters referred to as letters.

> The letter "m" is wider than the letter "i."
> Put an "x" in the right spot

However, such letters are more frequently italicized (or underlined), or left undifferentiated from the surrounding text where no confusion would result.

> How many *e*'s are in her name?
> a V-shaped blade
> He was happy to get a B in the course.

With Longer Quotations

10. Quotation marks are not used with longer passages of prose or poetry that are indented as separate paragraphs, called *extracts* or *block quotations.* Quoted text is usually set as an extract when it is longer than a sentence or runs to at least four lines, but individual requirements of consistency, clarity, or emphasis may alter these limits. Extracts are set off from the normal text by (1) indenting the passage on the left, and often on the right as well, and (2) usually setting it in smaller type. Extracts are usually preceded by a sentence ending with a colon, and they usually begin with a capitalized first word. The first line of an extract has no added indention; however, if the extract consists of more than one paragraph, the subsequent paragraphs are indented. (For the use of ellipsis points to show omissions within extracts, see the section beginning on page 66.)

> The chapter begins with a general description of memos:
>> The interoffice memorandum or memo is a means of informal communication within a firm or organization. It replaces the salutation, complimentary close, and written signature of the letter with identifying headings.

If the extract continues the flow of an incomplete sentence, no punctuation is required and the extract begins with a lowercase letter.

> They describe the memo as
>
> a means of informal communication within a firm or organization. It replaces the salutation, complimentary close, and written signature of the letter with identifying headings.

If the sentence preceding the extract does not refer directly to it, the sentence usually ends with a period, though a colon is also common.

> As of the end of April she believed that the product stood a good chance of success.
>
> Unit sales are strong, revenues are better than forecast, shipments are being made on schedule, and inventory levels are stable.

11. When an extract itself includes quoted material, double quotation marks enclose the material.

> The authors recommend the following procedure:
>
> The presiding officer will call for the appropriate report from an officer, board member, standing committee, or special committee by saying, "Will the chairperson of the Ways and Means Committee please present the committee's report?"

12. When poetry is set as an extract, the lines are divided exactly as in the original. A spaced slash separates lines of run-in poetry.

> The experience reminded them of Pope's observation:
>
> A little learning is a dang'rous thing;
> Drink deep, or taste not the Pierian spring:
> There shallow draughts intoxicate the brain,
> And drinking largely sobers us again.

> When Gerard Manley Hopkins wrote that "Nothing is so beautiful as spring— / When weeds, in wheels, shoot long and lovely and lush," he probably had my yard in mind.

13. Quotation marks are not used with epigraphs. However, they are generally used with advertising blurbs.

> The whole of science is nothing more than a refinement of everyday thinking.
> —Albert Einstein

> "A brutal irony, a slam-bang humor and a style of writing as balefully direct as a death sentence."—*Time*

With Other Punctuation

14. When a period or comma follows text enclosed in quotation marks, it is placed within the quotation marks, even if the original language quoted was not followed by a period or comma.

> He smiled and said, "I'm happy for you."
> But perhaps Pound's most perfect poem was "The Return."
> The cameras were described as "waterproof," but "moisture-resistant" would have been a better description.

In British usage, the period or comma goes outside the quoted matter whenever the original text did not include the punctuation.

15. When a colon or semicolon follows text enclosed in quotation marks, the colon or semicolon is placed outside the quotation marks.

> But they all chimed in on "O Sole Mio": raw adolescents, stately matrons, decrepit old pensioners, their voices soaring in passion together.
>
> She spoke of her "little cottage in the country"; she might better have called it a mansion.

16. The dash, question mark, and exclamation point are placed inside quotation marks when they punctuate the quoted matter only, but outside the quotation marks when they punctuate the whole sentence.

> "I can't see how—" he started to say.
>
> He thought he knew where he was going—he remembered her saying, "Take two lefts, then stay to the right"—but the streets didn't look familiar.
>
> He asked, "When did they leave?"
>
> What is the meaning of "the open door"?
>
> She collapsed in her seat with a stunned "Good God!"
>
> Save us from his "mercy"!

Single Quotation Marks

17. Single quotation marks replace double quotation marks when the quoted material occurs within quoted material.

> The witness said, "I distinctly heard him say, 'Don't be late,' and then I heard the door close."
>
> "We'd like to close tonight with that great Harold Arlen wee-hours standard, 'One for My Baby.'"
>
> This analysis is indebted to Del Banco's "Elizabeth Bishop's 'Insomnia': An Inverted View."

When both single and double quotation marks occur at the end of a sentence, the period falls within both sets of marks.

> The witness said, "I distinctly heard him say, 'Don't be late.'"

British usage often reverses American usage, enclosing quoted material in single quotation marks, and enclosing quotations within quotations in double quotation marks. In British usage, commas and periods following quoted material go inside only those quotation marks that enclose material that originally included the period or comma.

18. A quotation within a quotation within a quotation is usually enclosed in double quotation marks. (Such constructions are usually avoided by rewriting.)

> As the *Post* reported it, "Van Houten's voice can be clearly heard saying, 'She said "You wouldn't dare" and I said "I just did."'"
>
> *or*
>
> The *Post* reported that Van Houten's voice was clearly heard saying, "She said 'You wouldn't dare' and I said 'I just did.'"

SEMICOLON

The semicolon may be used much like the comma, period, or colon, depending on the context. Like a comma, it may separate elements in a series. Like a period or colon, it frequently marks the end of a complete clause, and like a colon it signals that the remainder of the sentence is closely related to the first part. However, in each case the semicolon is normally used in a distinctive way. It serves as a higher-level comma; it connects clauses, as a period does not; and it does not imply any following exemplification, amplification, or description, as a colon generally does.

Between Clauses

1. A semicolon separates related independent clauses joined without a coordinating conjunction.

   Cream the shortening and sugar; add the eggs and beat well.
   The river rose and overflowed its banks; roads became flooded and impassable; freshly plowed fields disappeared from sight.

2. A semicolon often replaces a comma between two clauses joined by a coordinating conjunction if the sentence might otherwise be confusing—for example, because of particularly long clauses or the presence of other commas.

   In a society that seeks to promote social goals, government will play a powerful role; and taxation, once simply a means of raising money, becomes, in addition, a way of furthering those goals.

3. A semicolon joins two clauses when the second includes a conjunctive adverb such as *accordingly, however, indeed,* or *thus,* or a phrase that acts like a conjunctive adverb such as *in that case, as a result,* or *on the other hand.*

   Most people are covered by insurance of some kind; indeed, many don't even see their medical bills.
   It won't be easy to sort out the facts; a decision must be made, however.
   The case could take years to work its way through the courts; as a result, many plaintiffs will accept settlements.

When *so* and *yet* are treated as conjunctive adverbs, they are often preceded by a semicolon and followed by a comma. When treated as coordinating conjunctions, as they usually are, they are generally only preceded by a comma.

   The new recruits were bright, diligent, and even enthusiastic; yet[,] the same problems persisted.
   His grades improved sharply, yet the high honor roll still eluded him.

4. A semicolon may join two statements when the second clause is elliptical, omitting essential words that are supplied by the first. In short sentences, a comma often replaces the semicolon.

   The conference sessions, designed to allow for full discussions, were much too long; the breaks between them, much too short.
   The aged Scotch was haunting, the Asiago piquant.

5. When a series of clauses are separated by semicolons and a coordinating conjunction precedes the final clause, the final semicolon is sometimes replaced with a comma.

> The bars had all closed hours ago; a couple of coffee shops were open but deserted[; *or* ,] and only a few lighted upper-story windows gave evidence of other victims of insomnia.

6. A semicolon is often used before introductory expressions such as *for example, that is,* and *namely,* in place of a colon, comma, dash, or parenthesis. (For more details, see paragraph 17 on pages 56–57.)

> On one point only did everyone agree; namely, too much money had been spent already.
> We were fairly successful on that project; that is, we made our deadlines and met our budget.

In a Series

7. A semicolon is used in place of a comma to separate phrases or items in a series when the phrases or items themselves contain commas. A comma may replace the semicolon before a conjunction that precedes the last item in a series.

> The assets in question include $22 million in land, buildings, and equipment; $34 million in cash, investments, and accounts receivable; and $8 million in inventory.
> The votes against were: Precinct 1, 418; Precinct 2, 332; Precinct 3, 256.
> The debate about the nature of syntactic variation continues to this day (Labov 1991; Dines 1991, 1993; Romaine 1995).
> The Pissarro exhibition will travel to Washington, D.C.; Manchester, N.H.; Portland, Ore., and Oakland, Calif.

When the items in a series are long or are sentences themselves, they are usually separated by semicolons even if they lack internal commas.

> Among the committee's recommendations were the following: more hospital beds in urban areas where there are waiting lines for elective surgery; smaller staff size in half-empty rural hospitals; and review procedures for all major purchases.

With Other Punctuation

8. A semicolon that punctuates the larger sentence is placed outside quotation marks and parentheses.

> I heard the senator on yesterday's "All Things Considered"; his views on Medicare are encouraging.
> She found him urbane and entertaining (if somewhat overbearing); he found her charmingly ingenuous.

SLASH

The slash (also known as the *virgule, diagonal, solidus, oblique,* and *slant*) is most commonly used in place of a short word or a hyphen or en dash, or to separate numbers or text elements. There is generally no space on either side of the slash.

1. A slash represents the words *per* or *to* when used between units of measure or the terms of a ratio.

    40,000 tons/year
    29 mi/gal
    price/earnings ratio   *or*   price–earnings ratio
    cost/benefit analysis   *or*   cost–benefit analysis
    a 50/50 split   *or*   a 50–50 split
    20/20 vision

2. A slash separates alternatives, usually representing the words *or* or *and/or.*

    alumni/ae
    his/her
    the *affect/effect* problem   *or*   the *affect-effect* problem

3. A slash replaces the word *and* in some compound terms.

    air/sea cruise   *or*   air-sea cruise
    the May/June issue   *or*   the May-June issue
    1996/97   *or*   1996–97
    travel/study trip   *or*   travel-study trip

4. A slash is sometimes used to replace certain prepositions such as *at, versus,* and *for.*

    U.C./Berkeley   *or*   U.C.–Berkeley
    parent/child issues   *or*   parent–child issues
    Vice President/Editorial   *or*   Vice President, Editorial

5. A slash punctuates a few abbreviations.

    w/o [*for* without]
    c/o [*for* care of]
    I/O [*for* input/output]
    d/b/a [*for* doing business as]
    w/w [*for* wall-to-wall]
    o/a [*for* on or about]

6. The slash separates the elements in a numerical date, and numerators and denominators in fractions.

    11/29/95
    2 3/16 inches wide   *or*   2 $\frac{3}{16}$ inches wide
    a 7/8-mile course   *or*   a $\frac{7}{8}$-mile course

7. The slash separates lines of poetry that are run in with the text around them. A space is usually inserted before and after the slash.

> Alexander Pope once observed: "'Tis with our judgments as our watches, none / Go just alike, yet each believes his own."

Capitals and Italics

Words and phrases are capitalized or italicized (underlining takes the place of italics in typed or handwritten text) to indicate that they have a special significance in particular contexts. (Quotation marks sometimes perform the same functions; see paragraphs 69–71 on pages 99–100 and the section on quotation marks beginning on page 75.)

BEGINNINGS

1. The first word of a sentence or sentence fragment is capitalized.

> They make a desert and call it peace.
> So many men, so many opinions.
> O times! O customs!

2. The first word of a sentence contained within parentheses is capitalized. However, a parentheticalal sentence occurring inside another sentence is not capitalized unless it is a complete quoted sentence.

> No one answered the telephone. (They were probably on vacation.)
> The road remains almost impassable (the locals don't seem to care), and the journey is only for the intrepid.
> After waiting in line for an hour (what else could we do?), we finally left.
> In the primary election Evans placed third ("My campaign started late").

3. The first word of a direct quotation is capitalized. However, if the quotation is interrupted in mid- sentence, the second part does not begin with a capital.

> The department manager explained, "We have no budget for new computers."
> "We have no budget for new computers," explained the department manager, "but we may next year."

4. When a quotation, whether a sentence fragment or a complete sentence, is syntactically dependent on the sentence in which it occurs, the quotation does not begin with a capital.

> The brochure promised a tour of "the most exotic ancient sites."
> His first response was that "there is absolutely no truth to the reports."

5. The first word of a sentence within a sentence that is not a direct quotation is usually capitalized. Examples include mottoes and rules, unspoken or imaginary dialogue, sentences referred to as sentences, and direct questions. (For the use of commas and quotation marks with such sentences, see paragraphs 30–31 on pages 59–60 and paragraphs 6–7 on pages 76–77.)

> You know the saying "Fools rush in where angels fear to tread."
> The first rule is, When in doubt, spell it out.
> One ballot proposition sought to enforce the sentencing rule of "Three strikes and you're out."
> My question is, When can we go?

6. The first word of a line of poetry is traditionally capitalized. However, in the poetry of this century line beginnings are often lowercased. The poem's original capitalization is always reproduced.

> Death is the mother of beauty, mystical,
> Within whose burning bosom we devise
> Our earthly mothers waiting, sleeplessly.
> —Wallace Stevens

>   If tributes cannot
> be implicit,
> give me diatribes and the fragrance of iodine,
> the cork oak acorn grown in Spain . . .
> —Marianne Moore

7. The first word following a colon is lowercased when it begins a list and usually lowercased when it begins a complete sentence. However, when the sentence introduced is lengthy and distinctly separate from the preceding clause, it is often capitalized.

> In the early morning they broadcast an urgent call for three necessities: bandages, antibiotics, and blood.
> The advantage of this system is clear: it's inexpensive.
> The situation is critical: This company cannot hope to recoup the fourth-quarter losses that were sustained in five operating divisions.

8. If a colon introduces a series of sentences, the first word of each sentence is capitalized.

> Consider the steps we have taken: A subcommittee has been formed to evaluate past performance. New sources of revenue are being explored. Several candidates have been interviewed for the new post of executive director.

9. The first words of items that form complete sentences in run-in lists are usually capitalized, as are the first words of items in vertical lists. However, numbered phrases within a sentence are lowercased. For details, see the section beginning on page 145.

10. The first word in an outline heading is capitalized.

    I. Editorial tasks
    II. Production responsibilities
       A. Cost estimates
       B. Bids

11. In minutes and legislation, the introductory words *Whereas* and *Resolved* are capitalized (and *Resolved* is also italicized). The word immediately following is also capitalized.

    Whereas, Substantial benefits . . .
    Resolved, That . . .

12. The first word and certain other words of the salutation of a letter and the first word of a complimentary close are capitalized.

    Dear Sir or Madam: Sincerely yours,
    Ladies and Gentlemen: Very truly yours,
    To whom it may concern:

13. The first word and each subsequent major word following a SUBJECT or TO heading in a memorandum are capitalized.

    SUBJECT: Pension Plans
    TO: All Department Heads and Editors

PROPER NOUNS AND ADJECTIVES

The following paragraphs describe the ways in which a broad range of proper nouns and adjectives are styled. Capitals are always employed, sometimes in conjunction with italics or quotation marks.

Abbreviations

1. Abbreviated forms of proper nouns and adjectives are capitalized, just as the spelled-out forms would be. (For details on capitalizing abbreviations, see the section beginning on page 125.)

    Jan. [*for* January]
    NATO [*for* North Atlantic Treaty Organization]

Abstractions and Personifications

2. Abstract concepts and qualities are sometimes capitalized when the concept or quality is being personified. If the term is simply used in conjunction with other words that allude to human characteristics or qualities, it is not capitalized.

    as Autumn paints each leaf in fiery colors
    the statue of Justice with her scales
    hoping that fate would lend a hand

Academic Degrees

3. The names of academic degrees are capitalized when they follow a person's name. The names of specific degrees used without a person's name are usually lowercased. More general names for degrees are lowercased.

> Lawton I. Byrne, Doctor of Laws
> earned his associate in science degree   *or*   earned his Associate in Science degree
> completed course work for his doctorate
> working for a master's degree

Abbreviations for academic degrees are always capitalized. (For details, see paragraphs 11–12 on pages 129–30.)

> Susan L. Wycliff, M.S.W.
> received her Ph.D. in clinical psychology

Animals and Plants

4. The common names of animals and plants are not capitalized unless they contain a proper noun, in which case the proper noun is usually capitalized and any name element preceding (but not following) it is often capitalized. When in doubt, consult a dictionary. (For scientific names, see the section on pages 97–98.)

> the springer spaniel   Queen Anne's lace
> Holstein cows   black-eyed Susan
> California condor   mayflower
> a Great Dane   jack-in-the-pulpit

Awards and Prizes

5. Names of awards and prizes are capitalized. Words and phrases that are not actually part of the award's name are lowercased.

> Academy Award   Nobel Prize winner
> Emmy   Nobel Prize in medicine
> Rhodes Scholarship   *but*
> Rhodes scholar   Nobel Peace Prize
> Pulitzer Prize–winning novelist

Derivatives of Proper Names

6. Derivatives of proper names are capitalized when used in their primary sense. If the derived term has taken on a specialized meaning, it is often lowercased. Consult a dictionary when in doubt.

> Roman sculpture   pasteurized milk
> Viennese culture   french fries
> Victorian prudery   *but*
> a Britishism   American cheese
> Hodgkins disease   Dutch door
> chinaware

Geographical and Topographical References

7. Terms that identify divisions of the earth's surface and distinct areas, regions, places, or districts are capitalized, as are derivative nouns and adjectives.

the Pacific Rim	Burgundy
the Great Lakes	Burgundians
Arnhem Land	the Highlands
the Golan Heights	Highland attitudes

8. Popular names of localities are capitalized.

Little Italy	the Sunbelt
the Left Bank	the Big Easy

9. Compass points are capitalized when they refer to a geographical region or form part of a street name. They are lowercased when they refer to a simple direction.

the Southwest	North Pole
West Coast	north of the Rio Grande
North Atlantic	born in the East
East Pleasant Street	driving east on I-90

10. Nouns and adjectives that are derived from compass points and that designate or refer to a specific geographical region are usually capitalized.

Southern hospitality	Southwestern recipes
Easterners	Northern Europeans

11. Words designating global, national, regional, and local political divisions are capitalized when they are essential elements of specific names. They are usually lowercased when they precede a proper name or are not part of a specific name.

the Roman Empire	the state of New York
British Commonwealth nations	the Third Precinct
New York State	voters in three precincts

In legal documents, such words are often capitalized regardless of position.

the State of New York

12. Common geographical terms (such as *lake, mountain, river,* or *valley*) are capitalized if they are part of a proper name.

Lake Tanganyika	Cape of Good Hope
Great Salt Lake	Massachusetts Bay
Atlas Mountains	Cayman Islands
Mount Everest	Yosemite Valley

13. Common geographical terms preceding names are usually capitalized.

> Lakes Huron and Erie
> Mounts McKinley and Whitney

When *the* precedes the common term, the term is lowercased.

> the river Nile

14. Common geographical terms that are not used as part of a single proper name are not capitalized. These include plural terms that follow two or more proper names, and terms that are used descriptively or alone.

> the Indian and South Pacific oceans
> the Mississippi and Missouri rivers
> the Pacific coast of Mexico
> Caribbean islands
> the river delta

15. The names of streets, monuments, parks, landmarks, well-known buildings, and other public places are capitalized. However, common terms that are part of these names (such as *street*, *park*, or *bridge*) are lowercased when they occur after multiple names or are used alone.

> State Street   Golden Gate Bridge
> the Lincoln Memorial   Empire State Building
> Statue of Liberty   Beverly Hills Hotel
> the Pyramids   back to the hotel
> Grant Park   Main and Oak streets

Well-known shortened forms of place-names are capitalized.

> the Hill [*for* Capitol Hill]
> the Channel [*for* English Channel]
> the Street [*for* Wall Street]

Governmental, Judicial, and Political Bodies

16. Full names of legislative, deliberative, executive, and administrative bodies are capitalized, as are easily recognizable short forms of these names. However, nonspecific noun and adjective references to them are usually lowercased.

> United States Congress   the Fed
> Congress   congressional hearings
> the House   a federal agency

When words such as *department, committee,* or *agency* are used in place of a full name, they are most often capitalized when the department or agency is referring to itself, but otherwise usually lowercased.

> This Department welcomes constructive criticism . . .
> The department claimed to welcome such criticism . . .

When such a word is used in the plural to describe more than one specific body, it is usually capitalized when it precedes the names and lowercased when it follows them.

> involving the Departments of State and Justice
> a briefing from the State and Justice department

17. Full names of high courts are capitalized. Short forms of such names are often capitalized in legal documents but lowercased otherwise.

> . . . in the U.S. Court of Appeals for the Ninth Circuit
> International Court of Justice
> The court of appeals [*or* Court of Appeals] held . . .
> the Virginia Supreme Court
> a federal district court
> the state supreme court

However, both the full and short names of the U.S. Supreme Court are capitalized.

> the Supreme Court of the United States
> the Supreme Court
> the Court

18. Names of city and county courts are usually lowercased.

> the Springfield municipal court   the county court
> small-claims court   juvenile court

19. The noun *court*, when it applies to a specific judge or presiding officer, is capitalized in legal documents.

> It is the opinion of this Court that . . .
> The Court found that . . .

20. The terms *federal* and *national* are capitalized only when they are essential elements of a name or title. (*Federal* is also capitalized when it refers to a historical architectural style, to members of the original Federalist party, or to adherents of the Union in the Civil War.)

> Federal Election Commission   National Security Council
> a federal commission   national security
> Federalist principles

21. The word *administration* is sometimes capitalized when it refers to the administration of a specific U.S. president, but is more commonly lowercased. Otherwise, it is lowercased except when it is a part of the official name of a government agency.

> the Reagan administration   *or*   the Reagan Administration
> the administration   *or*   the Administration
> from one administration to the next
> the Social Security Administration

22. Names of political organizations and their adherents are capitalized, but the word *party* is often lowercased.

   the Democratic National Committee
   the Republican platform
   the Christian Coalition
   most Republicans
   the Democratic party *or* the Democratic Party
   party politics

Names of less-distinct political groupings are usually lowercased, as are their derivative forms.

   the right wing
   the liberals
   the conservative agenda
      but often
   the Left
   the Right

23. Terms describing political and economic philosophies are usually lowercased; if derived from proper names, they are usually capitalized. Consult a dictionary for doubtful cases.

   authoritarianism   nationalism
   democracy   social Darwinist
   fascism *or* Fascism   Marxist

Historical Periods and Events

24. The names of some historical and cultural periods and movements are capitalized. When in doubt, consult a dictionary or encyclopedia.

   Bronze Age   Third Reich
   Middle Ages   the atomic age
   Prohibition   Victorian era
   the Renaissance   age of Pericles
   New Deal   the baby boom
   Fifth Republic

25. Century and decade designations are normally lowercased.

   the nineteenth century
   the twenties
   the turn of the century
   a 12th-century manuscript
      but
   Gay Nineties
   Roaring Twenties

26. The names of conferences, councils, expositions, and specific sporting, cultural, and historical events are capitalized.

Fourth World Conference on   Cannes Film Festival
  Women   Miss America Contest
Council of Trent   San Francisco Earthquake
New York World's Fair   Johnstown Flood
Super Bowl

27. Full names of specific treaties, laws, and acts are capitalized.

Treaty of Versailles
the Nineteenth Amendment
the Bill of Rights
Clean Air Act of 1990
  but
gun-control laws
an equal-rights amendment

28. The words *war, revolution,* and *battle* are capitalized when they are part of a full name. Official names of actions are capitalized. Descriptive terms such as *assault* and *siege* are usually lowercased even when used in conjunction with a place-name.

War of the Roses
World War II
the French Revolution
Battle of Gettysburg
Operation Desert Storm
between the two world wars
the American and French revolutions
the siege of Leningrad
Washington's winter campaign

Hyphenated Compounds

29. The second (third, etc.) element of a hyphenated compound is generally capitalized only if it is itself a proper noun or adjective. (For hyphenated titles, see paragraph 65 below.)

Arab-Israeli negotiations   Forty-second street
East-West trade agreements   twentieth-century architecture
French-speaking peoples

30. When joined to a proper noun or adjective, common prefixes (such as *pre-* or *anti-*) are usually lowercased, but geographical and ethnic combining forms (such as *Anglo-* or *Sino-*) are capitalized. (For details, see paragraphs 45 and 52 on pages 121 and 122.)

anti-Soviet forces
Sino-Japanese relations

Legal Material

31. The names of the plaintiff and defendant in legal case titles are italicized. The *v.* (for *versus*) may be roman or italic. Cases that do not involve two opposing parties are also italicized. When the party involved rather than the case itself is being discussed, the reference is not italicized. In running text, a case name involving two opposing parties may be shortened.

> *Jones* v. *Massachusetts*
> *Smith et al.* v. *Jones*
> *In re Jones*
> She covered the Jones trial for the newspaper.
> The judge based his ruling on a precedent set in the *Jones* decision.

Medical Terms

32. Proper names that are elements in terms designating diseases, symptoms, syndromes, and tests are capitalized. Common nouns are lowercased; however, abbreviations of such nouns are all-capitalized.

Alzheimer's disease	black lung disease
Tourette's syndrome	mumps
Schick test	AIDS

33. Scientific names of disease-causing organisms follow the rules discussed in paragraph 58 on page 97. The names of diseases or conditions derived from scientific names of organisms are lowercased and not italicized.

> a neurotoxin produced by *Clostridium botulinum*
> nearly died of botulism

34. Generic names of drugs are lowercased; trade names should be capitalized.

> retinoic acid
> Retin-A

Military Terms

35. The full titles of branches of the U.S. armed forces are capitalized, as are standard short forms.

U.S. Marine Corps	the Marines
the Marine Corps	the Corps

Those of other countries are capitalized when the precise title is used; otherwise they are usually lowercased. The plurals of *army, navy, air force,* and *coast guard* are lowercased.

> Royal Air Force
> the Guatemalan army
> the tiny armies of both countries

The modifiers *army, navy, marine coast, guard,* and *air force* are usually lower-cased; *naval* is lowercased unless it is part of an official name. The noun *marine* is usually lowercased.

an army helicopter   the first naval engagement
a career navy man   the Naval Reserves
the marine barracks   a former marine

Full or shortened names of specific units of a branch are usually capitalized.

U.S. Army Corps of Engineers
the Third Army
the Eighty-second [*or* 82nd] Airborne
the U.S. Special Forces, or Green Berets
. . . of the First Battalion. The battalion commander . . .

36. Military ranks are capitalized when they precede the names of their hold-ers, or replace the name in direct address. Otherwise they are lowercased.

Major General Smedley Butler
Please be seated, Admiral.
The major arrived precisely on time.

37. The names of decorations, citations, and medals are capitalized.

Medal of Honor
Purple Heart

Numerical Designations

38. A noun introducing a reference number is usually capitalized. The abbre-viation *No.* is usually omitted.

Order 704   Form 2E
Flight 409   Policy 118–4-Y

39. Nouns used with numbers or letters to refer to major reference entities or actual captions in books or periodicals are usually capitalized. Nouns that designate minor reference entities and do not appear in captions are lowercased.

Book II   Figure D.4
Volume 5   page 101
Chapter 2   line 8
Table 3   paragraph 6.1
Example 16.2   question 21

Organizations

40. Names of organizations, corporations, and institutions, and terms de-rived from those names to designate their members, are capitalized.

the League of Women Voters
General Motors Corporation

the Smithsonian Institution
the University of the South
the Rotary Club
all Rotarians

Common nouns used descriptively or occurring after the names of two or more organizations are lowercased.

enrolled at the university
Yale and Harvard universities
but
the Universities of Utah and Nevada

41. Words such as *agency, department, division, group,* or *office* that designate corporate and organizational units are capitalized only when used as part of a specific proper name. (For governmental units, see paragraph 16 on pages 88–89.)

head of the Sales Division of K2 Outfitters
a memo to the sales divisions of both companies

42. Nicknames for organizations are capitalized.

the Big Six accounting firms
referred to IBM as Big Blue
trading on the Big Board

People

43. The names and initials of persons are capitalized. If a name is hyphenated, both elements are capitalized. Particles forming the initial elements of surnames (such as *de, della, der, du, l', la, le, ten, ter, van,* and *von*) may or may not be capitalized, depending on the practice of the family or individual. However, the particle is always capitalized at the beginning of a sentence. The prefixes *Mac, Mc,* and *O'* are always capitalized.

Cecil Day-Lewis
Agnes de Mille
Cecil B. DeMille
Walter de la Mare
Mark deW. Howe
Martin Van Buren
. . . of van Gogh's life. Van Gogh's technique is . .

44. A nickname or epithet that either is added to or replaces the name of a person or thing is capitalized.

Babe Ruth	the Sun King
Stonewall Jackson	Deep Throat
Billy the Kid	Big Mama Thornton

A nickname or epithet placed between a person's first and last name is enclosed in quotation marks or parentheses or both. If it precedes the first name, it is sometimes enclosed in quotation marks but more often not.

> Charlie "Bird" [*or* ("Bird") *or* (Bird)] Parker
> Mother Maybelle Carter

45. Words of family relationship preceding or used in place of a person's name are capitalized; otherwise, they are lowercased.

> Uncle Fred   her uncle's book
> Mother's birthday   my mother's legacy

46. Words designating languages, nationalities, peoples, races, religious groups, and tribes are capitalized. Designations based on color are usually lowercased.

> Spanish   Muslims
> Spaniards   Assiniboin
> Chinese   both blacks and whites
> Asians   white, black, and Hispanic jurors

47. Corporate, professional, and governmental titles are capitalized when they immediately precede a person's name, unless the name is being used as an appositive.

> President John Tyler
> Professor Wendy Doniger of the University of Chicago
> Senator William Fulbright of Arkansas
> Arkansas's late former senator, William Fulbright

48. When corporate or governmental titles are used as part of a descriptive phrase to identify a person rather than as part of the name itself, the title is lowercased.

> Marcia Ramirez, president of Logex Corp.
> the president of Logex Corp., Marcia Ramirez
> *but*
> Logex Corp.'s prospects for the coming year were outlined by President Marcia Ramirez.

49. High governmental titles may be capitalized when used in place of individuals' names. In minutes and official records of proceedings, corporate or organizational titles are capitalized when used in place of individuals' names.

> The Secretary of State objected.
> The Judge will respond to questions in her chambers.
> The Treasurer then stated his misgivings about the project.
> *but*
> The report reached the senator's desk yesterday.
> The judge's rulings were widely criticized.
> The co-op's treasurer, it turned out, had twice been convicted of embezzlement.

50. The word *president* may be capitalized whenever it refers to the U.S. presidency, but more commonly is capitalized only when it refers to a specific U.S. president.

> It is the duty of the president [*or* President] to submit a budget to Congress. The President's budget, due out on Wednesday, is being eagerly awaited.

51. Titles are capitalized when they are used in direct address.

> Is it very contagious, Doctor?
> You may call your next witness, Counselor.

Religious Terms

52. Words designating the supreme being are capitalized. Plural forms such as *gods, goddesses,* and *deities* are not.

Allah	the Almighty
Brahma	the Trinity
Jehovah	in the eyes of God
Yahweh	the angry gods

53. Personal pronouns referring to the supreme being are often capitalized, especially in religious writing. Relative pronouns (such as *who, whom,* and *whose*) usually are not.

> God gave His [*or* his] Son
> Allah, whose Prophet, Muhammad . . .

54. Traditional designations of apostles, prophets, and saints are capitalized.

the Madonna	the Twelve
the Prophet	St. John of the Cross
Moses the Lawgiver	John the Baptist

55. Names of religions, denominations, creeds and confessions, and religious orders are capitalized, as are adjectives and nouns derived from these names.

Judaism	Eastern Orthodox
Church of England	Islamic
Apostles' Creed	Jesuit teachers
Society of Jesus	a Buddhist

Full names of specific places of worship are capitalized, but terms such as *church, synagogue,* and *mosque* are lowercased when used alone. The word *church* is sometimes capitalized when it refers to the worldwide Catholic Church.

Hunt Memorial Church	Beth Israel Synagogue
the local Baptist church	services at the synagogue

56. Names of the Bible and other sacred works, their books and parts, and versions or editions of them are capitalized but not italicized. Adjectives derived from the names of sacred books are capitalized, except for the words *biblical* and *scriptural.*

Bible	biblical
the Scriptures	Talmud
Revised Standard Version	Talmudic
Old Testament	Koran *or* Qur'an
Book of Revelation	Koranic *or* Qur'anic

57. The names of prayers and well-known passages of the Bible are capitalized.

the Ave Maria	Ten Commandments
Lord's Prayer	Sermon on the Mount
the Our Father	the Beatitudes

Scientific Terms

58. Genus names in biological binomial nomenclature are capitalized; species names are lowercased, even when derived from a proper name. Both names are italicized.

> Both the wolf and the domestic dog are included in the genus *Canis.*
> The California condor (*Gymnogyps californianus*) is facing extinction.

The names of races, varieties, or subspecies are lowercased and italicized.

> *Hyla versicolor chrysoscelis*
> *Otis asio naevius*

59. The New Latin names of classes, families, and all groups above the genus level in zoology and botany are capitalized but not italicized. Their derivative nouns and adjectives are lowercased.

Gastropoda	gastropod
Thallophyta	thallophytic

60. The names, both scientific and informal, of planets and their satellites, stars, constellations, and other specific celestial objects are capitalized. However, except in technical writing, the words *sun, earth,* and *moon* are usually lowercased unless they occur with other astronomical names. A generic term that follows the name of a celestial object is usually lowercased.

Jupiter	Mars, Venus, and Earth
the North Star	life on earth
Andromeda	a voyage to the moon
Ursa Major	Halley's comet
the Little Dipper	

Names of meterorological phenomena are lowercased.

> aurora australis
> northern lights
> parhelic circle

61. Terms that identify geological eons, eras, periods, systems, epochs, and strata are capitalized. The generic terms that follow them are lowercased.

Mesozoic era	in the Middle Ordovician
Upper Cretaceous epoch	the Age of Reptiles
Quaternary period	

62. Proper names that are elements of the names of scientific laws, theorems, and principles are capitalized, but the common nouns *law, theorem, theory,* and the like are lowercased. In the names of popular or fanciful theories or observations, such words are usually capitalized as well.

Mendel's law	Einstein's theory of relativity
the Pythagorean theorem	Murphy's Law
Occam's razor	the Peter Principle

63. The names of computer services and databases are capitalized. Some names of computer languages are written with an initial capital letter, some with all letters capitalized, and some commonly both ways. When in doubt, consult a dictionary.

America Online	BASIC
World Wide Web	Pascal *or* PASCAL
CompuServe	Internet *or* internet
Microsoft Word	

Time Periods and Dates

64. The names of the days of the week, months of the year, and holidays and holy days are capitalized. Names of the seasons are lowercased.

Tuesday	Ramadan
June	Holy Week
Yom Kippur	last winter's storm
Veterans Day	

Titles of Works

65. Words in titles of books, magazines, newspapers, plays, movies, long poems, and works of art such as paintings and sculpture are capitalized except for internal articles, coordinating conjunctions, prepositions, and the *to* of infinitives. Prepositions of four or more letters are often capitalized. The entire title is italicized. For sacred works, see paragraph 56 on page 97.

Far from [or *From*] *the Madding Crowd*
Wolfe's *Of Time and the River*
Publishers Weekly
USA Today
the original play *A Streetcar Named Desire*
All about [or *About*] *Eve,* with Bette Davis
Monet's *Water-Lily Pool,* in the Louvre
Rodin's *Thinker*

The elements of hyphenated compounds in titles are usually capitalized, but articles, coordinating conjunctions, and prepositions are lowercased.

> *The Post-Physician Era: Medicine in the Twenty-First Century*
> *Politics in Early Seventeenth-Century England*

66. The first word following a colon in a title is capitalized.

> *Jane Austen: A Literary Life*

67. An initial article that is part of a title is capitalized and italicized. It is often omitted if it would be awkward in context.

> *The Oxford English Dictionary*
> the 20-volume *Oxford English Dictionary*

68. In the titles of newspapers, the city or local name is usually italicized, but the preceding *the* is usually not italicized or capitalized.

> reported in the *New York Times*
> last Thursday's *Atlanta Constitution*

69. Many periodicals, especially newspapers, do not use italics for titles, but instead either simply capitalize the important words of the title or, more commonly, capitalize the words and enclose the title in quotation marks.

> the NB. column in the Times Literary Supplement
> The Nobel committee singled out Walcott's book-length epic "Omeros."

70. The titles of articles in periodicals, short poems, short stories, essays, lectures, dissertations, chapters of books, radio and television programs, and novellas published in a collection are capitalized and enclosed in quotation marks. The capitalization of articles, conjunctions, and prepositions follows the rules explained in paragraph 65 above.

> an article on Rwanda, "After the Genocide," in the *New Yorker*
> Robert Frost's "The Death of the Hired Man"
> O'Connor's story "Good Country People"
> "The Literature of Exhaustion," John Barth's seminal essay
> last Friday's lecture, "Labor's Task: A View for the Nineties"
> *The Jungle Book*'s ninth chapter is the well-known "Rikki-tikki-tavi."
> listening to "All Things Considered"
> watched "Good Morning America"

71. The titles of long musical compositions are generally capitalized and italicized; the titles of songs and other short compositions are capitalized and enclosed in quotation marks, as are the popular names of longer works. The titles of compositions identified primarily by their musical forms (such as *quartet, sonata,* or *mass*) are capitalized only, as are movements identified by their tempo markings.

> Mozart's *The Magic Flute*
> Frank Loesser's *Guys and Dolls*

"The Lady Is a Tramp"
Beethoven's "Für Elise"
the Piano Sonata in C-sharp minor, Op. 27, No. 2, or "Moonlight" Sonata
Symphony No. 104 in D major
Brahms's Violin Concerto in D
the Adagietto movement from Mahler's Fifth Symphony

72. Common titles of book sections (such as *preface, introduction,* or *index*) are usually capitalized when they refer to a section of the same book in which the reference is made. Otherwise, they are usually lowercased. (For numbered sections of books, see paragraph 39 on page 93).

See the Appendix for further information.
In the introduction to her book, the author explains her goals.

Trademarks

73. Registered trademarks, service marks, collective marks, and brand names are capitalized. They do not normally require any further acknowledgment of their special status.

Frisbee	Jacuzzi	Levi's
Coke	Kleenex	Vaseline
College Board	Velcro	Dumpster
Realtor	Xerox	Scotch tape
Walkman	Band-Aid	Teflon

Transportation

74. The names of individual ships, submarines, airplanes, satellites, and space vehicles are capitalized and italicized. The designations *U.S.S., S.S., M.V.,* and *H.M.S.* are not italicized.

Challenger
Enola Gay
H.M.S. *Bounty*

OTHER STYLING CONVENTIONS

1. Foreign words and phrases that have not been fully adopted into English are italicized. In general, any word that appears in the main section of *Merriam-Webster's Collegiate Dictionary* does not need to be italicized.

These accomplishments will serve as a monument, *aere perennius,* to the group's skill and dedication.
"The cooking here is *wunderbar!*"
The prix fixe lunch was $20.
The committee meets on an ad hoc basis.

A complete foreign-language sentence (such as a motto) can also be italicized. However, long sentences are usually treated as quotations; that is, they are set in roman type and enclosed in quotation marks. (For details, see paragraph 6 on page 76.)

The inscription *Honi soit qui mal y pense* encircles the seal.

2. In nonfiction writing, unfamiliar words or words that have a specialized meaning are set in italics on their first appearance, especially when accompanied by a short definition. Once these words have been introduced and defined, they are not italicized in subsequent references.

> *Vitiligo* is a condition in which skin pigment cells stop making pigment. Vitiligo usually affects . . .
>
> Another method is the *direct-to-consumer* transaction, in which the publisher markets directly to the individual by mail or door-to-door.

3. Italics are often used to indicate words referred to as words. However, if the word was actually spoken, it is usually enclosed in quotation marks instead.

> Purists still insist that *data* is a plural noun.
>
> *Only* can also be an adverb, as in "I *only* tried to help."
>
> We heard his warning, but we weren't sure what "repercussions" meant in that context.

4. Italics are often used for letters referred to as letters, particularly when they are shown in lowercase.

> You should dot your *i*'s and cross your *t*'s.

If the letter is being used to refer to its sound and not its printed form, slashes or brackets are used instead of italics in technical contexts.

> The pure /p/ sound is rarely heard in the mountain dialect.

A letter used to indicate a shape is capitalized but not italicized. Such letters are often set in sans-serif type.

> an A-frame house   Churchill's famous V sign
>
> the I beam   forming a giant X

5. Italics are often used to show numerals referred to as numerals. However, if there is no chance of confusion, they are usually not italicized.

> The first *2* and the last *1* are barely legible.
>
> Anyone whose ticket number ends in 4 or 6 will win a door prize.

6. Italics are used to emphasize or draw attention to words in a sentence.

> Students must notify the dean's office *in writing* of any added or dropped courses.
>
> It was not *the* model for the project, but merely *a* model.

7. Italics are used to indicate a word created to suggest a sound.

> Its call is a harsh, drawn-out *kreee-awww.*

8. Individual letters are sometimes italicized when used for lists within sentences or for identifying elements in an illustration.

> providing information about *(a)* typing, *(b)* transcribing, *(c)* formatting, and *(d)* graphics
>
> located at point A on the diagram

9. Commas, colons, and semicolons that follow italicized words are usually italicized.

> the Rabbit tetralogy (*Rabbit Run, Rabbit Redux, Rabbit Is Rich,* and *Rabbit at Rest*); *Bech: A Book; S;* and others

However, question marks, exclamation points, quotation marks, and apostrophes are not italicized unless they are part of an italicized title.

> Did you see the latest issue of *Newsweek?*
> Despite the greater success of *Oklahoma!* and *South Pacific,* Rodgers was fondest of *Carousel.*
> "Over Christmas vacation he finished *War and Peace.*"
> Students always mistake the old script *s*'s for *f*'s.

Parentheses and brackets may be italicized if most of the words they enclose are also italicized, or if both the first and last words are italicized.

> *(see also Limited Partnership)*
> [German, *wunderbar*]
> *(and* is replaced throughout by *&)*

10. Full capitalization is occasionally used for emphasis or to indicate that a speaker is talking very loudly. It is avoided in formal writing, where italics are far more often used for emphasis.

> Term papers received after Friday, May 18, WILL BE RETURNED UNREAD.
> Scalpers mingled in the noisy crowd yelling "SIXTY DOLLARS!"

11. The text of signs, labels, and inscriptions may be reproduced in various ways.

> a poster reading SPECIAL THRILLS COMING SOON
> a gate bearing the infamous motto "Arbeit macht frei"
> a Do Not Disturb sign
> a barn with an old CHEW MAIL POUCH ad on the side
> the stop sign

12. *Small capitals,* identical to large capitals but usually about the height of a lowercase *x*, are commonly used for era designations and computer commands. They may also be used for cross-references, for headings in constitutions and bylaws, and for speakers in a dramatic dialogue.

> The dwellings date from A.D. 200 or earlier.
> Press ALT + CTRL + PLUS + SIGN on the numeric keyboard.
> (See LETTERS AS LETTERS, page 162.)
> SECTION IV. The authority for parliamentary procedure in meetings of the Board . . .
> LADY WISHFORT. O dear, has my Nephew made his Addresses to Millamant? I order'd him.
> FOIBLE. Sir Wilfull is set in to drinking, Madam, in the Parlour.

13. *Underlining* indicates italics in typed material. It is almost never seen in typeset text.

14. *Boldface* type has traditionally been used primarily for headings and captions. It is sometimes also used in place of italics for terminology introduced in the text, especially for terms that are accompanied by definitions; for cross-references; for headwords in listings such as glossaries, gazetteers, and bibliographies; and for page references in indexes that locate a specific kind of material, such as illustrations, tables, or the main discussions of a given topic. (In mathematical texts, arrays, tensors, vectors, and matrix notation are standardly set bold as well.)

> **Application Forms and Tests** Many offices require applicants to fill out an employment form. Bring a copy . . .
> **Figure 4.2: The Electromagnetic Spectrum**
> The two axes intersect at a point called the **origin**.
> See **Medical Records**, page 123.
> **antecedent:** the noun to which a pronoun refers
> **appositive:** a word, phrase, or clause that is equivalent to a preceding noun
> Records, medical, **123–37**, 178, 243
> Referrals, **38–40**, 139

Punctuation that follows boldface type is set bold when it is part of a heading or heading-like text; otherwise it is generally set roman.

> **Table 9:** Metric Conversion
> **Warning:** This and similar medications . . .
> Excellent fourth-quarter earnings were reported by the pharmaceutical giants **Abbott Laboratories**, **Burroughs Wellcome**, and **Merck**.

Plurals and Possessives

The next sections describe the ways in which plurals, possessives, and compounds are most commonly formed.

In regard to plurals and compounds, consulting a dictionary will solve many of the problems discussed in this chapter. A good college dictionary, such as *Merriam-Webster's Collegiate Dictionary,* will provide plural forms for any common word, as well as a large number of permanent compounds. Any dictionary much smaller than the *Collegiate* will often be more frustrating in what it fails to show than helpful in what it shows.

PLURALS

The basic rules for writing plurals of English words, stated in paragraph 1, apply in the vast majority of cases. The succeeding paragraphs treat the categories of words whose plurals are most apt to raise questions.

Most good dictionaries give thorough coverage to irregular and variant plurals, and many of the rules provided here are reflected in the dictionary entries.

The symbol → is used here to link the singular and plural forms.

1. The plurals of most English words are formed by adding *-s* to the singular. If the noun ends in *-s*, *-x*, *-z*, *-ch*, or *-sh*, so that an extra syllable must be added in order to pronounce the plural, *-es* is added. If the noun ends in a *-y* preceded by a consonant, the *-y* is changed to *-i* and *-es* is added.

voter → voters	blowtorch → blowtorches
anticlimax → anticlimaxes	calabash → calabashes
blitz → blitzes	allegory → allegories

Abbreviations

2. The plurals of abbreviations are commonly formed by adding *-s* or *-'s;* however, there are some significant exceptions. (For details, see paragraphs 1–5 on pages 126–27.)

yr. → yrs.	M.B.A. → M.B.A.'s
TV → TVs	p. → pp.

Animals

3. The names of many fishes, birds, and mammals have both a plural formed with a suffix and one that is identical with the singular. Some have only one or the other.

bass → bass *or* basses	lion → lions
partridge → partridge *or* partridges	sheep → sheep
sable → sables *or* sable	

Many of the animals that have both plural forms are ones that are hunted, fished, or trapped; those who hunt, fish for, and trap them are most likely to use the unchanged form. The *-s* form is often used to emphasize diversity of kinds.

caught three bass
but
basses of the Atlantic Ocean
a place where antelope feed
but
antelopes of Africa and southwest Asia

Compounds and Phrases

4. Most compounds made up of two nouns—whether they appear as one word, two words, or a hyphenated word—form their plurals by pluralizing the final element only.

courthouse → courthouses
judge advocate → judge advocates
player-manager → player-managers

5. The plural form of a compound consisting of an *-er* noun and an adverb is made by pluralizing the noun element only.

   runner-up → runners-up   diner-out → diners-out
   onlooker → onlookers   passerby → passersby

6. Nouns made up of words that are not nouns form their plurals on the last element.

   show-off → show-offs
   pushover → pushovers
   tie-in → tie-ins
   lineup → lineups

7. Plurals of compounds that consist of two nouns separated by a preposition are normally formed by pluralizing the first noun.

   sister-in-law → sisters-in-law   chief of staff → chiefs of staff
   attorney-at-law → attorneys-at-law   grant-in-aid → grants-in-aid
   power of attorney → powers of
     attorney

8. Compounds that consist of two nouns separated by a preposition and a modifier form their plurals in various ways.

   snake in the grass → snakes in the grass
   justice of the peace → justices of the peace
   jack-in-the-box → jack-in-the-boxes *or* jacks-in-the-box
   will-o'-the wisp → will-o'-the-wisps

9. Compounds consisting of a noun followed by an adjective are usually pluralized by adding *-s* to the noun. If the adjective tends to be understood as a noun, the compound may have more than one plural form.

   attorney general → attorneys general *or* attorney generals
   sergeant major → sergeants major *or* sergeant majors
   poet laureate → poets laureate *or*   poet laureates
   heir apparent → heirs apparent
   knight-errant → knights-errant

Foreign Words and Phrases

10. Many nouns of foreign origin retain the foreign plural. However, most also have a regular English plural.

    alumnus → alumni
    genus → genera
    crisis → crises
    criterion → criteria
    appendix → appendixes *or* appendices
    concerto → concerti *or* concertos
    symposium → symposia *or* symposiums

11. Phrases of foreign origin may have a foreign plural, an English plural, or both.

> pièce de résistance → pièces de résistance
> hors d'oeuvre → hors d'oeuvres
> beau monde → beau mondes   *or*   beaux mondes

Irregular Plurals

12. A few English nouns form their plurals by changing one or more of their vowels, or by adding *-en* or *-ren*.

> foot → feet   woman → women
> goose → geese   tooth → teeth
> louse → lice   ox → oxen
> man → men   child → children
> mouse → mice

13. Some nouns do not change form in the plural. (See also paragraph 3 above.)

> series → series   corps → corps
> politics → politics   species → species

14. Some nouns ending in *-f*, *-fe*, and *-ff* have plurals that end in *-ves*. Some of these also have regularly formed plurals.

> elf → elves   wife → wives
> loaf → loaves   staff → staffs   *or*   staves
> scarf → scarves   *or*   scarfs

Italic Elements

15. Italicized words, phrases, abbreviations, and letters are usually pluralized by adding *-s* or *-'s* in roman type. (See also paragraphs 16, 21, and 26 below.)

> three *Fortune*s missing from the stack
> a couple of *Gravity's Rainbow*s in stock
> used too many *etc.*'s in the report
> a row of *x*'s

Letters

16. The plurals of letters are usually formed by adding *-'s*, although capital letters are often pluralized by adding *-s* alone.

> p's and q's
> V's of migrating geese   *or*   Vs of migrating geese
> dot your *i*'s
> straight As   *or*   straight A's

Numbers

17. Numerals are pluralized by adding *-s* or, less commonly, *-'s*.

> two par 5s   *or*   two par 5's
> 1990s   *or*   1990's
> in the 80s   *or*   in the 80's   *or*   in the '80s
> the mid-$20,000s   *or*   the mid-$20,000's

18. Written-out numbers are pluralized by adding *-s*.

> all the fours and eights
> scored three tens

Proper Nouns

19. The plurals of proper nouns are usually formed with *-s* or *-es*.

> Clarence → Clarences
> Jones → Joneses
> Fernandez → Fernandezes

20. Plurals of proper nouns ending in *-y* usually retain the *-y* and add *-s*.

> Sunday → Sundays
> Timothy → Timothys
> Camry → Camrys

Words ending in *-y* that were originally proper nouns are usually pluralized by changing *-y* to *-i* and adding *-es*, but a few retain the *-y*.

> bobby → bobbies   Tommy → Tommies
> johnny → johnnies   Bloody Mary → Bloody Marys

Quoted Elements

21. The plural of words in quotation marks are formed by adding *-s* or *-'s* within the quotation marks, or *-s* outside the quotation marks. (See also paragraph 26 below.)

> too many "probably's" [*or* "probablys"] in the statement
> one "you" among millions of "you"s
> a record number of "I can't recall"s

Symbols

22. When symbols are referred to as physical characters, the plural is formed by adding either *-s* or *-'s*.

> printed three *s
> used &'s instead of *and*'s
> his π's are hard to read

Words Ending in *-ay, -ey,* and *-oy*

23. Words that end in *-ay, -ey,* or *-oy,* unlike other words ending in *-y,* are pluralized by simply adding *-s*.

> castaways
> donkeys
> envoys

Words Ending in *-ful*

24. Any noun ending in *-ful* can be pluralized by adding *-s,* but most also have an alternative plural with *-s-* preceding the suffix.

> handful → handfuls
> teaspoonful → teaspoonfuls
> armful → armfuls *or* armsful
> bucketful → bucketfuls *or* bucketsful

Words Ending in *-o*

25. Most words ending in *-o* are normally pluralized by adding *-s.* However, some words ending in *-o* preceded by a consonant take *-es* plurals.

solo → solos	cargo → cargoes *or* cargos
photo → photos	proviso → provisos *or* provisoes
tomato → tomatoes	halo → haloes *or* halos
potato → potatoes	echo → echoes
hobo → hoboes	motto → mottoes
hero → heroes	

Words Used as Words

26. Words referred to as words and italicized usually form their plurals by adding *-'s* in roman type. (See also paragraph 21 above.)

> five *and*'s in one sentence
> all those *wherefore*'s and *howsoever*'s

When a word referred to as a word has become part of a fixed phrase, the plural is usually formed by adding *-s* without the apostrophe.

> oohs and aahs
> dos and don'ts *or* do's and don'ts

POSSESSIVES

Common Nouns

1. The possessive of singular and plural common nouns that do not end in an *s* or *z* sound is formed by adding *-'s* to the end of the word.

the child's skates	this patois's range
women's voices	people's opinions
the cat's dish	the criteria's common theme

2. The possessive of singular nouns ending in an *s* or *z* sound is usually formed by adding *-'s.* A less common alternative is to add *-'s* only when it is easily pronounced; if it would create a word that is difficult to pronounce, only an apostrophe is added.

> the witness's testimony
> the disease's course
> the race's sponsors
> the prize's recipient
> rickets's symptoms *or* rickets' symptoms

A multisyllabic singular noun that ends in an *s* or *z* sound drops the -*s* if it is followed by a word beginning with an *s* or *z* sound.

> for appearance' sake
> for goodness' sake

3. The possessive of plural nouns ending in an *s* or *z* sound is formed by adding only an apostrophe. However, the possessive of one-syllable irregular plurals is usually formed by adding -*'s*.

> dogs' leashes   buyers' guarantees
> birds' migrations   lice's lifespans

Proper Names

4. The possessives of proper names are generally formed in the same way as those of common nouns. The possessive of singular proper names is formed by adding -*'s*.

> Jane's rules of behavior   Tom White's presentation
> three books of Carla's   Paris's cafes

The possessive of plural proper names, and of some singular proper names ending in an *s* or *z* sound, is made by adding just an apostrophe.

> the Stevenses' reception   New Orleans' annual festival
> the Browns' driveway   the United States' trade deficit
> Massachusetts' capital   Protosystems' president

5. The possessive of singular proper names ending in an *s* or *z* sound may be formed by adding either -*'s* or just an apostrophe. Adding -*'s* to all such names, without regard for the pronunciation of the resulting word, is more common than adding just the apostrophe. (For exceptions see paragraph 6 below).

> Jones's car   *or*   Jones' car
> Bliss's statue   *or*   Bliss' statue
> Dickens's novels   *or*   Dickens' novels

6. The possessive form of classical and biblical names of two or more syllables ending in -*s* or -*es* is usually made by adding just an apostrophe. If the name has only one syllable, the possessive form is made by adding -*'s*.

> Socrates' students   Elias' prophecy
> Claudius' reign   Zeus's warnings
> Ramses' kingdom   Cis's sons

The possessives of the names *Jesus* and *Moses* are always formed with just an apostrophe.

> Jesus' disciples
> Moses' law

7. The possessive of names ending in a silent -*s*, -*z*, or -*x* are usually formed with -'*s*.

   Des Moines's recreation department
   Josquin des Prez's music
   Delacroix's painting

8. When the possessive ending is added to an italicized name, it is not italicized.

   East of Eden's main characters
   the *Spirit of St. Louis*'s historic flight
   Brief Encounter's memorable ending

Pronouns

9. The possessive of indefinite pronouns is formed by adding -'*s*.

anyone's rights	somebody's wedding
everybody's money	one's own
someone's coat	either's preference

   Some indefinite pronouns usually require an *of* phrase to indicate possession.

   the rights of each
   the inclination of many
   the satisfaction of all

10. Possessive pronouns do not include apostrophes.

mine	hers
ours	his
yours	theirs
its	

Miscellaneous Styling Conventions

11. No apostrophe is generally used today with plural nouns that are more descriptive than possessive.

weapons systems	steelworkers union
managers meeting	awards banquet
singles bar	

12. The possessive form of a phrase is made by adding an apostrophe or -'*s* to the last word in the phrase.

    his father-in-law's assistance
    board of directors' meeting
    from the student of politics' point of view
    after a moment or so's though

Constructions such as these are often rephrased.

> from the point of view of the student of politics
> after thinking for a moment or so

13. The possessive form of words in quotation marks can be formed in two ways, with -'s placed either inside the quotation marks or outside them.

> the "Marseillaise"'s [*or* "Marseillaise's"] stirring melody

Since both arrangements look awkward, this construction is usually avoided.

> the stirring melody of the "Marseillaise"

14. Possessives of abbreviations are formed like those of nouns that are spelled out. The singular possessive is formed by adding -'s; the plural possessive, by adding an apostrophe only.

> the IRS's ruling
> AT&T's long-distance service
> IBM Corp.'s annual report
> Eli Lilly & Co.'s chairman
> the HMOs' lobbyists

15. The possessive of nouns composed of numerals is formed in the same way as for other nouns. The possessive of singular nouns is formed by adding -'s; the possessive of plural nouns is formed by adding an apostrophe only.

> 1996's commencement speaker
> the 1920s' greatest jazz musicians

16. Individual possession is indicated by adding -'s to each noun in a sequence. Joint possession may be indicated in the same way, but is most commonly indicated by adding an apostrophe or -'s to the last noun in the sequence.

> Joan's and Emily's friends
> Jim's, Ed's, and Susan's reports
> her mother and father's anniversary
> Peter and Jan's trip   *or*   Peter's and Jan's trip

Compounds

A compound is a word or word group that consists of two or more parts that work together as a unit to express a specific concept. Compounds can be formed by combining two or more words (as in *double-check, cost-effective, farmhouse, graphic equalizer, park bench, around-the-clock,* or *son of a gun*), by combining prefixes or suffixes with words (as in *ex-president, shoeless, presorted,* or *uninterruptedly*), or by combining two or more word elements (as in *macrophage* or *photochromism*). Compounds are written in one of three ways: solid (as in *cottonmouth*), hyphenated (*screenwriter-director*), or open (*health care*). Because of the variety of standard practice, the choice among these styles for a given compound represents one of the most common and vexing of all style issues that writers encounter.

A good dictionary will list many *permanent compounds,* compounds so commonly used that they have become permanent parts of the language. It will not list *temporary compounds,* those created to meet a writer's need at a particular moment. Most compounds whose meanings are self-evident from the meanings of their component words will not be listed, even if they are permanent and quite widely used. Writers thus cannot rely wholly on dictionaries to guide them in writing compounds.

One approach is to hyphenate all compounds not in the dictionary, since hyphenation immediately identifies them as compounds. But hyphenating all such compounds runs counter to some well-established American practice and can therefore call too much attention to the compound and momentarily distract the reader. Another approach (which applies only to compounds whose elements are complete words) is to leave open any compound not in the dictionary. Though this is widely done, it can result in the reader's failing to recognize a compound for what it is. A third approach is to pattern the compound after other similar ones. Though this approach is likely to be more complicated, it can make the compound look more familiar and thus less distracting or confusing. The paragraphs that follow are intended to help you use this approach.

As a general rule, writing meant for readers in specialized fields usually does not hyphenate compounds, especially technical terminology.

Compound Nouns

Compound nouns are combinations of words that function in a sentence as nouns. They may consist of two or more nouns, a noun and a modifier, or two or more elements that are not nouns.

Short compounds consisting of two nouns often begin as open compounds but tend to close up as they become familiar.

1. **noun + noun**   Compounds composed of two nouns that are short and commonly used, of which the first is accented, are usually written solid.

farmhouse	lifeboat	football
hairbrush	paycheck	workplace

2. When a noun + noun compound is short and common but pronounced with nearly equal stress on both nouns, it is more likely to be open.

fuel oil	health care
park bench	desk lamp

3. Noun + noun compounds that consist of longer nouns and are self-evident or temporary are usually written open.

> costume designer
> computer terminal
> billiard table

4. When a noun + noun compound describes a double title or double function, the compound is hyphenated.

> hunter-gatherer
> secretary-treasurer
> bar-restaurant

Sometimes a slash is used in place of the hyphen.

> bar/restaurant

5. Compounds formed from a noun or adjective followed by *man, woman, person,* or *people* and denoting an occupation are normally solid.

anchorman	spokesperson
congresswoman	salespeople

6. Compounds that are units of measurement are hyphenated.

foot-pound	column-inch
kilowatt-hour	light-year

7. **adjective + noun**   Most adjective + noun compounds are written open.

municipal court	minor league
genetic code	nuclear medicine
hazardous waste	basic training

8. Adjective + noun compounds consisting of two short words are often written solid when the first word is accented. However, some are usually written open, and a few are hyphenated.

notebook	shortcut	steel mill
bluebird	dry cleaner	two-step

9. **participle + noun**   Most participle + noun compounds are written open.

landing craft	sounding board	preferred stock
frying pan	barbed wire	informal consent

10. **noun's + noun**   Compounds consisting of a possessive noun followed by another noun are usually written open; a few are hyphenated. Compounds of this type that have become solid have lost the apostrophe.

fool's gold	Queen Anne's lace	foolscap
hornet's nest	cat's-paw	menswear
seller's market	bull's-eye	

11. **noun + verb + *-er* or *-ing*** Compounds in which the first noun is the object of the verb or gerund to which the suffix has been added are most often written open but sometimes hyphenated. Permanent compounds like these are sometimes written solid.

problem solver	street-sweeping	air conditioner
deal making	fund-raiser	lifesaving
ticket-taker	gene-splicing	

12. **object + verb** Noun compounds consisting of a verb preceded by a noun that is its object are written in various ways.

fish fry	bodyguard
eye-opener	roadblock

13. **verb + object** A few, mostly older compounds are formed from a verb followed by a noun that is its object; they are written solid.

cutthroat	carryall
breakwater	pickpocket

14. **noun + adjective** Compounds composed of a noun followed by an adjective are written open or hyphenated.

sum total	president-elect
consul general	secretary-general

15. **particle + noun** Compounds consisting of a particle (usually a preposition or adverb) and a noun are usually written solid, especially when they are short and the first syllable is accented.

downturn	outpatient	afterthought
outfield	undertone	onrush
input	upswing	

A few particle + noun compounds, especially when composed of longer elements or having equal stress on both elements, are hyphenated or open.

on-ramp	off year
cross-reference	cross fire

16. **verb + particle; verb + adverb** These compounds may be hyphenated or solid. Compounds with particles such as *to, in,* and *on* are often hyphenated. Compounds with particles such as *up, off,* and *out* are hyphenated or solid with about equal frequency. Those with longer particles or adverbs are usually solid.

lean-to	backup	time-out
trade-in	spin-off	turnout
add-on	payoff	hideaway
start-up		

17. **verb + -*er* + particle; verb + -*ing* + particle**   Except for *passerby,* these compounds are hyphenated.

runner-up	listener-in	talking-to
diners-out	carrying-on	falling-out

18. **letter + noun**   Compounds formed from a single letter (or sometimes a combination of them) followed by a noun are either open or hyphenated.

T square	T-shirt
B vitamin	ƒstop
V neck	H-bomb
Rh factor	A-frame
D major	E-mail *or* e-mail

19. **Compounds of three or four elements**   Compounds of three or four words may be either hyphenated or open. Those incorporating prepositional phrases are more often open; others are usually hyphenated.

editor in chief	right-of-way
power of attorney	jack-of-all-trades
flash in the pan	give-and-take
base on balls	rough-and-tumble

20. **Reduplication compounds**   Compounds that are formed by reduplication and so consist of two similar-sounding elements are hyphenated if each element has more than one syllable. If each element has only one syllable, the compound is often written solid. Very short words and newly coined words are more often hyphenated.

namby-pamby	crisscross	sci-fi
razzle-dazzle	singsong	hip-hop

Compound Adjectives

Compound adjectives are combinations of words that work together to modify a noun—that is, they work as *unit modifiers.* As unit modifiers they can be distinguished from other strings of adjectives that may also precede a noun.

For instance, in "a low, level tract of land" the two adjectives each modify the noun separately; the tract is both low and level. These are *coordinate* (i.e., equal) *modifiers.* In "a low monthly fee" the first adjective modifies the noun plus the second adjective; the phrase denotes a monthly fee that is low. It could not be revised to "a monthly and low fee" without altering or confusing its meaning. Thus, these are *noncoordinate modifiers.* However, "low-level radiation" does not mean radiation that is low and level or level radiation that is low, but rather radiation that is at a low level. Both words work as a unit to modify the noun.

Unit modifiers are usually hyphenated, in order to help readers grasp the relationship of the words and to avoid confusion. The hyphen in "a call for more-specialized controls" removes any ambiguity as to which word *more* modifies. By contrast, the lack of a hyphen in a phrase like "graphic arts exhibition" may give it an undesirable ambiguity.

21. **Before the noun (attributive position)** Most two-word compound adjectives are hyphenated when placed before the noun.

> the fresh-cut grass
> its longer-lasting effects
> her lace-trimmed dress
> a made-up excuse
> his best-selling novel
> projected health-care costs

22. Compounds whose first word is an adverb ending in *-ly* are usually left open.

> a privately chartered boat
> politically correct opinions
> its weirdly skewed perspective
> a tumultuously cascading torrent

23. Compounds formed of an adverb not ending in *-ly* followed by a participle (or sometimes an adjective) are usually hyphenated when placed before a noun.

> the well-worded statement
> more-stringent measures
> his less-exciting prospects
> their still-awaited assignments
> her once-famous uncle

24. The combination of *very* + adjective is not a unit modifier. (See also paragraph 33 below.)

> a very happy baby

25. When a compound adjective is formed by using a compound noun to modify another noun, it is usually hyphenated.

> a hazardous-waste site
> the basic-training period
> a minor-league pitcher
> a roll-call vote
> their problem-solving abilities

Some familiar open compound nouns are frequently left open when used as adjectives.

> a high school diploma   *or*   a high-school diploma
> a real estate license   *or*   a real-estate license
> an income tax refund   *or*   an income-tax refund

26. A proper name used as a modifier is not hyphenated. A word that modifies the proper name is attached by a hyphen (or an en dash in typeset material).

> the Civil War era
> a New England tradition
> a *New York Times* article
> the Supreme Court decision
> the splendid *Gone with the Wind* premiere
> a Los Angeles-based company
> a Pulitzer Prize–winning author
> pre–Bull Run skirmishes

27. Compound adjectives composed of foreign words are not hyphenated when placed before a noun unless they are hyphenated in the foreign language itself.

> per diem expenses
> an ad hoc committee
> her *faux-naif* style
> a comme il faut arrangement
> the a cappella chorus
> a ci-devant professor

28. Compounds that are quoted, capitalized, or italicized are not hyphenated.

> a "Springtime in Paris" theme
> the book's "I'm OK, you're OK" tone
> his AMERICA FIRST sign
> the *No Smoking* notice

29. Chemical names and most medical names used as modifiers are not hyphenated.

> a sodium hypochlorite bleach
> the amino acid sequence
> a new Parkinson's disease medication

30. Compound adjectives of three or more words are hyphenated when they precede the noun.

> step-by-step instructions
> state-of-the-art equipment
> a wait-and-see attitude
> a longer-than-expected list
> turn-of-the-century medicine

31. Following the noun When a compound adjective follows the noun it modifies, it usually ceases to be a unit modifier and is therefore no longer hyphenated.

> instructions that guide you step by step
> a list that was longer than expected

However, a compound that follows the noun it modifies often keeps its hyphen if it continues to function as a unit modifier, especially if its first element is a noun.

> hikers who were ill-advised to cross the glacier
> an actor too high-strung to relax
> industries that could be called low-tech
> metals that are corrosion-resistant
> tends to be accident-prone

32. Permanent compound adjectives are usually written as they appear in the dictionary even when they follow the noun they modify.

> for reasons that are well-known
> a plan we regarded as half-baked
> The problems are mind-boggling.

However, compound adjectives of three or more words are normally not hyphenated when they follow the noun they modify, since they usually cease to function as adjectives.

> These remarks are off the record.
> medical practice of the turn of the century

When compounds of three or more words appear as hyphenated adjectives in dictionaries, the hyphens are retained as long as the phrase is being used as a unit modifier.

> The candidate's position was middle-of-the-road

33. When an adverb modifies another adverb that is the first element of a compound modifier, the compound may lose its hyphen. If the first adverb modifies the whole compound, however, the hyphen is retained.

> a very well developed idea
> *but*
> a delightfully well-written book
> a most ill-timed event

34. Adjective compounds that are color names in which each element can function as a noun are almost always hyphenated.

> red-orange fabric
> The fabric was red-orange.

Color names in which the first element can only be an adjective are often unhyphenated before a noun and usually unhyphenated after.

> a bright red tie
> the pale yellow-green chair
> reddish orange fabric   *or*   reddish-orange fabric
> The fabric was reddish orange.

35. Compound modifiers that include a number followed by a noun (except for the noun *percent*) are hyphenated when they precede the noun they modify, but usually not when they follow it. (For details on measurement, see paragraph 42 on pages 149–50.)

> the four-color press
> a 12-foot-high fence
> a fence 12 feet high
> a 300-square-mile area
> an area of 300 square miles
> *but*
> a 10 percent raise

  If a currency symbol precedes the number, the hyphen is omitted.

> an $8.5 million deficit

36. An adjective composed of a number followed by a noun in the possessive is not hyphenated.

> a nine days' wonder
> a two weeks' wait
> *but*
> a two-week wait

Compound Adverbs

37. Adverb compounds consisting of preposition + noun are almost always written solid. However, there are a few important exceptions.

> downstairs
> uphill
> offshore
> overnight
> *but*
> in-house
> off-key
> on-line

38. Compound adverbs of more than two words are usually written open, and they usually follow the words they modify.

> here and there
> more or less
> head and shoulders
> hand in hand
> every which way
> once and for all
> *but*
> a more-or-less certain result

A few three-word adverbs are usually hyphenated, but many are written open even if the corresponding adjective is hyphenated.

> placed back-to-back
> met face-to-face
> *but*
> a word-for-word quotation
> quoted word for word
> software bought off the shelf

Compound Verbs

39. Two-word verbs consisting of a verb followed by an adverb or a preposition are written open.

follow up	strike out	run across
roll back	take on	set back

40. A compound composed of a particle followed by a verb is written solid.

overlook	undercut
outfit	download

41. A verb derived from an open or hyphenated compound noun is hyphenated.

double-space	water-ski
rubber-stamp	field-test

42. A verb derived from a solid noun is written solid.

mastermind	brainstorm
highlight	sideline

Compounds Formed with Word Elements

Many new and temporary compounds are formed by adding word elements to existing words or by combining word elements. There are three basic kinds of word elements: prefixes (such as *anti-, non-, pre-, post-, re-, super-*), suffixes (such as *-er, -fold, -ism, -ist, -less, -ness*), and combining forms (such as *mini-, macro-, pseudo-, -graphy, -logy*). Prefixes and suffixes are usually attached to existing words; combining forms are usually combined to form new words.

43. prefix + word Except as specified in the paragraphs below, compounds formed from a prefix and a word are usually written solid.

anticrime	subzero
nonaligned	superheroine
premedical	transnational
reorchestration	postdoctoral

44. If the prefix ends with a vowel and the word it is attached to begins with the same vowel, the compound is usually hyphenated.

anti-incumbent	semi-independent
de-escalate	intra-arterial
co-organizer	pre-engineered

However, there are many exceptions.

reelect
preestablished
cooperate

45. If the base word or compound to which a prefix is added is capitalized, the resulting compound is almost always hyphenated.

pre-Victorian
anti-Western
post-Darwinian
non-English-speaking
but
transatlantic
transalpine

If the prefix and the base word together form a new proper name, the compound may be solid with the prefix capitalized.

Postimpressionists
Precambrian
but
Pre-Raphaelite

46. Compounds made with *ex-*, in its "former" sense, and *self-* are hyphenated.

ex-mayor   self-control
ex-husband   self-sustaining

Compounds formed from *vice-* are usually hyphenated. Some permanent compounds are open.

vice-chair   vice president
vice-consul   vice admiral

A temporary compound with *quasi(-)* or *pseudo(-)* may be written open (if *quasi* or *pseudo* is being treated as a modifier) or hyphenated (if it is being treated as a combining form).

quasi intellectual   *or*   quasi-intellectual
pseudo liberal   *or*   pseudo-liberal

47. If a prefix is added to a hyphenated compound, it may be either followed by a hyphen or closed up solid to the next element. Permanent compounds of this kind should be checked in a dictionary.

unair-conditioned   non-self-governing
ultra-up-to-date   unself-confident

48. If a prefix is added to an open compound, the hyphen is often replaced by an en dash in typeset material.

ex–campaign treasurer
post–World War I era

49. A compound that would be identical with another word if written solid is usually hyphenated to prevent misreading.

> a re-creation of the setting
> shopped at the co-op
> multi-ply fabric

50. Compounds that might otherwise be solid are often hyphenated in order to clarify their formation, meaning, or pronunciation.

tri-city	re-oil	anti-fur
de-iced	non-news	pro-choice

51. When prefixes are attached to numerals, the compounds are hyphenated.

> pre-1995 models
> post–1945 economy
> non-19th-century architecture

52. Compounds created from proper ethnic or national combining forms are hyphenated when the second element is an independent word, but solid when it is a combining form.

Anglo-Saxon	Anglophile
Judeo-Christian	Francophone
Sino-Japanese	Sinophobe

53. Prefixes that are repeated in the same compound are separated by a hyphen.

> re-refried
> post-postmodern

54. Compounds consisting of different prefixes or adjectives with the same base word which are joined by *and* or *or* are shortened by pruning the first compound back to a hyphenated prefix.

> pre- and postoperative care
> anti- or pro-Revolutionary sympathies
> over- and underachievers
> early- and mid-20th-century painters
> 4-, 6-, and 8-foot lengths

55. word + suffix Except as noted in the paragraphs below, compounds formed by adding a suffix to a word are written solid.

Fourierism	characterless
benightedness	custodianship
yellowish	easternmost

56. Compounds made with a suffix or a terminal combining form are often hyphenated if the base word is more than two syllables long, if it ends with the same letter the suffix begins with, or if it is a proper name.

industry-wide   jewel-like
recession-proof   Hollywood-ish
American-ness   Europe-wide

57. Compounds made from a number + *-odd* are hyphenated. A number + *-fold* is written solid if the number is spelled out but hyphenated if it is in numerals.

fifty-odd   tenfold
50-odd   10-fold

58. Most compounds formed from an open or hyphenated compound + a suffix do not separate the suffix with a hyphen. But combining forms that also exist as independent words, such as *-like, -wide, -worthy,* and *-proof,* are attached by a hyphen.

self-righteousness
middle-of-the-roadism
bobby-soxer
a Red Cross-like approach
a New York-wide policy

Open compounds often become hyphenated when a suffix is added unless they are proper nouns.

flat-taxer
Ivy Leaguer
World Federalist

59. combining form + combining form   New terms in technical fields created with one or more combining forms are normally written solid.

cyberworld
macrographic

Abbreviations

Abbreviations may be used to save space and time, to avoid repetition of long words and phrases, or simply to conform to conventional usage.

The contemporary styling of abbreviations is inconsistent and arbitrary, and no set of rules can hope to cover all the possible variations, exceptions, and peculiarities encountered in print. The form abbreviations take—capitalized vs. lowercased, punctuated vs. unpunctuated—often depends on a writer's preference or a publisher's or organization's policy. However, the following paragraphs provide a number of useful guidelines to contemporary practice. In doubtful cases, a good general dictionary or a dictionary of abbreviations will usually show standard forms for common abbreviations.

The present discussion deals largely with general, nontechnical writing. In scientific writing, abbreviations are almost never punctuated.

An abbreviation is not divided at the end of a line.

Abbreviations are almost never italicized. An abbreviation consisting of single initial letters, whether punctuated or not, never standardly has spacing between the letters. (Initials of personal names, however, normally are separated by spaces.)

The first reference to any frequently abbreviated term or name that could be confusing or unfamiliar is commonly spelled out, often followed immediately by its abbreviation in parentheses. Later references employ the abbreviation alone.

PUNCTUATION

1. A period follows most abbreviations that are formed by omitting all but the first few letters of a word.

   cont. [*for* continued]   Oct. [*for* October]
   enc. [*for* enclosure]   univ. [*for* university]

Former abbreviations that are now considered words do not need a period.

   lab   photo
   gym   ad

2. A period follows most abbreviations that are formed by omitting letters from the middle of a word.

   govt. [*for* government]   bros. [*for* brothers]
   atty. [*for* attorney]   Dr. [*for* Doctor]

Some abbreviations, usually called *contractions,* replace the omitted letters with an apostrophe. Such contractions do not end with a period. (In American usage, very few contractions other than two-word contractions involving verbs are in standard use.)

   ass'n   *or*   assn. [*for* association]
   dep't   *or*   dept.   [*for* department]
   nat'l   *or*   natl. [*for* national]
   can't [*for* cannot]

3. Periods are usually omitted from abbreviations made up of single initial letters. However, for some of these abbreviations, especially uncapitalized ones, the periods are usually retained. No space follows an internal period.

   GOP [*for* Grand Old Party]
   PR [*for* public relations]
   CEO   *or*   C.E.O. [*for* chief executive officer]
   a.m. [*for* ante meridiem]

4. A few abbreviations are punctuated with one or more slashes in place of periods. (For details on the slash, see the section beginning on page 81.)

c/o [*for* care of]
d/b/a *or* d.b.a. [*for* doing business as]
w/o [*for* without]
w/w [*for* wall-to-wall]

5. Terms in which a suffix is added to a numeral are not genuine abbreviations and do not require a period. (For details on ordinal numbers, see the section on pages 136–37.)

1st	3d
2nd	8vo

6. Isolated letters of the alphabet used to designate a shape or position in a sequence are not abbreviations and are not punctuated.

T square
A1
F minor

7. When a punctuated abbreviation ends a sentence, its period becomes the terminal period.

For years she claimed she was "the oldest living fossil at Briggs & Co."

CAPITALIZATION

1. Abbreviations are capitalized if the words they represent are proper nouns or adjectives.

F [*for* Fahrenheit]
IMF [*for* International Monetary Fund]
Jan. [*for* January]
Amer. [*for* American]
LWV [*for* League of Women Voters]

2. Abbreviations are usually all-capitalized when they represent initial letters of lowercased words. However, some common abbreviations formed in this way are often lowercased.

IQ [*for* intelligence quotient]
U.S. [*for* United States]
COLA [*for* cost-of-living allowance]
FYI [*for* for your information]
f.o.b. *or* FOB [*for* free on board]
c/o [*for* care of]

3. Most abbreviations formed from single initial letters that are pronounced as words, rather than as a series of letters, are capitalized. Those that are not proper nouns and have been assimilated into the language as words in their own right are most often lowercased.

OSHA	snafu
NATO	laser
CARE	sonar
NAFTA	scuba

4. Abbreviations that are ordinarily capitalized are commonly used to begin sentences, but abbreviations that are ordinarily uncapitalized are not.

Dr. Smith strongly disagrees.
OSHA regulations require these new measures.
Page 22 [*not* P. 22] was missing.

PLURALS, POSSESSIVES, AND COMPOUNDS

1. Punctuated abbreviations of single words are pluralized by adding -*s* before the period.

yrs. [*for* years]
hwys. [*for* highways]
figs. [*for* figures]

2. Punctuated abbreviations that stand for phrases or compounds are usually pluralized by adding -*'s* after the last period.

M.D.'s   *or*   M.D.s
Ph.D.'s   *or*   Ph.D.s
LL.B.'s   *or*   LL.B.s
v.p.'s

3. All-capitalized, unpunctuated abbreviations are usually pluralized by adding a lowercase -*s*.

IRAs	CPAs
PCs	SATs

4. The plural form of a few lowercase one-letter abbreviations is made by repeating the letter.

ll. [*for* lines]
pp. [*for* pages]
nn. [*for* notes]
vv. [*for* verses]
ff.   *or*   ff [*for* and the following ones *or* folios]

5. The plural form of abbreviations of units of measurement (including one-letter abbreviations) is the same as the singular form. (For more on units of measurement, see the section beginning on page 149.)

> 10 cc *or* cc. [*for* cubic centimeters]
> 30 m *or* m. [*for* meters]
> 15 mm *or* mm. [*for* millimeters]
> 24 h. [*for* hours]
> 10 min. [*for* minutes]
> 45 mi. [*for* miles]

However, in informal nontechnical text several such abbreviations are pluralized like other single-word abbreviations.

> lbs.   qts.
> gals.   hrs.

6. Possessives of abbreviations are formed like those of spelled-out nouns: the singular possessive is formed by adding -'s, the plural possessive simply by adding an apostrophe.

> the CEO's speech   the PACs' influence
> Apex Co.'s profits   Brown Bros.' ads

7. Compounds that consist of an abbreviation added to another word are formed in the same way as compounds that consist of spelled-out nouns.

> an FDA-approved drug
> an R&D-driven company
> the Eau Claire, Wisc.–based publisher

Compounds formed by adding a prefix or suffix to an abbreviation are usually hyphenated.

> pre-CD recordings   a CIA-like operation
> non-IRA deductions   a PCB-free product

SPECIFIC STYLING CONVENTIONS

A and *An*

1. The choice of the article *a* or *an* before abbreviations depends on the sound, rather than the actual letter, with which the abbreviation begins. If it begins with a consonant sound, *a* is normally used; if with a vowel sound, *an* is used.

> a CD-ROM version   an FDA-approved drug
> a YAF member   an M.D. degree
> a U.S. Senator   an ABA convention

A.D. and B.C.

2. The abbreviations A.D. and B.C. and other abbreviated era designations usually appear in books and journals as small capitals; in newspapers and in typed or keyboarded material, they usually appear as full capitals. The abbreviation B.C. follows the date; A.D. usually precedes the date, though in many publications A.D. follows the date as well. In references to whole centuries, A.D. follows the century. (For more on era designations, see paragraph 12 on page 143.)

> A.D. 185   *but also*   185 A.D.
> 41 B.C.
> the fourth century A.D.

Agencies, Associations, Organizations, and Companies

3. The names of agencies, associations, and organizations are usually abbreviated after being spelled out on their first occurrence in a text. If a company is easily recognizable from its initials, the abbreviation is likewise usually employed after the first mention. The abbreviations are usually all-capitalized and unpunctuated. (In contexts where the abbreviation will be recognized, it often replaces the full name throughout.)

> Next, the president of the Pioneer Valley Transit Authority presented the annual PVTA award.
> . . . at the American Bar Association (ABA) meeting in June. The ABA's new officers . . .
> International Business Machines released its first-quarter earnings figures today. An IBM spokesperson . . .

4. The words *Company, Corporation, Incorporated,* and *Limited* in company names are commonly abbreviated even at their first appearance, except in quite formal writing.

> Procter & Gamble Company   *or*   Procter & Gamble Co.
> Brandywine Corporation   *or*   Brandywine Corp.

Ampersand

5. The ampersand (&), representing the word *and,* is often used in the names of companies.

> H&R Block
> Standard & Poor's
> Ogilvy & Mather

It is not used in the names of federal agencies.

> U.S. Fish and Wildlife Service
> Office of Management and Budget

Even when a spelled-out *and* appears in a company's official name, it is often replaced by an ampersand in writing referring to the company, whether for the sake of consistency or because of the writer's inability to verify the official styling.

6. When an ampersand is used in an abbreviation, there is usually no space on either side of the ampersand.

> The Barkers welcome all guests to their B&B at 54 West Street.
> The S&P 500 showed gains in technology stocks.
> The Texas A&M Aggies prevailed again on Sunday.

7. When an ampersand is used between the last two elements in a series, the comma is omitted.

> Jones, Kuhn & Malloy, Attorneys at Law

Books of the Bible

8. Books of the Bible are spelled out in running text but generally abbreviated in references to chapter and verse.

> The minister based his first Advent sermon on Matthew.
> Ye cannot serve God and mammon.—Matt. 6:24

Compass Points

9. Compass points are normally abbreviated when they follow street names; these abbreviations may be punctuated and are usually preceded by a comma.

> 1600 Pennsylvania Avenue[,] NW [N.W.]

When a compass point precedes the word *Street, Avenue,* etc., or when it follows the word but forms an integral part of the street name, it is usually spelled out.

> 230 West 43rd Street
> 50 Park Avenue South

Dates

10. The names of days and months are spelled out in running text.

> at the Monday editorial meeting
> the December issue of *Scientific American*
> a meeting held on August 1, 1995

The names of months usually are not abbreviated in datelines of business letters, but they are often abbreviated in government and military correspondence.

> *business dateline:*   November 1, 1995
> *military dateline:*   1 Nov 95

Degrees and Professional Ratings

11. Abbreviations of academic degrees are usually punctuated; abbreviations of professional ratings are slightly more commonly unpunctuated.

> Ph.D.
> B.Sc.
> M.B.A.
> PLS   *or*   P.L.S. [*for* Professional Legal Secretary]
> CMA   *or*   C.M.A. [*for* Certified Medical Assistant]
> FACP   *or*   F.A.C.P. [*for* Fellow of the American College of Physicians]

12. Only the first letter of each element in abbreviations of degrees and professional ratings is generally capitalized.

> D.Ch.E. [*for* Doctor of Chemical Engineering]
> Litt.D. [*for* Doctor of Letters]
> D.Th. [*for* Doctor of Theology]
>   *but*
> LL.B. [*for* Bachelor of Laws]
> LL.M. [*for* Master of Laws]
> LL.D. [*for* Doctor of Laws]

Geographical Names

13. When abbreviations of state names are used in running text immediately following the name of a city or county, the traditional state abbreviations are often used.

> Ellen White of 49 Lyman St., Saginaw, Mich., has been chosen . . .
> the Dade County, Fla., public schools
>   *but*
> Grand Rapids, in western Michigan, . . .

Official postal service abbreviations for states are used in mailing addresses.

> 6 Bay Rd.
> Gibson Island, MD 21056

14. Terms such as *Street, Road,* and *Boulevard* are often written as punctuated abbreviations in running text when they form part of a proper name.

> an accident on Windward Road [*or* Rd.]
> our office at 1234 Cross Blvd. [*or* Boulevard]

15. Names of countries are usually spelled in full in running text.

> South Africa's president urged the United States to impose meaningful sanctions.

Abbreviations for country names (in tables, for example), are usually punctuated. When formed from the single initial letters of two or more individual words, they are sometimes unpunctuated.

Mex.	Ger.	U.K. *or* UK
Can.	Scot.	U.S. *or* US

16. *United States* is normally abbreviated when used as an adjective or attributive. When used as a noun, it is generally spelled out.

> the U.S. Department of Justice
> U.S. foreign policy
> The United States has declined to participate.

17. *Saint* is usually abbreviated when it is part of a geographical or topographical name. *Mount, Point,* and *Fort* may be either spelled out or abbreviated. (For the abbreviation of *Saint* with personal names, see paragraph 25 below.)

> St. Paul, Minnesota   *or*   Saint Paul, Minnesota
> St. Thomas, U.S.V.I.   *or*   Saint Thomas
> Mount Vernon   *or*   Mt. Vernon
> Point Reyes   *or*   Pt. Reyes
> Fort Worth   *or*   Ft. Worth
> Mt. Kilimanjaro   *or*   Mount Kilimanjaro

Latin Words and Phrases

18. Several Latin words and phrases are almost always abbreviated. They are punctuated, lowercased, and usually not italicized.

etc.	viz.	q.v.
i.e.	et al.	c. *or* ca.
e.g.	ibid.	fl.
cf.	op. cit.	et seq.

Versus is usually abbreviated *v.* in legal writing, *vs.* otherwise.

> *Da Costa* v. *United States*
> good vs. evil   *or*   good versus evil

Latitude and *Longitude*

19. The words *latitude* and *longitude* are abbreviated in tables and in technical contexts but often written out in running text.

> *in a table:*   lat. 10°20′N *or* lat. 10–20N
> *in text:*   from 10°20′ north latitude to 10°30′ south latitude
>   *or*   from lat. 10°20′N to lat. 10°30′S

Military Ranks and Units

20. Official abbreviations for military ranks follow specific unpunctuated styles for each branch of the armed forces. Nonmilitary writing usually employs a punctuated and less concise style.

> *in the military:*   BG Carter R. Stokes, USA
>   LCDR Dawn Wills-Craig, USN
>   Col S. J. Smith, USMC
>   LTJG Carlos Ramos, USCG
>   Sgt Bernard P. Brodkey, USAF
> *outside the military:*   Brig. Gen. Carter R. Stokes
>   Lt. Comdr. Dawn Wills-Craig
>   Col. S. J. Smith
>   Lt. (j.g.) Carlos Ramos
>   Sgt. Bernard P. Brodkey

21. Outside the military, military ranks are usually given in full when used with a surname only but abbreviated when used with a full name.

> Major Mosby
> Maj. John S. Mosby

Number

22. The word *number*, when followed by a numeral, is usually abbreviated to *No.* or *no.*

> The No. 1 priority is to promote profitability.
> We recommend no. 6 thread.
> Policy No. 123–5-X
> Publ. Nos. 12 and 1

Personal Names

23. When initials are used with a surname, they are spaced and punctuated. Unspaced initials of a few famous persons, which may or may not be punctuated, are sometimes used in place of their full names.

> E. M. Forster
> C. P. E. Bach
> JFK   *or*   J.F.K.

24. The abbreviations *Jr.* and *Sr.* may or may not be preceded by a comma.

> Martin Luther King Jr.   *or*   Martin Luther King, Jr.

Saint

25. The word *Saint* is often abbreviated when used before the name of a saint. When it forms part of a surname or an institution's name, it follows the style used by the person or institution. (For the styling of *Saint* in geographical names, see paragraph 17 above.)

> St. [*or* Saint] Teresa of Avila   St. Martin's Press
> Augustus Saint-Gaudens   St. John's College
> Ruth St. Denis

Scientific Terms

26. In binomial nomenclature, a genus name may be abbreviated to its initial letter after the first reference. The abbreviation is always capitalized, punctuated, and italicized.

> . . . its better-known relative *Atropa belladonna* (deadly nightshade).
> Only *A. belladonna* is commonly found in . . .

27. Abbreviations for the names of chemical compounds and the symbols for chemical elements and formulas are unpunctuated.

> MSG   Pb   NaCl
> PCB   O   FeS

28. Abbreviations in computer terms are usually unpunctuated.

PC	I/O	Ctrl
RAM	DOS	ASCII
MB	Esc	EBCDIC
CD-ROM	Alt	

Time

29. When time is expressed in figures, the abbreviations *a.m. (ante meridiem)* and *p.m. (post meridiem)* are most often written as punctuated lowercase letters, sometimes as punctuated small capital letters. In newspapers, they usually appear in full-size capitals. (For more on *a.m.* and *p.m.*, see paragraph 39 on page 149.)

> 8:30 a.m.   *or*   8:30 A.M.   *or*   8:30 A.M.
> 10:00 p.m.   *or*   10:00 P.M.   *or*   10:00 P.M.

Time-zone designations are usually capitalized and unpunctuated.

> 9:22 a.m. EST [*for* eastern standard time]
> 4:45 p.m. CDT [*for* central daylight time]

Titles and Degrees

30. The courtesy titles *Mr., Ms., Mrs.,* and *Messrs.* occur only as abbreviations today. The professional titles *Doctor, Professor, Representative,* and *Senator* are often abbreviated.

> Ms. Lee A. Downs
> Messrs. Lake, Mason, and Nambeth
> Doctor Howe   *or*   Dr. Howe

31. Despite some traditional objections, the honorific titles *Honorable* and *Reverend* are often abbreviated, with and without *the* preceding the titles.

> the Honorable Samuel I. O'Leary   *or*   [the] Hon. Samuel I. O'Leary
> the Reverend Samuel I. O'Leary   *or*   [the] Rev. Samuel I. O'Leary

32. When an abbreviation for an academic degree, professional certification, or association membership follows a name, no courtesy or professional title precedes it.

> Dr. Jesse Smith   *or*   Jesse Smith, M.D.   *but not*   Dr. Jesse Smith, M.D.
> Katherine Fox Derwinski, CLU
> Carol W. Manning, M.D., FACPS
> Michael B. Jones II, J.D.
> Peter D. Cohn, Jr., CPA

33. The abbreviation *Esq.* (for *Esquire*) often follows attorneys' names in correspondence and in formal listings, and less often follows the names of certain other professionals, including architects, consuls, clerks of court, and justices of the peace. It is not used if a degree or professional rating follows the name, or if a courtesy title or honorific (*Mr., Ms., Hon., Dr.,* etc.) precedes the name.

> Carolyn B. West, Esq.   *not*   Ms. Carolyn B. West, Esq.   *and not*   Carolyn B. West, J.D., Esq.

Units of Measurement

34. A unit of measurement that follows a figure is often abbreviated, especially in technical writing. The figure and abbreviation are separated by a space. If the numeral is written out, the unit should also be written out.

> 15 cu. ft.   *but*   fifteen cubic feet
> What is its capacity in cubic feet?

35. Abbreviations for metric units are usually unpunctuated; those for traditional units are usually punctuated in nonscientific writing. (For more on units of measurement, see the section beginning on page 149.)

> 14 ml   50 m   4 sec.
> 12 km   8 ft.   20 min.

Numbers

The treatment of numbers presents special difficulties because there are so many conventions to follow, some of which may conflict in a particular passage. The major issue is whether to spell out numbers or to express them in figures, and usage varies considerably on this point.

NUMBERS AS WORDS OR FIGURES

At one style extreme—usually limited to proclamations, legal documents, and some other types of very formal writing—all numbers (sometimes even including dates) are written out. At the other extreme, some types of technical writing may contain no written-out numbers. Figures are generally easier to read than spelled-out numbers; however, the spelled-out forms are helpful in certain circumstances, and are often felt to be less jarring than figures in nontechnical writing.

Basic Conventions

1. Two alternative basic conventions are in common use. The first and more widely used system requires that numbers up through nine be spelled out, and that figures be used for exact numbers greater than nine. (In a variation of this system, the number ten is spelled out.) Round numbers that consist of a whole number between one and nine followed by *hundred, thousand, million,* etc., may either be spelled out or expressed in figures.

The museum includes four rooms of early American tools and implements, 345 pieces in all.

He spoke for almost three hours, inspiring his audience of 19,000 devoted followers.

They sold more than 700 [*or* seven hundred] TVs during the 10-day sale.

She'd told him so a thousand times.

2. The second system requires that numbers from one through ninety-nine be spelled out, and that figures be used for all exact numbers above ninety-nine. (In a variation of this system, the number one hundred is spelled out.) Numbers that consist of a whole number between one and ninety-nine followed by *hundred, thousand, million,* etc., are also spelled out.

Audubon's engraver spent nearly twelve years completing these four volumes, which comprise 435 hand-colored plates.

In the course of four hours, she signed twenty-five hundred copies of her book.

3. Written-out numbers only use hyphens following words ending in *-ty*. The word *and* before such words is usually omitted.

twenty-two
five-hundred ninety-seven
two thousand one hundred forty-nine

Sentence Beginnings

4. Numbers that begin a sentence are written out. An exception is occasionally made for dates. Spelled-out numbers that are lengthy and awkward are usually avoided by restructuring the sentence.

Sixty-two new bills will be brought before the committee.
or There will be 62 new bills brought before the committee.
Nineteen ninety-five was our best earnings year so far.
or occasionally 1995 was our best earnings year so far.
One hundred fifty-seven illustrations, including 86 color plates, are contained in the book.
or The book contains 157 illustrations, including 86 color plates.

Adjacent Numbers and Numbers in Series

5. Two separate figures are generally not written adjacent to one another in running text unless they form a series. Instead, either the sentence is rephrased or one of the figures is spelled out—usually the figure with the shorter written form.

sixteen ½-inch dowels
worked five 9-hour days in a row
won twenty 100-point games
lost 15 fifty-point matches
By 1997, thirty schools . . .

6. Numbers paired at the beginning of a sentence are usually written alike. If the first word of the sentence is a spelled-out number, the second number is also spelled out. However, each number may instead be styled independently, even if that results in an inconsistent pairing.

> Sixty to seventy-five copies will be required.
> *or* Sixty to 75 copies will be required.

7. Numbers that form a pair or a series within a sentence or a paragraph are often treated identically even when they would otherwise be styled differently. The style of the largest number usually determines that of the others. If one number is a mixed or simple fraction, figures are used for all the numbers in the series.

> She wrote one proposal and thirteen [*or* 13] memos that week.
> His total record sales came to a meager 8 [*or* eight] million; Bing Crosby's, he mused, may have surpassed 250 million.
> The three jobs took 5, 12, and 4½ hours, respectively.

Round Numbers

8. Approximate or round numbers, particularly those that can be expressed in one or two words, are often spelled out in general writing. In technical and scientific writing, they are expressed as numerals.

> seven hundred people   *or*   700 people
> five thousand years   *or*   5,000 years
> four hundred thousand volumes   *or*   400,000 volumes
> *but not*   400 thousand volumes
>> *but in technical writing*
> 200 species of fish
> 50,000 people per year
> 300,000 years

9. Round (and round-appearing) numbers of one million and above are often expressed as figures followed by the word *million, billion,* and so forth. The figure may include a one- or two-digit decimal fraction; more exact numbers are written entirely in figures.

> the last 600 million years
> about 4.6 billion years old
> 1.2 million metric tons of grain
> $7.25 million
> $3,456,000,000

Ordinal Numbers

10. Ordinal numbers generally follow the styling rules for cardinal numbers. In technical writing, ordinal numbers are usually written as figure-plus-suffix combinations. Certain ordinal numbers—for example, those for percentiles and latitudes—are usually set as figures even in nontechnical contexts.

entered the seventh grade
wrote the 9th [*or* ninth] and 12th [*or* twelfth] chapters
in the 21st [*or* twenty-first] century
the 7th percentile
the 38th parallel

11. In figure-plus-suffix combinations where the figure ends in 2 or 3, either a one- or a two-letter suffix may be used. A period does not follow the suffix.

2d   *or*   2nd
33d   *or*   33rd
102d   *or*   102nd

Roman Numerals

12. Roman numerals are traditionally used to differentiate rulers and popes with identical names.

King George III
Henri IV
Innocent X

13. When Roman numerals are used to differentiate related males with the same name, they are used only with the full name. Ordinals are sometimes used instead of Roman numerals. The possessive is formed in the usual way. (For the use of *Jr.* and *Sr.*, see paragraph 24 on page 132.)

James R. Watson II
James R. Watson 2nd *or* 2d
James R. Watson II's [*or* 2nd's *or* 2d's] alumni gift

14. Lowercase Roman numerals are generally used to number book pages that precede the regular Arabic sequence (often including a table of contents, acknowledgments, foreword, or other material).

on page iv of the preface
See Introduction, pp. ix–xiii.

15. Roman numerals are used in outlines; see paragraph 23 on page 146.

16. Roman numerals are found as part of a few established scientific and technical terms. Chords in the study of music harmony are designated by capital and lowercase Roman numerals (often followed by small Arabic numbers). Most technical terms that include numbers, however, express them in Arabic form.

blood-clotting factor VII
quadrant III
the cranial nerves II and IX
HIV-III virus
Population II stars

type I error
vii$_6$ chord
   but
adenosine 3′,5′-monophosphate
cesium 137
PL/1 programming language

17. Miscellaneous uses of Roman numerals include the Articles, and often the Amendments, of the Constitution. Roman numerals are still sometimes used for references to the acts and scenes of plays and occasionally for volume numbers in bibliographic references.

Article IX
Act III, Scene ii   *or*   Act 3, Scene 2
(III, ii)   *or*   (3, 2)
Vol. XXIII, No. 4   *but usually*   Vol. 23, No. 4

PUNCTUATION

These paragraphs provide general rules for the use of commas, hyphens, and en dashes with compound and large numbers. For specific categories of numbers, such as dates, money, and decimal fractions, see Specific Styling Conventions, beginning on page 141.

Commas in Large Numbers

1. In general writing, figures of four digits may be written with or without a comma; including the comma is more common. If the numerals form part of a tabulation, commas are necessary so that four-digit numerals can align with numerals of five or more digits.

2,000 cases   *or less commonly*   2000 cases

2. Whole numbers of five digits or more (but not decimal fractions) use a comma to separate three-digit groups, counting from the right.

a fee of $12,500
15,000 units
a population of 1,500,000

3. Certain types of numbers of four digits or more do not contain commas. These include decimal fractions and the numbers of policies and contracts, checks, street addresses, rooms and suites, telephones, pages, military hours, and years.

2.5544	Room 1206
Policy 33442	page 145
check 34567	1650 hours
12537 Wilshire Blvd.	in 1929

4. In technical writing, the comma is frequently replaced by a thin space in numerals of five or more digits. Digits to the right of the decimal point are also separated in this way, counting from the decimal point.

> 28 666 203
> 209.775 42

Hyphens

5. Hyphens are used with written-out numbers between 21 and 99.

> forty-one years old
> his forty-first birthday
> Four hundred twenty-two visitors were counted.

6. A hyphen is used in a written-out fraction employed as a modifier. A nonmodifying fraction consisting of two words only is usually left open, although it may also be hyphenated. (For details on fractions, see the section beginning on page 144.)

> a one-half share
> three fifths of her paycheck   *or*   three-fifths of her paycheck
>   *but*
> four five-hundredths

7. Numbers that form the first part of a modifier expressing measurement are followed by a hyphen. (For units of measurement, see the section on pages 149–50.)

> a 5-foot board
> a 28-mile trip
> an eight-pound baby
>   *but*
> a $6 million profit

8. Serial numbers, Social Security numbers, telephone numbers, and extended zip codes often contain hyphens that make lengthy numerals more readable or separate coded information.

> 020–42–1691
> 413–734–3134   *or*   (413) 734–3134
> 01102–2812

9. Numbers are almost never divided at the end of a line. If division is unavoidable, the break occurs only after a comma.

Inclusive Numbers

10. Inclusive numbers—those that express a range—are usually separated either by the word *to* or by a hyphen or en dash, meaning "(up) to and including."

> spanning the years 1915 to 1941
> the fiscal year 1999–2000

the decade 1920–1929
pages 40 to 98
pp. 40–98

Inclusive numbers separated by a hyphen or en dash are not used after the words *from* or *between*.

from page 385 to page 419   *not*   from page 385–419
from 9:30 to 5:30   *not*   from 9:30–5:30
between 1997 and 2000   *not*   between 1997–2000
between 80 and 90 percent   *not*   between 80–90 percent

11. Inclusive page numbers and dates may be either written in full or elided (i.e., shortened) to save space or for ease of reading.

pages 523–526   *or*   pages 523–26
1955–1969   *or*   1955–69

However, inclusive dates that appear in titles and other headings are almost never elided. Dates that appear with era designations are also not elided.

England and the French Revolution 1789–1797
1900–1901   *not*   1900–01   *and not*   1900–1
872–863 B.C.   *not*   872–63 B.C.

12. The most common style for the elision of inclusive numbers is based on the following rules: Never elide inclusive numbers that have only two digits.

24–28   *not*   24–8
86–87   *not*   86–7

Never elide inclusive numbers when the first number ends in 00.

100–103   *not*   100–03   *and not*   100–3
300–329   *not*   300–29

In other numbers, do not omit the tens digit from the higher number. *Exception:* Where the tens digit of both numbers is zero, write only one digit for the higher number.

234–37   *not*   234–7
3,824–29   *not*   3,824–9
605–7   *not*   605–07

13. Units of measurement expressed in words or abbreviations are usually used only after the second element of an inclusive number. Symbols, however, are repeated.

ten to fifteen dollars
30 to 35 degrees Celsius
an increase in dosage from 200 to 500 mg
  but
45° to 48° F
$50–$60 million   *or* $50 million to $60 million

14. Numbers that are part of an inclusive set or range are usually styled alike: figures with figures, spelled-out words with other spelled-out words.

> from 8 to 108 absences
> five to twenty guests
> 300,000,000 to 305,000,000   *not*   300 million to 305,000,00

SPECIFIC STYLING CONVENTIONS

The following paragraphs, arranged alphabetically, describe styling practices commonly followed for specific situations involving numbers.

Addresses

1. Numerals are used for all building, house, apartment, room, and suite numbers except for *one,* which is usually written out.

> 6 Lincoln Road   Apartment 609   Suite 2000
> 1436 Fremont Street   Room 982   One Bayside Drive

When the address of a building is used as its name, the number in the address is often written out.

> the sophisticated elegance of Ten Park Avenue

2. Numbered streets have their numbers written as ordinals. Street names from First through Tenth are usually written out, and numerals are used for all higher-numbered streets. Less commonly, all numbered street names up to and including One Hundredth are spelled out.

> 167 Second Avenue
> 19 South 22nd Street   *or less commonly*   19 South Twenty-second Street
> 145 East 145th Street
> in the 60s   *or*   in the Sixties [streets from 60th to 69th]
> in the 120s [streets from 120th to 129th]

When a house or building number immediately precedes the number of a street, a spaced hyphen may be inserted between the two numbers, or the street number may be written out, for the sake of clarity.

> 2018 - 14th Street
> 2018 Fourteenth Street

3. Arabic numerals are used to designate highways and, in some states, county roads.

> Interstate 90   *or*   I-90   Texas 23
> U.S. Route 1   *or*   U.S. 1   County 213

Dates

4. Year numbers are written as figures. If a year number begins a sentence, it may be left as a figure but more often is spelled out; the sentence may also be rewritten to avoid beginning it with a figure.

> the 1997 edition
> Nineteen thirty-seven marked the opening of the Golden Gate Bridge.
> *or*   The year 1937 marked the opening of the Golden Gate Bridge.
> *or*   The Golden Gate Bridge opened in 1937.

5. A year number may be abbreviated to its last two digits when an event is so well known that it needs no century designation. In these cases an apostrophe precedes the numerals.

> the blizzard of '88
> class of '91   *or*   class of 1991
> the Spirit of '76

6. Full dates are traditionally written in the sequence month-day-year, with the year set off by commas that precede and follow it. An alternative style, used in the military and in U.S. government publications, is the inverted sequence day-month-year, which does not require commas.

> *traditional:*   July 8, 1976, was a warm, sunny day in Philadelphia.
>   the explosion on July 16, 1945, at Alamogordo
> *military:*   the explosion on 16 July 1945 at Alamogordo
>   the amendment ratified on 18 August 1920

7. Ordinal numbers are not used in full dates. Ordinals are sometimes used, however, for a date without an accompanying year, and they are always used when preceded in a date by the word *the.*

> December 4, 1829
> on December 4th   *or*   on December 4
> on the 4th of December

8. All-figure dating, such as 6–8–00 or 6/8/00, is usually avoided except in informal writing. For some readers, such dates are ambiguous; the examples above generally mean June 8, 2000, in the United States, but in almost all other countries mean August 6, 2000.

9. Commas are usually omitted from dates that include the month and year but not the day. The word *of* is sometimes inserted between the month and year.

> in October 1997
> back in January of 1981

10. References to specific centuries may be either written out or expressed in figures.

> in the nineteenth century   *or*   in the 19th century
> a sixteenth-century painting   *or*   a 16th-century painting

11. The name of a specific decade often takes a short form, usually with no apostrophe and uncapitalized. When the short form is part of a set phrase, it is capitalized.

> a song from the sixties
>   *occasionally*   a song from the 'sixties   *or*   a song from the Sixties
> tunes of the Gay Nineties

The name of a decade is often expressed in numerals, in plural form. The figure may be shortened, with an apostrophe to indicate the missing numerals; however, apostrophes enclosing the figure are generally avoided. Any sequence of such numbers is generally styled consistently.

> the 1950s and 1960s *or* the '50s and '60s
> *but not*
> the '50's and '60's
> the 1950s and '60s
> the 1950s and sixties

12. Era designations precede or follow words that specify centuries or numerals that specify years. Era designations are unspaced abbreviations, punctuated with periods. They are usually typed or keyboarded as regular capitals, and typeset in books as small capitals and in newspapers as full-size capitals. The abbreviation B.C. (before Christ) is placed after the date, while A.D. (*anno Domini,* "in the year of our Lord") is usually placed before the date but after a century designation. Any date given without an era designation or context is understood to mean A.D.

> 1792–1750 B.C.
> between 600 and 400 B.C.
> from the fifth or fourth millennium to c. 250 B.C.
> between 7 B.C. and A.D. 22
> c. A.D. 100 to 300
> the second century A.D.
> the 17th century

13. Less common era designations include A.H. (*anno Hegirae,* "in the year of [Muhammad's] Hegira," or *anno Hebraico,* "in the Hebrew year"); B.C.E. (before the common era; a synonym for B.C.); C.E. (of the common era; a synonym for A.D.); and B.P. (before the present; often used by geologists and archeologists, with or without the word *year*). The abbreviation A.H. is usually placed before a specific date but after a century designation, while B.C.E., C.E., and B.P.,. are placed after both a date and a century.

> the tenth of Muharram, A.H. 61 (October 10, A.D. 680)
> the first century A.H.
> from the 1st century B.C.E. to the 4th century C.E.
> 63 B.C.E.
> the year 200 C.E.
> 5,000 years B.P.
> two million years B.P.

Degrees of Temperature and Arc

14. In technical writing, a quantity expressed in degrees is generally written as a numeral followed by the degree symbol (°). In the Kelvin scale, neither the word *degree* nor the symbol is used with the figure.

a 45° angle
6°40′10″N
32° F
0° C
Absolute zero is zero kelvins or 0 K.

15. In general writing, the quantity expressed in degrees may or may not be written out. A figure may be followed by either the degree symbol or the word *degree;* a spelled-out number is always followed by the word *degree.*

   latitude 43°19″N
   latitude 43 degrees N
   a difference of 43 degrees latitude
   The temperature has risen about thirty degrees.

Fractions and Decimal Fractions

16. In nontechnical prose, fractions standing alone are usually written out. Common fractions used as nouns are usually unhyphenated, although the hyphenated form is also common. When fractions are used as modifiers, they are hyphenated.

   lost three quarters of its value   *or*   lost three-quarters of its value
   had a two-thirds chance of winning

Multiword numerators and denominators are usually hyphenated, or written as figures.

   one one-hundredth of an inch   *or*   1/100 of an inch

17. Mixed fractions (fractions with a whole number, such as 3½) and fractions that form part of a modifier are usually expressed in figures in running text.

   waiting 2½ hours
   a 7/8-mile course
   2½-pound weights

Fractions that are not on the keyboard or available as special characters on a computer may be typed in full-sized digits; in mixed fractions, a space is left between the whole number and the fraction.

   a 7/8-mile course
   waiting 2 3/4 hours

18. Fractions used with units of measurement are usually expressed in figures, but common short words are often written out.

¹⁄₁₀ km	half a mile
⅓ oz.	a half-mile walk
⅞ inch	a sixteenth-inch gap

19. Decimal fractions are always set as figures. In technical writing, a zero is placed to the left of the decimal point when the fraction is less than a whole number; in general writing, the zero is usually omitted. Commas are not used in numbers following a decimal point.

> An example of a pure decimal fraction is 0.375, while 1.402 is classified as a mixed decimal fraction.
>
> a .22-caliber rifle
>
> 0.142857

20. Fractions and decimal fractions are usually not mixed in a text.

> weights of 5½ lbs., 3¼ lbs., and ½ oz.
> *or* weights of 5.5 lbs., 3.25 lbs., and .5 oz.
> *not* weights of 5.5 lbs., 3¼ lbs., and ½ oz.

Lists and Outlines

21. Both run-in and vertical lists are often numbered. In run-in numbered lists—that is, numbered lists that form part of a normal-looking sentence—each item is preceded by a number (or, less often, an italicized letter) enclosed in parentheses. The items are separated by commas if they are brief and unpunctuated; if they are complex or punctuated, they are separated by semicolons. The entire list is introduced by a colon if it is preceded by a full clause, and often when it is not.

> I will try to establish (1) the immediate historical background, (2) the chronological sequence of events in the critical two days, and (3) the likely cause-and-effect relations of the key decisions and actions.
>
> The new medical dictionary has several special features: *(a)* common variant spellings; *(b)* examples of words used in context; *(c)* abbreviations, combining forms, prefixes, and suffixes; and *(d)* brand names for drugs and their generic equivalents.

22. In vertical lists, each number is followed by a period; the periods align vertically. Run-over lines usually align under the item's first word. Each item may be capitalized, especially if the items are syntactically independent of the words that introduce them.

> The English peerage consists of five ranks, listed here in descending order:
> 1. Duke (duchess)
> 2. Marquess (marchioness)
> 3. Earl (countess)
> 4. Viscount (viscountess)
> 5. Baron (baroness)

The listed items end with periods (or question marks) when they are complete sentences, and also often when they are not.

> We require answers to the following questions:
> 1. Does the club intend to engage heavy-metal bands to perform in the future?

2. Will any such bands be permitted to play past midnight on week-
   ends?
3. Are there plans to install proper acoustic insulation?

Items that are syntactically dependent on the words that introduce them
often begin with a lowercase letter and end with a comma or semicolon
just as in a run-in series in an ordinary sentence.

The signed consent may be given by
1. the patient,
2. a legally qualified representative (such as a parent or guardian) of the
   patient,
3. an executor or administrator of an estate, or
4. an agency designated by the court as a guardian.

A vertical list may also be unnumbered, or may use bullets (•) in place of
numerals, especially where the order of the items is not important.

Chief among the important advances
in communication were these 19th-
century inventions:
Morse's telegraph
Daguerre's camera
Bell's telephone
Edison's phonograph

This book covers in detail:
• Punctuation
• Capitalization and italicization
• Numbers
• Abbreviations
• Grammar and composition

23. Outlines standardly use Roman numerals, capitalized letters, Arabic numerals, and lowercase letters, in that order. Each numeral or letter is
followed by a period, and each item is capitalized.

I. Using health information
A. Confidentiality
B. Insurance billing
   1. Requirements for health information
   2. Diagnosis coding
   3. Procedure coding
II. Managing health information
A. Storage and retrieval
   1. Filing systems
      a. Numerical
      b. Color-coded
   2. Retrieval systems
B. Record disposal

Money

24. A sum of money that can be expressed in one or two words is usually
written out in running text, as is the unit of currency. But if several sums
are mentioned in the sentence or paragraph, all are usually expressed
as figures and are used with the unspaced currency symbol.

The scalpers were asking eighty dollars.
Grandfather remembered the days of the five-cent cigar.
The shoes on sale are priced at $69 and $89.
Jill wanted to sell the lemonade for 25¢, 35¢, and 45¢.

25. Monetary units of mixed dollars-and-cents amounts are expressed in figures.

    $16.75
    $307.02

26. Even-dollar amounts are often expressed in figures without a decimal point and zeros. But when even-dollar amounts appear near amounts that include cents, the decimal point and zeros are usually added for consistency. The dollar sign is repeated before each amount in a series or inclusive range.

    They paid $500 for the watercolor.
    The price had risen from $8.00 to $9.95.
    bids of $80, $90, and $100
    in the $80–$100 range

27. Sums of money in the millions or above rounded to no more than one decimal place are usually expressed in a combination of figures and words.

    a $10-million building program
    $4.5 billion

28. In legal documents a sum of money is usually written out fully, often capitalized, with the corresponding figures in parentheses immediately following.

    Twenty-five Thousand Dollars ($25,000)

Organizations and Governmental Entities

29. Ordinal numbers in the names of religious organizations and churches are usually written out.

    Seventh-Day Adventists
    Third Congregational Church

30. Local branches of labor unions and fraternal organizations are generally identified by a numeral, usually placed after the name.

    Motion Picture Studio Mechanics Local 476
    Loyal Order of Moose No. 220
    Local 4277 Communications Workers of America

31. In names of governmental bodies and electoral, judicial, and military units, ordinal numbers of one hundred or below are usually written out but often not.

    Second Continental Congress
    Fifth Republic
    First Congressional District
    Court of Appeals for the Third Circuit
    U.S. Eighth Army
    Twelfth Precinct   *or*   12th Precinct
    Ninety-eighth Congress   *or*   98th Congress

Percentages

32. In technical writing, and often in business and financial writing, percentages are written as a figure followed by an unspaced % symbol. In general writing, the word *percent* normally replaces the symbol, and the number may either be written out (if it does not include a decimal) or expressed as a figure.

technical:	15%
	13.5%
general:	15 percent
	87.2 percent
	Fifteen percent of the applicants were accepted.
	a four percent increase *or* a 4% increase

33. In a series or range, the percent sign is usually included with all numbers, even if one of the numbers is zero.

rates of 8.3%, 8.8%, and 9.1%
a variation of 0% to 10% *or* a 0%–10% variation

Plurals

34. The plurals of written-out numbers, including fractions, are formed by adding *-s* or *-es*.

at sixes and sevens	ever since the thirties
divided into eighths	still in her thirties

35. The plurals of figures are formed by adding *-s* or less commonly *-'s,* especially where the apostrophe can prevent a confusing typographic appearance.

in the '80s
since the 1980s [*or less commonly* 1980's]
temperatures in the 80s and 90s [*or* 80's and 90's]
the *1*'s looked like *l*'s

Ratios

36. Ratios are generally expressed in figures, usually with the word *to*; in technical writing the figures may be joined by a colon or a slash instead. Ratios expressed in words use a hyphen (or en dash) or the word *to.*

odds of 10 to 1	29 mi/gal
a proportion of 1 to 4	a fifty-fifty chance
a 3:1 ratio	a ratio of ten to four

Time of Day

37. In running text, the time of day is usually spelled out when expressed in even, half, or quarter hours or when it is followed by *o'clock.*

around four-thirty
arriving by ten
planned to leave at half past five
now almost a quarter to two
arrived at nine o'clock

38. Figures are generally used when specifying a precise time.

> an appointment at 9:30 tomorrow morning
> buses at 8:42, 9:12, and 10:03 a.m.

39. Figures are also used when the time of day is followed by *a.m.* and *p.m.* These are usually written as punctuated lowercase letters, sometimes as small capital letters. They are not used with *o'clock* or with other words that specify the time of day.

> 8:30 a.m.   *or*   8:30 A.M.
> 10:30 p.m.   *or*   10:30 P.M.
> 8 a.m.   *or*   8 A.M.
> home by nine o'clock
> 9:15 in the morning
> eleven in the evening

With *twelve o'clock* or *12:00,* it is helpful to specify *midnight* or *noon* rather than the ambiguous *a.m.* or *p.m.*

> The third shift begins at 12:00 (midnight).

40. Even-hour times are generally written with a colon and two zeros when used in a series or pairing with any times not ending in two zeros.

> started at 9:15 a.m. and finished at 2:00 p.m.
> worked from 8:30 to 5:00

41. The 24-hour clock system—also called *military time*—uses no punctuation and omits *o'clock, a.m., p.m.* or any other additional indication of the time of day. The word *hours* sometimes replaces them.

> from 0930 to 1100
> at 1600 hours

Units of Measurement

42. In technical writing, all numbers used with units of measurement are written as numerals. In nontechnical writing, such numbers often simply follow the basic conventions explained on page 134; alternatively, even in nontechnical contexts all such numbers often appear as numerals.

> In the control group, only 8 of the 90 plants were affected.
> picked nine quarts of berries
> chugging along at 9 [*or* nine] miles an hour
> a pumpkin 5 [*or* five] feet in diameter
> weighing 7 pounds 9 ounces
> a journey of 3 hours and 45 minutes

The singular form of units of measurement is used in a modifier before a noun, the plural form in a modifier that follows a noun.

> a 2- by 9-inch board   *or*   a two-inch by nine-inch board   *or*   a two- by nine-inch board

measured 2 inches by 9 inches   *or*   measured two inches by nine inches
a 6-foot 2-inch man
is 6 feet 2 inches tall   *or*   is six feet two inches tall
is six feet two   *or*   is 6 feet 2

43. When units of measurement are written as abbreviations or symbols, the adjacent numbers are always figures. (For abbreviations with numerals, see the section on page 134.)

6 cm	$4.25	4′
1 mm	67.6 fl. oz.	98.6°

44. When two or more quantities are expressed, as in ranges or dimensions or series, an accompanying symbol is usually repeated with each figure.

4″ × 6″ cards
temperatures of 30°, 55°, 43°, and 58°
$450–$500 suits

Other Uses

45. Figures are generally used for precise ages in newspapers and magazines, and often in books as well.

Taking the helm is Colin Corman, 51, a risk-taking high roller.
At 9 [*or* nine] she mastered the Mendelssohn Violin Concerto.
the champion 3[*or* three]-year-old filly
for anyone aged 62 and over

46. Figures are used to refer to parts of a book, such as volume, chapter, illustration, and table numbers.

vol. 5, p. 202
Chapter 8   *or*   Chapter Eight
Fig. 4

47. Serial, policy, and contract numbers use figures. (For punctuation of these numbers, see paragraph 3 on page 138.)

Serial No. 5274
Permit No. 63709

48. Figures are used to express stock-market quotations, mathematical calculations, scores, and tabulations.

Industrials were up 4.23.
3 × 15 = 45
a score of 8 to 2   *or*   a score of 8–2
the tally: 322 ayes, 80 nays

Grammar Glossary

The following list defines and illustrates more than 80 of the most important grammatical terms, many of which are used in the preceding discussion of English style.

active voice A verb form indicating that the subject of a sentence is performing the action *(A bird was singing; Interest rates rose)*; compare **passive voice**.

adjective A word that describes or modifies a noun *(red balloon; torrential rain; extensive damage; nine kittens; other voices; those nights)*.

adverb A word that modifies a verb, adjective, adverb, preposition, phrase, clause, or sentence *(walking slowly; the very popular movie; very patiently; just over; almost on time; Luckily, it worked)*.

antecedent The noun or noun equivalent to which a pronoun refers *(Judy wrote to say she is coming; They saw Bob and called to him)*.

appositive A word, phrase, or clause that is equivalent to an adjacent noun *(My husband, Larry, told them)*.

article One of three words *(a, an, and the)* used with a noun to indicate definiteness *(the blue car)* or indefiniteness *(a simple task; an explanation)*.

case A form of a noun or pronoun indicating its relation to other words. See **nominative**, **objective**, **possessive**.

clause A group of words having its own subject and predicate but forming only part of a compound or complex sentence. A **main** or **independent clause** could stand alone as a sentence; a **subordinate** or **dependent clause** requires a main clause.

comma fault Mistaken use of a comma instead of a semicolon to link two independent clauses *(We'd heard the stories, however, apparently no one else had)*.

comparison Change in the form of an adjective or adverb to show different levels of quality, quantity, or relation. The **comparative** form shows relation between two items, usually by adding *-er* or *more* or *less* to the adjective or adverb *(He's shorter than I am; This book sold more quickly than that)*. The **superlative** form expresses an extreme among three or more items, usually by adding *-est* or *most* or *least* to the adjective or adverb *(The cheetah is the fastest mammal; It is the least compelling reason)*.

compound A combination of words or word elements that work together in various ways *(farmhouse, cost-effective, ex-husband, shoeless, figure out, in view of that, real estate agent, greenish white powder, carefully tended garden, great white shark)*.

conjunction A word or phrase that joins together words, phrases, clauses, or sentences. **Coordinating conjunctions** (such as *and, or, but*) join elements of equal weight; **correlative conjunctions** (such as *either . . . or, neither . . .*

nor) are used in pairs and link alternatives; **subordinating conjunctions** (such as *unless, whether*) join subordinate clauses to main clauses.

conjunctive adverb A transitional adverb that expresses relationship between two independent clauses, sentences, or paragraphs (*also, however, therefore*).

count noun A noun that identifies things that can be counted (*two tickets; a motive*); compare **mass noun**.

dangling modifier A modifying phrase that lacks a normally expected grammatical relation to the rest of the sentence (*Taking the dog out for a walk, the leash got caught in the revolving door*).

direct object A word or phrase denoting the goal or result of the action of the verb (*He closed the window; They'll do whatever it takes*); compare **indirect object**.

direct question A question quoted exactly as spoken, written, or imagined (*Will it work?*); compare **indirect question**.

direct quotation Text that is quoted exactly as spoken or written (*I heard her say, "I'll be there at two o'clock"*); compare **indirect quotation**.

gender A characteristic of certain nouns and pronouns that distinguishes them as masculine, feminine, or neuter (*duke, duchess; chairman, chairwoman, chair; him, her, it*).

gerund A word having the characteristics of both verb and noun, usually ending in *-ing* (*The ice made skiing impossible*).

imperative The form (mood) of a verb that expresses a command or makes a request (*Come here; Please open the window*).

indicative The form (mood) of a verb that states a fact or asks a question (*The train stopped; Has the rain begun?*).

indirect object A person or thing indirectly affected by the action of the verb (*She gave the dog a bone*); compare **direct object**.

indirect question A statement of the substance of a question without using the speaker's exact words (*He wondered whether it would work*); compare **direct question**.

indirect quotation A statement of the substance of a quotation without using the speaker's exact words (*I heard her say she'd be there at two o'clock*); compare **direct quotation**.

infinitive A verb form having the characteristics of both verb and noun and usually used with *to* (*We had to stop; To err is human*).

inflection The change in form that words undergo to mark **case**, **gender**, **number**, **tense**, **person**, **mood**, or **voice** (*he, his, him; actor, actress; rat, rats; blame, blames, blamed, blaming; who, whom; she is careful, if she were careful, be careful; like, likes, is liked*).

interjection An exclamatory word or phrase (*Ouch!; Oh, you're probably right*).

intransitive verb A verb lacking an object (*He ran away; Snow was falling*); compare **transitive verb**.

linking verb A verb that links a subject with its predicate without indicating action (*Lisa is right, It all became clear, This feels firmer, He seemed calm*).

mass noun A noun that identifies a thing or concept without subdivisions (*some money; great courage; the study of politics*); compare **count noun**.

modifier A word or phrase that qualifies, limits, or restricts the meaning of another word or phrase. See **adjective**, **adverb**.

mood The form of a verb that shows the manner of the action or state it expresses. See **indicative**, **imperative**, **subjunctive**.

nominative A form (case) of a noun or pronoun indicating its use as the subject of a verb (*We ate dinner*).

nonrestrictive or **nonessential clause** A dependent or subordinate clause, set off by commas, that could be omitted without changing the meaning of the main clause (*The author, who turned out to be charming, autographed my book*).

noun A word that is the name of a person, place, or thing (*boy, America, table, commotion, poetry*).

number A characteristic of a noun, pronoun, or verb that signifies whether it is either singular or plural. See **singular**, **plural**.

object A noun or noun phrase that directly or indirectly receives the action of a verb or follows a preposition (*She rocked the baby; I gave him the news; over the rainbow*). See **direct object**, **indirect object**.

objective A form (case) of a noun or pronoun indicating its use as the object of a verb or preposition (*We spoke to them yesterday; He's a man whom everyone should know*).

parenthetical element A word, phrase, or sentence inserted in a passage to explain or modify the thought; set off by parentheses, commas, or dashes (*a ruling by the FCC (Federal Communications Commission); All of us, to tell the truth, were amazed; The examiner chose—God knows why—to ignore it*).

participle A word derived from a verb that may stand alone as an adjective or may be combined with helping verbs such as *be* or *have* to form a different tense. The **present participle** ends in *-ing* (*fascinating*), the **past participle** usually ends in *-ed* (*seasoned*); the **perfect participle** combines *having* with the past participle (*having escaped*).

parts of speech Eight classes into which words are grouped according to their uses in a sentence. See **adjective**, **adverb**, **conjunction**, **interjection**, **noun**, **preposition**, **pronoun**, **verb**.

passive voice A verb form indicating that the subject of a sentence is being acted upon (*He is respected by others; The dinner will be cooked by Grandmother*).

person A characteristic of a word that indicates whether a person is speaking (**first person**), is spoken to (**second person**), or is spoken about (**third person**).

personal pronoun A pronoun that refers to beings and objects and reflects their person, number, and gender (*You and I will attend; She gave him the book; They're just old rags*).

phrase A group of two or more words that does not contain both a subject and a verb, and functions as a noun, adjective, or adverb (*the old sinner; stretching for miles; without a limp*).

plural A word form used to denote more than one person, thing, or instance (*the children's toys; seven deer; these kinds*).

possessive A form (case) of a noun or pronoun denoting ownership (*the president's message; their opinions; the poem's meter*).

predicate The part of a sentence or clause, usually including everything that follows the subject, that expresses what is said of the subject (*The pitcher threw a spitball; The teachers from the surrounding towns were invited to the dinner*).

prefix A letter, syllable, or word attached to the beginning of a word to change its meaning (*ahistorical, presort, anti-imperialist, posthypnotic*).

preposition A word or compound that expresses direction, motion, position, or relationship and takes a noun or pronoun as its object (*on the table; outside himself; because of that*).

pronoun A word used in place of a noun (*he, it, herself, whose, which, those*).

proper noun A capitalized noun that names a particular person, place, or thing (*Susan, New York, December, General Motors, Mormon, Library of Congress, Middle Ages*).

restrictive or **essential clause** A subordinate clause, not set off by commas, that cannot be omitted without changing the meaning of the main clause (*Textbooks that are not current should be returned*).

sentence A group of words representing a complete thought and containing a subject and a verb. A **simple sentence** consists of one independent clause; a **compound sentence** consists of two or more independent clauses; and a **complex sentence** consists of one independent clause and one or more dependent clauses. A **declarative sentence** makes a statement; an **exclamatory sentence** expresses strong feeling; an **interrogative sentence** asks a question; and an **imperative sentence** expresses a command or request.

singular A word form denoting a single person, thing, or instance (*man, tattoo, eventuality*).

split infinitive An infinitive interrupted by at least one adverb (*to ultimately avoid trouble; to utterly and without mercy crush their opponents*).

subject A word or group of words, normally preceding the verb, that names the person, place, or thing about which something is said (*He stopped; He was stopped; It's clouding up; All sixty members voted; The teachers from the surrounding towns were invited*).

subjunctive The form (mood) of a verb that expresses a condition contrary to fact or follows clauses of necessity, demand, or wishing *(If he were here, he could answer that; I wish they would come soon).*

subordinate clause A group of words that contains both a subject and a predicate but cannot stand alone and must be either preceded or followed by a **main clause** *(He is a man who will succeed).*

suffix A letter, syllable, or word added to the end of a word to modify its meaning *(editors, countywide, umbrella-like).*

superlative See **comparison**.

tense The characteristic of a verb that expresses time present, past, or future *(see, saw, will see, is seeing, has seen, had seen, will have seen, had been seeing).*

transitive verb A verb that acts upon a direct object *(She contributed money; He runs the store; Express your opinion)*; compare **intransitive verb**.

verb A word or phrase used to express action or state of being *(leap, carry out, feel, be).*

voice The property of a verb that indicates whether the subject acts (active voice) or is acted upon (passive voice). See **active voice**, **passive voice**.

Composition and Word Usage

Whereas the preceding chapter dealt with what is often called the "mechanics" of writing, this chapter is devoted to such substantive issues of business writing as structuring a communication, achieving a desired tone, choosing appropriate language, and revising an initial draft.

Letter-Writing Guidelines

All business letters should not sound alike. The tone of each letter—formal or informal, objective or partial, friendly or critical, and so on—will depend on your relationship with your recipient. However, the language should almost always be polite and pleasant, and *never* less than civil. Always keep the reader's point of view and possible reactions in mind, even when you are intent on setting forth your own objectives. Except when special formality is required or when you are very friendly with the recipient, try to use language that is slightly more formal and concise than your everyday speech.

Highlight or underscore significant facts and requests in any letter you are responding to. If necessary, make your own notes in the margin of the previous letter—meeting dates, appointments, brochure titles, and so on.

Jot down in order the topics you have to cover, producing a basic outline before beginning to write, even if the outline amounts to no more than four or five scrawled subject headings.

Bear in mind that your degree of familiarity with the subject matter will often be different from your reader's. Avoid writing on too low a level to experts in a given field, and avoid writing over the heads of nonexperts.

Feel free to vary the length of your paragraphs. Generally keep them as short as appropriate, with few longer than five sentences. However, breaking all your paragraphs up into one- and two-sentence lengths defeats the purpose of paragraphing, which is to organize the material for the sake of easier comprehension.

Open most paragraphs with a topic sentence, which should usually correspond to a heading in your outline. This will greatly assist the reader to scan the material initially and later to absorb it more easily and thoroughly. It will also help you keep your paragraphs focused in an appropriately narrow way.

Use natural, easy-to-understand language, while avoiding overly casual or slangy expressions. Short, clear, direct words are easier to read and understand than long words and should generally be used in place of their longer synonyms except where they risk making the tone too abrupt or the sentence too graceless. They will also prevent your sounding self-important, insecure, or bureaucratic.

Prefer the active voice to the passive. Active voice usually sounds more natural, direct, and honest and takes fewer words. However, the passive can sometimes be useful, particularly for disguising the identity of the person doing something, whether for reasons of tact or prudence.

Avoid clichés. Business-letter clichés (see the list in this chapter) have unfortunately become fixtures in the prose of many writers who think they are somehow appropriate and desirable. A busy reader can easily become impatient with them. However, there is no need to avoid many standard phrases that are as useful and irreplaceable as individual words.

Employ the personal pronouns—*I, we, you, my, our, your,* etc.—in order to give a communication a warmer tone. Avoiding them can make a letter less cordial—which in certain cases may be desirable.

Use contractions when you want to achieve a somewhat informal tone. Sometimes contractions will be all that is needed to soften a letter's formality.

Avoid padding your letter with overlong or repetitious material. Your reader will be grateful.

Give accurate and adequate information, and respond to any questions that have been raised. Neglecting to answer a question from previous correspondence is a serious omission; double-check by rereading the previous correspondence against your response.

Avoid ambiguous language, and scan your prose for unintended ambiguity. If a statement *can* be misunderstood, it *will* be.

Use specifics rather than abstractions where possible. Abstractions not only tend to bore the reader but may indicate that the writer hasn't actually visualized the subject adequately or is generalizing beyond his or her knowledge.

Exercise tact. Try to introduce unfavorable comments with favorable ones and to present the positive aspects of a situation before making any negative observations. Soften your language with euphemisms, if necessary, to avoid a negative tone.

Use humor where it seems natural and appropriate; there is no law that business and professional letters have to be humorless. For some writers, however, it is hard to find a good humorous tone, and there is often the possibility that the recipient won't think the humor successful or, more seriously, will fail to understand that it is even intended as humor. If you are uncertain about its effect, be sure to put the letter aside before rereading it.

Avoid sexist and other biased language. You risk offending or at least distracting many readers today if you are not attentive to problems of discriminatory usage. In particular, try to avoid using *he, him,* or *his* when referring to a person who could be either male or female.

State or restate any request clearly and pleasantly in the last paragraph. If no request is being made, use the final paragraph of an informal letter for a pleasant closing thought (for instance, an allusion to the season or to a recent or upcoming event in the recipient's life).

Edit your first draft. Ask yourself if each word is necessary or desirable and cross out all those that aren't. (See also the section on editing later in this chapter.)

Set your letter aside for a while, if possible, so that you can come back to it with a fresh eye. Pretend that you are the recipient and have just opened it. (To make the exercise more realistic, you could even try putting it in an envelope and then opening the envelope to read it.)

When giving your letter a final rereading, ask yourself the following questions:

- Has every question, request, and issue raised in the preceding communication been dealt with, or at least acknowledged?
- Is the tone appropriate, given the particular relationship between writer (or signer) and reader?
- Will the recipient be able to grasp the essence of the letter almost immediately?
- Is it obvious why each paragraph *is* a paragraph? Does it hang together, or does it instead contain material that really belongs elsewhere or omit material that instead shows up in another paragraph?
- Is the meaning of each sentence unambiguous?
- Is there still any unnecessary or undesirable verbiage?
- Have you used the word *I* too much?
- Is any intended humor both appropriate and funny?
- Have you actually enclosed all the enclosures referred to?

Be sure you know whose signature is to appear at the end. Normally, only letters of general information and routine requests may bear a secretary's or assistant's signature, except when special authorization has been given.

Proofread the letter for misspelled words, incorrect figures and dates, lack of agreement between subject and verb, misplaced commas, and other such pitfalls. Check to see that each of the necessary parts or elements of the letter has been included. (See also the section on proofreading later in this chapter.)

Problems in Word Usage

The following list discusses words that present a variety of problems to writers. Review it from time to time to keep yourself alert to potential usage issues in your own writing. (See also the next two sections, which provide lists of easily confused words and business clichés.)

aggravate *Aggravate* is used chiefly in two meanings: "to make worse" ("aggravated her shoulder injury," "their financial position was aggravated by the downturn") and "to irritate, annoy" ("The President was aggravated by the French intransigence"). The latter is not often seen in writing. However, *aggravation* usually means "irritation," and *aggravating* almost always expresses annoyance.

almost, most *Most* is often used like *almost* in speech ("Most everyone was there"), but it is rarely seen in business writing.

alot, a lot *Alot* hardly ever appears in print and is usually regarded as an error.

alright Though the business community has been using the one-word *alright* since the 1920s, it is only gradually gaining acceptance and is still often regarded as an error. It is rarely seen in published works outside of newspaper writing.

amount, number *Number* is normally used with nouns that can form a plural and can be used with a numeral ("a large number of orders," "any number of times"). *Amount* is mainly used with nouns that denote a substance or concept that can't be divided and counted up ("the annual amount of rainfall," "a large amount of money"). The use of *amount* with count nouns, usually when the number of things can be thought of as a mass or collection ("a substantial amount of job offers"), is often criticized; and many people will regard it as an error.

apt, liable Both *liable* and *apt*, when followed by an infinitive, are used nearly interchangeably with *likely* ("more liable to get tired easily," "roads are apt to be slippery"). This use of *apt* is widely accepted, but some people think *liable* should be limited to situations risking an undesirable outcome ("If you speed, you're liable to be caught") and it is generally used this way in writing.

as, as if, like *Like* used as a conjunction in the sense of *as* ("just like I used to do") or *as if* ("It looks like it will rain") has been frequently criticized, especially since its use in a widely publicized cigarette commercial slogan. Though *like* has been used in these ways for nearly 600 years, it is safer to use *as* or *as if* instead.

as far as "As far as clothes, young people always know best" is an example of *as far as* used as a preposition. This use developed from the more common conjunction use ("As far as clothes are concerned . . .") by omitting the following verb or verb phrase; it is very widely used in speech but is often regarded as an error in print.

awful It has been traditional to criticize any use of *awful* and *awfully* that doesn't convey the original sense of being filled with awe. However, *awful* has long been acceptable in the meanings "extremely objectionable" ("What an awful color") and "exceedingly great" ("an awful lot of money") in speech and casual writing. Use of *awful* and *awfully* as intensifiers ("I'm awful tired," "he's awfully rich") is likewise common in informal prose, but it is safer to avoid them in formal business writing.

between, among It is often said that *between* can only be used when dealing with two items ("between a rock and a hard place"), and that *among* must be used for three or more items ("strife among Croats, Serbs, and Muslims"). However, *between* is actually quite acceptable in these latter cases, especially when specifying one-to-one relationships, regardless of the number of items ("between you and me and the lamppost").

can, may Both *can* and *may* are used to refer to possibility ("Can the deal still go through?" "It may still happen"). Since the possibility of someone's doing something may depend on someone else's agreeing to it, the two words have become interchangeable when they refer to permission ("You can [may] go now if you like"). Though the use of *can* to ask or grant permission has been common since the last century, *may* is more appropriate in formal correspondence. However, this meaning of *may* is relatively rare in negative constructions, where *cannot* and *can't* are more usual ("They can't [may not] use it without paying").

comprise The sense of *comprise* meaning "to compose or constitute" ("the branches that comprise our government") rather than "to include or be made up of" ("Our government comprises various branches") has been attacked as wrong, for reasons that are unclear. Until recently, it was used chiefly in scientific and technical writing; today it has become the most widely used sense. But it still may be safer to use *compose* or *make up* instead.

contact Though some regard *contact* as only a noun and an adjective, its use as a verb, especially to mean "get in touch with" ("Contact your local dealer"), has long been widely accepted.

data *Data* has firmly established itself with a meaning independent of its use as the plural form of *datum*. It is used in one of two ways: as a plural noun (like *earnings*), taking a plural verb and plural modifiers (such as *these* or *many*) but not cardinal numbers ("These data show that we're out of the recession"); or as an abstract mass noun (like *information*), taking a singular verb and singular modifiers (such as *this, much,* or *little*) ("The data on the subject is plentiful"). Both constructions are standard, but many people are convinced that only the plural form is correct, and thus the plural form is somewhat more common in print. What you want to avoid is mixing in signs of the singular (like *this* or *much*) when you use a plural verb.

different from, different than Both of these phrases are standard; however, some people dislike the latter and will insist that, for example, "different than the old proposal" be changed to "different from the old proposal.". *Different from* works best when you can take advantage of the *from* ("The new proposal is very different from the old one"). *Different than* works best when a clause follows ("very different in size than it was two years ago").

disinterested, uninterested *Disinterested* has basically two meanings: "unbiased" ("a disinterested decision," "disinterested intellectual curiosity"), and "not interested," which is also the basic meaning of *uninterested*. Though this second use of *disinterested* is widespread, some people object to it and it may be safer to avoid it.

due to When the *due* of *due to* is clearly an adjective ("absences due to the flu") no one complains about the phrase. When *due to* is a preposition ("Due to the holiday, our office will be closed"), some people object and call for *owing to* or *because of*. Both uses of *due to* are entirely standard, but in formal writing one of the alternatives for the prepositional use may be safer.

each other, one another The traditional rules call for *each other* to be used in reference to two ("The two girls looked at each other in surprise") and *one another* to be used in reference to three or more ("There will be time for people to talk with one another after the meeting"). In fact, however, they are employed interchangeably.

finalize Though avoided by many writers, *finalize* occurs frequently in business and government contexts ("The budget will be finalized," "finalizing the deal"), where it is regarded as entirely standard.

good, well Both *good* and *well* are acceptable when used to express good health ("I feel good," "I feel well"), and *good* may also connote good spirits. However, the adverb *good* has been much criticized, with people insisting that *well* be used instead ("The orchestra played well this evening"), and this adverbial use should be avoided in writing.

hardly *Hardly* meaning "certainly not" is sometimes used with *not* for added emphasis ("Just another day at the office? Not hardly"). *Hardly* is also used like *barely* or *scarcely* to emphasize a minimal amount ("I hardly knew her," "Almost new—hardly a scratch on it"). When *hardly* is used with a negative verb (such as *can't, couldn't, didn't*) it is often called a double negative, though it is really a weaker negative. *Hardly* with a negative is a spoken form, and should be avoided in writing (except when quoting someone directly).

hopefully When used to mean "I hope" or "We hope" ("Hopefully, they'll reach an agreement"), as opposed to "full of hope" ("We continued our work hopefully and cheerfully"), *hopefully* is often criticized, even though other similar sentence adverbs (such as *frankly, clearly,* and *interestingly)* are accepted by everyone. Despite the objections, this sense of *hopefully* is now in standard use.

I, me In informal speech and writing, such phrases as "It's me," "Susan is taller than me," "He's as big as me," "Who, me?" and "Me too" are generally accepted. In formal writing, however, it is safer to use *I* after *be* ("It was

I who discovered the mistake'') and after *as* and *than* when the first term of the comparison is the sentence's subject (''Susan is taller than I,'' ''He is as big as I'').

imply, infer *Infer* is mostly used to mean ''to draw a conclusion, to conclude'' and is commonly followed by *from* (''I infer from your comments that . . . ''). *Imply* is used to mean ''to suggest'' (''The letter implies that our service was not satisfactory''). The use of *infer,* with a personal subject, as a synonym of *imply* (''Are you inferring that I made a mistake?'') is not widely accepted in print and is best avoided.

irregardless *Irregardless,* though a real word (and not uncommon in speech), is still a long way from general acceptance; use *regardless* (or *irrespective*) instead.

lay, lie Though *lay* has long been used as an intransitive verb meaning ''lie'' (''tried to make the book lay flat,'' ''lay down on the job''), it is generally condemned. In business writing it is safer to keep the two words distinct, and to keep their various easily confused forms *(lie, lying, lay, lain; lay, laying, laid)* distinct as well.

lend, loan Some people still object to the use of *loan* as a verb (''loaned me the book'') and insist on *lend*. Nevertheless, *loan* is in standard use. *Loan* is used only literally (''loans large sums of money''), however, while *lend* can be used both literally (''lends large sums of money'') and figuratively (''Would you please lend me a hand?'').

less, fewer The traditional view is that *less* is used for matters of degree, value, or amount, and that it modifies nouns that refer to uncountable things (''less hostility,'' ''less clothing'') while *fewer* modifies numbers and plural nouns (''fewer students,'' ''fewer than eight trees''). However, *less* has been used to modify plural nouns for centuries. Today *less* is actually more likely than *fewer* to modify plural nouns when distances, sums of money, and certain common phrases are involved (''less than 100 miles,'' ''less than $2000,'' ''in 25 words or less'') and just as likely to modify periods of time (''in less [fewer] than four hours''). But phrases such as ''less bills,'' ''less vacation days,'' and ''less computers'' should be avoided in business writing.

like, such as Should you write ''cities like Chicago and Des Moines'' or ''cities such as Chicago and Des Moines''? You are in fact free to use either one, or change the latter to ''such cities as Chicago and Des Moines.''

media *Media* is the plural of *medium*. With all the references to the mass media today, *media* is often used as a singular mass noun (''The media always wants a story''). But this singular use is not as well established as the similar use of *data,* and, except in the world of advertising, you will probably want to keep *media* plural in most writing.

memorandum *Memorandum* is a singular noun with two acceptable plurals: *memorandums* and *memoranda*. *Memoranda* is not yet established as a singular form.

neither The use of *neither* to refer to more than two nouns, though sometimes criticized, has been standard for centuries ("Neither the post office, the bank, nor City Hall is open today"). Traditionally, the pronoun *neither* is used with a singular verb ("Neither is ideal"). However, when a prepositional phrase follows *neither,* a plural verb is common and acceptable ("Neither of those solutions are ideal").

one The use of *one* to indicate a generic individual lends formality to writing, since it suggests distance between the writer and the reader ("One never knows" is more formal than "You never know"). Using *one* in place of *I* or *me* ("I'd like to read more, but one doesn't have the time") is common in British English but may be thought odd or objectionable in American English.

people, persons *People* is used to designate an unspecified number of persons ("People everywhere are talking about the new show"), and *persons* is commonly used when a definite number is specified ("Occupancy by more than 86 persons is prohibited"). However, the use of *people* where numbers are mentioned is also acceptable nowadays ("Ten people were questioned").

per *Per,* meaning "for each," is most commonly used with figures, usually in relation to price ("$150 per performance"), vehicles ("25 miles per gallon," "55 miles per hour"), or sports ("15 points per game"). Avoid inserting words like *a* or *each* between *per* and the word or words it modifies ("could type 70 words per each minute").

phenomena *Phenomena* is the usual plural of *phenomenon*. Use of *phenomena* as a singular ("St. Elmo's Fire is an eerie phenomena") is encountered in speech and now and then in writing, but it is nonstandard and it is safer to avoid it.

plus The use of *plus* to mean "and" ("a hamburger plus french fries for lunch") or "besides which" ("We would have been on time, but we lost the car keys. Plus, we forgot the map") is quite informal and is avoided in business writing.

presently The use of *presently* to mean "at the present time" ("I am presently working up a report") rather than "soon" ("He'll be with you presently"), while often criticized, is standard and acceptable.

pretty *Pretty,* when used as an adverb to tone down or moderate a statement ("pretty cold weather"), is avoided in formal writing, so using it in correspondence will lend an informal tone.

prior to *Prior to,* a synonym of *before,* most often appears in fairly formal contexts. It is especially useful in suggesting anticipation ("If all specifications are finalized prior to system design, cost overruns will be avoided").

proved, proven Both *proved* and *proven* are past participles of *prove*. Earlier in this century, *proved* was more common than *proven,* but today they are about equally common. As a past participle, either is acceptable ("has been proved [proven] effective"), but *proven* is more frequent as an adjective ("proven gas reserves").

providing, provided Although *providing* in the sense of "if" or "on condition that" has occasionally been disapproved ("providing he finds a buyer"), both *providing* and *provided* are well established, and either may be used. *Provided* is somewhat more common.

real The adverb *real* is used interchangeably with *really* only as an intensifier ("a real tough assignment"). This use is very common in speech and casual writing, but you should not use it in anything more formal.

set, sit *Set* generally takes an object ("Set the lamp over there") and *sit* does not ("sat for an hour in the doctor's office"). There are exceptions when *set* is used intransitively ("The sun will set soon," "The hen was setting") and *sit* takes an object ("I sat her down by her grandfather"). When used of people, however, intransitive *set* is a spoken use that should be avoided in writing.

shall, will *Shall* and *will* are generally interchangeable in present-day American English. In recent years, *shall* has been regarded as somewhat affected; *will* is much more common. However, *shall* is more appropriate in questions to express simple choice ("Shall we go now?") because *will* in such a context suggests prediction ("Will the prototype be ready next week?").

slow, slowly *Slow* used as an adverb (meaning "slowly") has often been called an error. *Slow* is almost always used with verbs indicating motion or action, and it typically follows the verb it modifies ("a stew cooked long and slow"). *Slowly* can be used in the same way ("drove slowly"), but it also is used before the verb ("The winds slowly subsided"), with adjectives formed from verbs ("the slowly sinking sun"), and in places where *slow* would sound inappropriate ("turned slowly around").

so The use of the adverb *so* to mean "very" or "extremely" is widely disapproved of in formal writing, except in negative contexts ("not so long ago") or when followed by an explaining clause ("cocoa so hot that I burned my tongue"). The use of the conjunction *so* to introduce clauses of result ("The acoustics are good, so every note is clear") and purpose ("Be quiet so I can sleep") is sometimes criticized, but these uses are standard. In the latter case (when used to mean "in order that"), *so that* is more common in formal and business writing ("to cut spending so that the deficit will be reduced").

such Some people disapprove of the using *such* as a pronoun ("such was the result," "sorting out glass and newspapers and such"), but dictionaries recognize it as standard.

Frequently Confused and Misused Words

Misusing one word for another in one's writing is a common source of confusion, embarrassment, and unintentional humor. Computer spell checkers will not identify a word that is being wrongly used in place of the proper word. Try to review the following list periodically in order to avert word confusions you may be overlooking.

abjure to reject solemnly
adjure to command

abrogate to nullify
arrogate to claim

abstruse hard to understand
obtuse dull, slow

accede to agree
exceed to go beyond

accent to emphasize
ascent climb
assent to agree to something

access right or ability to enter
excess intemperance

ad advertisement
add to join to something; to find a sum

adapt to adjust to something
adept highly skilled
adopt to take as one's child; to take up

addenda additional items
agenda list of things to be done

addition part added
edition publication

adjoin to be next to
adjourn to suspend a session
adjure to command

adverse unfavorable
averse disinclined

advert to refer
avert to avoid
overt unconcealed

advice counsel or information
advise to give advice

affect to act upon or influence
effect result; to bring about

agenda *see* ADDENDA
alimentary relating to nourishment
elementary simple or basic

allude to refer indirectly
elude to evade

allusion indirect reference
illusion misleading image

amenable accountable, agreeable
amendable modifiable

amend to alter in writing
emend to correct

ante- prior to or earlier than
anti- opposite or against

anymore any longer, now
any more more

appraise to set a value on
apprise to give notice of
apprize to appreciate or value

arraign to bring before a court
arrange to come to an agreement
arrogate *see* ABROGATE

ascent *see* ACCENT

assay to test for valuable content
essay to try tentatively

assent *see* ACCENT

assure to give confidence to
ensure to make certain
insure to guarantee against loss

aural relating to the ear or hearing
oral relating to the mouth, spoken

averse *see* ADVERSE

avert *see* ADVERT

bail security given
bale bundle of goods

base bottom
bass fish; deep voice

biannual usu. twice a year; sometimes every two years

biennial every two years

bloc group working together
block tract of land

born produced by birth
borne carried

breadth width
breath breathed air
breathe to draw in air

callous hardened
callus hard area on skin

canvas strong cloth; oil painting
canvass to solicit votes or opinions

capital city that is the seat of government
capitol state legislature building
Capitol U.S. Congress building

casual not planned
causal relating to or being a cause

casually by chance or accident
casualty one injured or killed

censor to examine for improper content
censure to express disapproval of

cession a yielding
session meeting

cite to summon; to quote
sight payable on presentation
site piece of land

collaborate to work or act jointly
corroborate to confirm

collision act of colliding
collusion secret cooperation for deceit

complacent self-satisfied
complaisant amiable

complement remainder
compliment admiring remark

concert to act in harmony or conjunction
consort to keep company

consul diplomatic official
council administrative body
counsel legal representative; to give advice

corespondent joint respondent
correspondent one who communicates

corroborate *see* COLLABORATE

council *see* CONSUL

councilor member of a council
counselor lawyer

counsel *see* COUNCIL

credible worthy of being believed
creditable worthy of praise
credulous gullible

currant raisinlike fruit
current stream; belonging to the present

cynosure one that attracts
sinecure easy job

decent good or satisfactory
descent downward movement
dissent difference of opinion

decree official order
degree extent or scope

defuse to make less harmful
diffuse to pour out or spread widely

deluded misled or confused
diluted weakened in consistency

demur to protest
demure shy

deposition testimony
disposition personality; outcome

depraved corrupted
deprived divested or stripped

deprecate to disapprove of
depreciate to lower the worth of

descent *see* DECENT

desperate having lost hope
disparate distinct

detract to disparage or reduce
distract to draw attention away

device piece of equipment or tool
devise to invent, to plot

diffuse *see* DEFUSE

diluted *see* DELUDED

disassemble to take apart
dissemble to disguise feelings or intentions

disburse to pay out
disperse to scatter

discreet capable of keeping a secret
discrete individually distinct

disparate *see* DESPERATE

disperse *see* DISBURSE

disposition *see* DEPOSITION

dissemble *see* DISASSEMBLE

dissent *see* DECENT

distract *see* DETRACT

edition *see* ADDITION

effect *see* AFFECT

e.g. for example
i.e. that is

elementary *see* ALIMENTARY

elicit to draw or bring out
illicit not lawful

eligible qualified to have
illegible not readable

emanate to come out from a source
eminent standing above others
immanent inherent
imminent ready to take place

emend *see* AMEND

emigrate to leave a country
immigrate to come into a place

eminence prominence or superiority
immanence restriction to one domain
imminence state of being imminent

ensure *see* ASSURE

envelop to surround
envelope letter container

equable free from unpleasant extremes
equitable fair

erasable removable by erasing
irascible hot-tempered

essay *see* ASSAY

every day each day
everyday ordinary

exceed *see* ACCEDE

excess *see* ACCESS

extant currently existing
extent size, degree, or measure

flaunt to display ostentatiously
flout to scorn

flounder to struggle
founder to sink

forego to precede
forgo to give up

formally in a formal manner
formerly at an earlier time

forth forward, out of
fourth 4th

gage security deposit
gauge to measure

gait manner of walking
gate opening in a wall or fence

generic general
genetic relating to the genes

gibe to tease or mock
jibe to agree
jive foollish talk

guarantee to promise to be responsible for
guaranty something given as a security

hail to greet
hale to compel to go; healthy

hearsay rumor
heresy dissent from a dominant theory

i.e. *see* E.G.

illegible *see* ELIGIBLE

illicit *see* ELICIT

illusion *see* ALLUSION

immanence *see* EMINENCE

immanent *see* EMANATE

immigrate *see* EMIGRATE

imminence *see* EMINENCE

imminent *see* EMANATE

imply hint, indicate
infer conclude, deduce

impracticable not feasible
impractical not practical

inapt not suitable
inept unfit or foolish

incite to urge on
insight discernment

incredible unbelievable
incredulous disbelieving, astonished

incurable not curable
incurrable capable of being
incurred

inept *see* INAPT

inequity lack of equity
iniquity wickedness

infer *see* IMPLY

ingenious very clever
ingenuous innocent and candid

inherent intrinsic
inherit to receive from an ancestor

iniquity *see* INEQUITY

insight *see* INCITE

install to set up for use
instill to impart gradually

insure *see* ASSURE

interment burial
internment confinement or
impounding

interstate involving more than one
state
intestate leaving no valid will
intrastate existing within a state

irascible *see* ERASABLE

it's it is
its belonging to it

jibe *see* GIBE
jive *see* GIBE

lead to guide; heavy metal
led guided

lean to rely on for support
lien legal claim on property

lesser smaller
lessor grantor of a lease

levee embankment to prevent
flooding
levy imposition or collection of a
tax

liable obligated by law
libel to make libelous statements;
false publication

lien *see* LEAN

material having relevance or
importance; matter
matériel equipment and supplies

median middle value in a range
medium intermediate; means of
communication

meet to come into contact with
mete to allot

meretricious falsely attractive
meritorious deserving reward or
honor
meticulous extremely careful about
details

militate to have effect
mitigate to make less severe

miner mine worker
minor one of less than legal age;
not important or serious

moot having no practical
significance
mute a person unable to speak; to
tone down or muffle

naval relating to a navy
navel belly button

obtuse *see* ABSTRUSE

oral *see* AURAL

ordinance law, rule, or decree
ordnance military supplies
ordonnance compilation of laws

overt *see* ADVERT

parlay to bet again a stake and its
winnings
parley discussion of disputed points

peer one of equal standing
pier bridge support

peremptory ending a right of action, debate or delay
preemptory preemptive

perpetrate to be guilty of
perpetuate to make perpetual

perquisite a right or privilege
prerequisite a necessary preliminary

persecute to harass injuriously
prosecute to proceed against at law

personal relating to a particular person
personnel body of employees

perspective view of things
prospective relating to the future
prospectus introductory description of an enterprise

perspicacious very discerning
perspicuous easily understood

pier *see* PEER

plain ordinary
plane airplane; surface

plaintiff complaining party in litigation
plaintive sorrowful

plat plan of a piece of land
plot small piece of land

pole long slender piece of wood or metal
poll sampling of opinion

pore to read attentively
pour to dispense from a container

practicable feasible
practical capable of being put to use

precede to go or come before
proceed to go to law

precedence priority
precedents previous examples to follow

preemptory *see* PEREMPTORY

preposition part of speech
proposition proposal

prerequisite *see* PERQUISITE

prescribe to direct to use; to assert a prescriptive right
proscribe to forbid

preview advance view
purview part or scope of a statute

principal main body of an estate; chief person or matter
principle basic rule or assumption

proceed *see* PRECEDE

proposition *see* PREPOSITION

proscribe *see* PRESCRIBE

prosecute *see* PERSECUTE

prospective *see* PERSPECTIVE

prostate gland
prostrate prone; to reduce to helplessness

purview *see* PREVIEW

raise to lift, to increase
raze to destroy or tear down

reality the quality or state of being real
realty real property

rebound to spring back or recover
redound to have an effect

recession ceding back
recision cancellation
rescission act of rescinding or abrogating

respectfully with respect
respectively in order

resume to take up again
résumé summary

role part, function
roll turn

session *see* CESSION

shear to cut off
sheer very thin or transparent

sight *see* CITE

sinecure *see* CYNOSURE

site *see* CITE

stationary still
stationery writing material

statue piece of sculpture
stature natural height or achieved
status
statute law enacted by a legislature

tack course of action
tact sense of propriety

tenant one who occupies a rental
dwelling
tenet principle

therefor for that
therefore thus

tortuous lacking in
straightforwardness

torturous very painful or distressing

track path or course
tract stretch of land; system of body
organs

trustee one entrusted with
something
trusty convict allowed special
privileges

venal open to bribery
venial excusable

waive to give up voluntarily
wave to motion with the hands

waiver act of waiving a right
waver to be irresolute

who's who is
whose of whom

your belonging to you
you're you are

Expressions to Avoid in Business Writing

The effectiveness of your business communications can be markedly increased by avoiding the padding and clichés that so often fill such writing.
A busy reader can become bored by tired language or exasperated at having
to wade through superfluous verbiage to get to the gist of a communication.
Some of these expressions are redundant, and some are merely long and
unwieldy. Some are genuinely antiquated, and some are simply stale. Some
may be appropriate in legal writing but sound stiff and awkward elsewhere.
Writers seeking clarity, brevity, and freshness in their prose should at least
consider alternatives to many of the expressions in the following list, a list
which should be reviewed periodically.

above Since this word may be used as a noun ("the above"), an adjective
("the above material"), and an adverb ("see above"), it can easily be over-
used; consider alternative expressions.

> *not:*   the above figure
> See the above.

> *instead:*   this figure
> the figure on page 27
> See the earlier illustration.

abovementioned/aforementioned/aforesaid These words can sound pompous outside of legal contexts, and can usually be replaced by *this, that, these,* and *those.*

> *not:* the abovementioned company
> the aforesaid dispute
>
> *instead:* this company
> the company in question
> the dispute mentioned earlier
> this dispute

acknowledge receipt of/are in receipt of These expressions can be replaced by the shorter *have received.*

> *not:* We acknowledge receipt of your check.
> We are in receipt of your check.
>
> *instead:* We have received your check.

afford (one) the opportunity This wordy expression can usually be replaced with *allow* or *permit.*

> *not:* This ruling affords us the opportunity to move ahead.
>
> *instead:* This ruling allows us to move ahead.

and etc. This phrase is redundant, because the Latin *et cetera* means "and the rest." Omit the *and.*

> *not:* calls, letters, faxes, and etc.
>
> *instead:* calls, letters, faxes, etc.

and/or This expression is best restricted to use between two alternatives: "A and/or B" means "A or B or both." In "A, B, and/or C," *and/or* will likely be either ambiguous or unnecessary.

any and all Except in legal documents, this phrase should be shortened to either *any* or *all.*

as per This expression has been overworked when meaning "as," "in accordance with," and "following."

> *not:* as per your request
> as per our telephone conversation of
> as per our agreement
>
> *instead:* as you requested
> according to your request
> in accordance with your request
> as a follow-up to our telephone conversation
> as we agreed

as regards/in regards to/with regard to These expressions can often be replaced with *concerning, regarding,* or *about.*

> *not:* We have written to them in regard to their unpaid balance.
>
> *instead:* We have written to them about their unpaid balance.

at an early (a later) date   This phrase can usually be replaced by *soon* (or *later*).

> *not:*   We expect to be able to present our case at an early date.
>
> *instead:*   We expect to be able to present our case soon.

at this juncture   This is best used only when referring to a crucial moment ("At this critical juncture in the negotiations"), and can usually be replaced by *at this point, now, currently,* or *at present.*

> *not:*   The department is not considering any changes at this juncture.
>
> At this juncture we are considering our options.
>
> *instead:*   The department is not considering any changes at present.
>
> Currently we are considering our options.

at this (that) point in time   These phrases may be replaced by briefer alternatives.

> *not:*   At this point in time we are not contemplating any changes.
>
> We did not feel any need for it at that point in time.
>
> *instead:*   We are not currently contemplating any changes.
>
> We did not then feel any need for it.

at this writing   This phrase may be replaced by *currently, now,* or *at present.*

attached/enclosed hereto/herewith   These phrases are rather formal, and the sentences in which they occur can often be recast.

> *not:*   Attached hereto is
>
> *instead:*   Attached is/are
>
> We are attaching
>
> I have enclosed
>
> You'll find enclosed

at your earliest convenience   This expression can often be replaced by the more direct *as soon as possible, immediately, by (January),* or *within (6) days.*

awaiting your instructions   Sentences using this phrase can usually be recast.

> *not:*   We are awaiting your instructions regarding this matter.
>
> *instead:*   Please let us know how you would like us to handle this matter.

deem   This rather stiff word can often be avoided.

> *not:*   We deem it advisable that you
>
> *instead:*   We advise you to
>
> We think it in your best interest to

despite the fact that   Substitute *although* or *though.*

due to/due to the fact that   *Because (of)* or *since* can often be substituted.

duly   This word is usually unnecessary and can almost always be omitted.

> *not:*   Your request has been duly forwarded.
>
> *instead:*   Your request has been forwarded.
>
> We have forwarded your request.

during the time that/at the time when   These expressions can usually be replaced by *while, when,* or *as.*

not:	During the time that the injunction was in force, At the time when she was suffering from seizures,
instead:	While the injunction was in force, When she was suffering from seizures,

each and every   Shorten to either *each* or *every.*

endeavor   This formal verb can be replaced by *try* or *attempt.*

not:	We shall endeavor to
instead:	We will attempt to We will make every effort to We will do everything we can to

for the reason that   Substitute *because* or *since.*

forward . . . on   Shorten to simply *forward.*

not:	We have forwarded your complaint on to the proper authorities.
instead:	We have forwarded your complaint to the proper authorities.

hold in abeyance   This expression often sounds stilted and can usually be avoided.

not:	We are holding our final decision in abeyance.
instead:	We are deferring our final decision. We are delaying our final decision. We are holding up our final decision.

I (we) call your attention to   This phrase can usually be replaced with *please note* or simply *note.*

not:	I call your attention to paragraph 15.
instead:	Please note paragraph 15. Note the wording in paragraph 15.

if and when   This phrase can usually be shortened to either *if* or *when.*

in a . . . manner   This phrase can usually be replaced by an adverb ending in *-ly.*

not:	He approached his work in a careless manner.
instead:	He approached his work carelessly.

in connection with   This is usually a wordy way of saying *about, on,* or *concerning.*

not:	They received numerous compliments in connection with their efforts.
instead:	They received numerous compliments on their efforts.

in many cases   This can usually be replaced by *often* or *frequently.*

not:	In many cases you can avoid litigation.
instead:	You can often avoid litigation.

in order that   This can usually be replaced with *so that*.

    not: in order that we may process your forms

    instead: so that we may process your forms

in the amount of   This is a long way of saying *for*.

    not: We are sending you a check in the amount of $50.95.

    instead: We are sending you a check for $50.95.

in the course of   The more concise *during* may often be substituted.

    not: in the course of the negotiations

    instead: during the negotiations

in the event that   This phrase may often be replaced by *if* or *in case*.

    not: In the event that you cannot meet with me next week,

    instead: If you cannot meet with me next week,

in the process of   This overworked phrase can usually be replaced with *currently* or *now*.

    not: We are in the process of reviewing these plans.

    instead: We are currently reviewing these plans.

in view of the fact that   This expression can be replaced by *because (of)*, *since*, or *as*.

    not: In view of the fact that he is now president,

                     He was terminated in view of the fact that he had been negligent.

    instead: Since he is now president,

                     He was terminated because he had been negligent.

in view of the foregoing   This expression can often be replaced by *thus*, *therefore*, or *consequently*.

    not: In view of the foregoing, we cannot accept these terms.

    instead: Therefore, we cannot accept these terms.

it has been brought to our notice   Substitute *We note, We notice, We see,* or *We have learned*.

it is interesting to note that   This expression can often be either dropped or replaced with a transitional word or short phrase.

    not: It is interesting to note that, by this time last year, all January orders had been met.

    instead: By this time last year, all orders received in January had been met.

                     Moreover, by this time last year, all January orders had been met.

it may be said that   This phrase can often be omitted.

    not: Indeed, it may be said that without the support of this department, this project would not have succeeded

    instead: Indeed, without the support of this department, this project would not have succeeded.

kindly   This expression can be replaced with *please.*

make the necessary inquiries/make inquiry   This hackneyed expression can usually be replaced with *look into, research,* or *investigate.*

not:	We will make the necessary inquiries.
instead:	We will look into the matter for you.
	We will research the matter for you.

meet with (one's) approval   This stiff phrase can often be avoided by recasting the sentence.

not:	If the plan meets with your approval,
instead:	If the plan is acceptable to you,
	If you approve the plan,

not within (one's) power to   Sentences using this phrase can often be recast.

not:	It is not within our power to pursue such a questionable goal.
instead:	We cannot pursue such a questionable goal.

notwithstanding the fact that   This wordy phrase can be replaced with *although* or *even though.*

not:	notwithstanding the fact that her basic complaint is well-founded
instead:	even though her basic complaint is well-founded

of a . . . nature/of this nature   This phrase can usually be avoided by using an adjective or by recasting the sentence.

not:	The court does not normally hear cases of a probate nature.
instead:	The court does not normally hear probate cases.

of the opinion that   This stiff phrase can often be avoided.

not:	We are of the opinion that
instead:	We think (*or* believe) that
	Our opinion is that

on a . . . basis/on the basis of   Though these phrases are sometimes useful and unavoidable, they can often be replaced.

not:	On the basis of what we have learned so far,
	They accepted the case on the basis of its merits.
	We will provide services on an as-needed basis.
instead:	From what we have learned so far,
	They accepted the case because of its merits.
	We will provide services as needed.

on or about   Outside of legal contexts, this phrase can often be shortened to either *on* or *about.*

period of time   This can often be shortened to either *period* or *time.*

not:	during this period of time
instead:	during this period

pursuant to   This stiff phrase, which unfortunately occurs at the very beginning of many follow-up letters and memorandums, can be replaced with *According to, Following up, As a follow-up to,* or *In accordance with.*

not:	Pursuant to discussions held in this office on June 1,
instead:	Following up our June 1 meeting,

reason is because   Replace *because* with *that.*

receipt . . . is acknowledged   This impersonal passive construction can be replaced by *We received* or *We have received.*

reduce to a minimum   Replace with *minimize.*

not:	This tack reduces to a minimum the possibility of error.
instead:	This tack minimizes the possibility of error.

refuse and decline   Shorten to either *refuse* or *decline.*

not:	We must refuse and decline any further dealings
instead:	We must refuse any further dealings
	We must decline to have any further dealings

regarded as being   Omit *being.*

not:	The witness is regarded as being hostile.
instead:	The witness is regarded as hostile.

reiterate again   Omit *again.*

said   Though standard in legal documents, this adjective sounds stiff in other contexts. Use *the, this, that, these,* or *those* instead.

not:	the complaints of said clients
instead:	the complaints of these clients
	these clients' complaints

same   This is often an awkward substitute for *it* or *them,* or for the noun it replaces.

not:	We have your check and we thank you for same.
	Your July 2 inquiry has been received and same is being researched.
instead:	Thank you for your check.
	Your July 2 inquiry has been received and is being researched.

subsequent to   This phrase may usually be replaced by one beginning with *after* or *following.*

not:	Subsequent to her acceptance of the job,
instead:	After accepting the job,

therefor/therein/thereon   Though common in legal documents, these words sound stiff in general business contexts.

not:	The order is enclosed herewith with payment therefor.
	The safe is in a secure area with the blueprints kept therein.
	Enclosed please find Form X; please affix your signature thereon.
instead:	We're enclosing a check with our order.
	The blueprints are kept in the safe, which is located in a secure area.
	Please sign the enclosed Form X.

to all intents and purposes   This phrase can usually be replaced by *in effect* or *really*.

> *not:*   Their response was, to all intents and purposes, no response at all.
>
> *instead:* Their response was, in effect, no response at all.

until such time as   This legalism may usually be replaced by *until* or *unless*.

> *not:*   Until such time as we receive new instructions from you,
>
> *instead:* Until we receive new instructions from you,

up to the present writing   This stilted expression can be replaced with briefer alternatives.

> *not:*   Up to the present writing, we have not received your answer.
>
> *instead:* We have not yet received your answer.
> We still haven't received your answer.
> To date, we have not received your answer.

we would appreciate your advising us   This long phrase can usually be replaced by *please let us know*.

> *not:*   We would appreciate your advising us of any changes.
>
> *instead:* Please let us know of any changes.

whosoever/whomsoever   These highly formal words can be replaced by *whoever/whomever* or *anyone who*.

with reference to/with respect to   These phrases can usually be replaced by *as to, concerning,* or *about*.

> *not:*   He called with reference to a complaint that was received.
> With respect to your second point,
>
> *instead:* He called about a complaint that was received.
> Concerning your second point,

with the exception of   This phrase can usually be replaced by *except* or *except for*.

> *not:*   With the exception of SoundStorm, all parties have agreed in principle.
>
> *instead:* All parties except SoundStorm have agreed in principle.

would   This verbal auxiliary should not be unnecessarily repeated.

> *not:*   I would think that our chances would improve if we accepted arbitration.
>
> *instead:* I think our chances would improve if we accepted arbitration.

Editing and Proofreading

Basic editing primarily requires checking a manuscript for grammar, spelling, punctuation, stylistic consistency, and factual accuracy, and may also involve moving or even rewriting entire sentences and paragraphs. Such basic editing is often called *copyediting*. Good editing requires a firm grasp of English style and usage and a strong sense of organizational logic.

Proofreading, in its narrow sense, is the late-stage correcting of material that has already been typeset—that is, professionally set in type by a typesetter. The word means literally the reading and checking of *proofs*—copies of newly typeset material sent back from the typesetter to the editor for correction—against the original manuscript. But the term *proofreading* is generally used today to mean the final checking of *any* written material.

In the era of word processors, laser printers, and desktop publishing systems, the line between editing and proofreading has become blurred. There is, however, still a distinction to be made between the initial critical editing done on any letter or manuscript and the final checking for errors in revised and rekeyboarded material—even when you are simultaneously the author, editor, and proofreader of a given document, and thus communicating only with yourself when you mark it up.

Both editing and proofreading require that you have at hand a good desk dictionary. In addition, it can be very useful to have a style manual (such as Chapter 2 of this book), a thesaurus, and possibly other specialized reference books. If your company has its own style guide, the rules stated there must be followed.

The principal difference in marking between editing and proofreading is that, in formal proofreading (that is, when checking typeset proofs), each error must be marked both where it occurs and in the margin immediately to the left or right. Whereas manuscript for editing is normally double-spaced, allowing room for handwritten additions, lines of typeset material (or keyboarded material in final form) are usually set close together, so only small marks can be made within the text. Thus, the margins provide room for larger marks and the insertion of omitted material; just as important, marginal notations make the corrections more visible so that the typist or typesetter will not overlook them. The corrections in the margins for a given line must be shown in the same order (reading from left to right) as they are marked in the text itself; that is, if the first correction is shown in the left margin, the second must either follow it immediately (with a slash in between) or be written in the right margin. Instructions—such as "cap" (for "capitalize") or "sp" for ("spell out")—are generally circled, but added or substituted text is not.

Figures 3.1, 3.2, and 3.3 show, respectively, an edited manuscript page, a table of proofreading marks, and a sheet of proof that has been proofread. (The number of errors in the proof is unrealistically high.) Most of the marks shown within the text area in Fig. 3.1 can be used equally for editing and for proofreading, but in formal proofreading each mark must be accompanied in the margin by the mark or notation shown there in the illustration.

When proofreading, move a ruler, an index card, or a blank sheet of paper slowly down the newly set or keyboarded page to keep your eye focused on each successive line, and use your finger to keep your place on the manu-

Figure 3.1. An Edited Memo

PAYNE SAPERSTEIN INC.

❖ ❖

MEMORANDUM

DATE: February 29, 20--

TO: The Employees of Questron Datalabs

FROM: Peter Tamposi, Executive Vice President

RE: Transition

As you have already been ~~advised,~~ *informed,* Gregory Christensen has ~~elected~~ *decided* to leave Questron to take the position of V.P. *for Research* at DeltaX in Los Angeles. Greg has made many *significant* contributions to ~~the development of~~ *creative energies and his* Questron, and the loss of his insights about our industry will be missed.

It is with *(rom)* ~~great~~ pleasure that I can announce that the board of directors of Payne Saperstein has approved the promotion of Kenneth Borland, one of Questron's own, to be ~~the~~ *its* new president. He exemplifies the employee-oriented management style that makes *the special company* Questron ~~what it is.~~ In his more than 15 years here, Ken has been a leader in shaping the quality of Questron's existing products and he has served as well as a skilful advocate for moving into the electronic future.

Ken's appointment ~~is~~ *represents* a vote of confidence in the past achievements of Questron and its promising future as a new and welcome Member of the growing corporate family of Payne Saperstein. Please give Ken your congratulations and cooperation. ~~Ken~~ *He* will be coming to Houston shortly to discuss the company's new direction *with the Payne Saperstein management,* and I hope to be in Phoenix myself next week to visit with Ken and his team on their home ground.

Figure 3.2. Proofreaders' Marks

ℰ or ℰ or ℰ	delete; take it out	: or ⊙	colon
ℭ	close up; print as one word	ℰ ℰ or ℰ ℰ	quotation marks
ℰ	delete and close up	(/)	parentheses
∧ or > or ∧	caret; insert here (something	[/]	brackets
#	insert a space	↑	comma
eq #	space evenly where indicated	↓	apostrophe
stet	let marked text stand as set	⊙	period
tr	transpose; change order the	; or ;/	semicolon
⊏ ⌞	set farther to the left		
⌉ set⌉	farther to the right		
=	straighten alignment		
‖ ‖	straighten or align		
X	imperfect or broken character		
☐	indent or insert em quad space		
¶	begin a new paragraph		
⑤ℙ	spell out ⟨set 5 lbs as five pounds⟩		
cap	set in capitals ⟨CAPITALS⟩		
sm cap or s.c.	set in small capitals ⟨SMALL CAPITALS⟩		
lc	set in lowercase ⟨lowercase⟩		
ital	set in italic ⟨italic⟩		
rom	set in roman ⟨roman⟩		
bf	set in boldface ⟨boldface⟩		
= or -/ or ⌃ or /H/	hyphen		
$\frac{1}{N}$ or en or /N/	en dash ⟨1965–72⟩		
$\frac{1}{M}$ or em or /M/	em — or long — dash		
∨	superscript or superior ⟨3 as in πr^2⟩		
∧	subscript or inferior ⟨2 as in H_2O⟩		
⌃∨ or X	centered ⟨· for a centered dot in $p \cdot q$⟩		

script beside it. Read a few words at a time from the manuscript before immediately reading the same words on the new version or proof. Train yourself to read word by word, or even character by character. Otherwise, you will fail to notice omitted words and letters, transposed words and letters, and misspellings in general, since you will tend to unconsciously "correct" them as you read.

After proofreading the final version against the original manuscript, go back and reread it all by itself for its content as if you were its intended recipient. You may discover important errors, omissions, or repetitions that you missed when doing your more "mechanical" proofreading.

Though word processing has facilitated writing in many ways, it has also facilitated the making of certain kinds of errors. In word-processed manuscripts, be especially alert for unintentional deletions, symbols introduced

Figure 3.3. A Proofread Paragraph

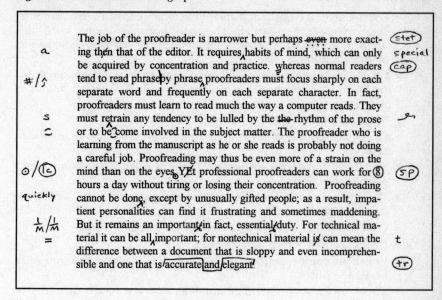

accidentally, italic and boldface type that runs on past where it should have ended, and material that was not properly deleted at its original location after new material was substituted. Perhaps the main reason for an increase in errors in word-processed writing is that checking for errors on the computer screen is far less effective than doing so on the printed page.

Word-processing programs today standardly include spelling-, grammar- and style-checking features, as well as dictionaries and thesauruses. Use a spell checker when you want to check an entire document for misspellings or typographical errors. Spell checkers are popular and can be very useful; however, they will not recognize when a word has been mistakenly used in place of another, similar word (for example, *there* in place of *their*). Grammar and style checkers are designed to check for correct sentence structure, punctuation, and mechanical errors such as mixed capitalization or transposed words. However, because of the complexities of language, grammar and style checkers have been found problematic by many users. No software can substitute for a sound knowledge of English style, and the deficiencies in grammar and style checkers are such that you may well be better off ignoring them.

The following checklists may be useful as reminders for the editor and proofreader.

EDITING CHECKLIST

- For the sake of consistency when editing large manuscripts, consider creating a *style sheet*—an alphabetical list of troublesome words that occur in the manuscript, showing their proper spelling, punctuation, or capitalization.
- Check the organization of the document. If there are headings and subheadings, they should by themselves form a coherent outline of the contents.
- Make sure the paragraphing is logical.
- Check the spelling of every word about which you are not absolutely certain.
- Be alert to errors involving similar words (e.g., *it/if/is*) and homophones *(hear/here)*.
- Check all proper names. This can be a sensitive area, and errors can slip through very easily.
- Check that list entries are grammatically parallel.
- Check for noun/verb agreement.
- Check all number sequences, particularly numbered lists and numbered footnotes.
- Check *and recheck* any other numbers that are used—they may be extremely important. It may be wise to check any arithmetic using the computer's calculator function.
- Be sure that all dates are correct.
- Check that all alphabetical lists are in proper alphabetical order.
- Be sure that all punctuation is in place and consistent. Be especially alert to paired punctuation marks—parentheses, quotation marks, dashes, and brackets.
- Be sure that capitalization is consistent, particularly in headings, in unusual terms, and in lists and tables.
- Check any bibliographical references for consistency and accuracy.

PROOFREADING CHECKLIST

- In letters, check especially that the dateline, reference line, initials, enclosure line, and carbon-copy notation have been included.
- Check that all headings and other separate elements are consistent in style and properly positioned.
- Check that any table of contents is accurate as to both titles and page numbers.
- Check all cross-references.
- Check that all margins are proper.
- Check tables for horizontal and vertical alignment.

- Check that no footnotes have been omitted.
- Be alert for unintentional repetition of small words (*and and, the the,* etc.).
- Check that page numbers are correct. Check any running heads (headers) or running feet (footers).
- Check any headings and captions separately.

CHAPTER 4

Forms of Address

The following pages contain a chart of forms of address for individuals whose offices, ranks, or professions warrant special courtesy. (For information about complimentary closes, see Chapter 1.) The main categories in the chart are listed below in the order of their appearance.

1. Government Officials—Federal
2. Government Officials—State
3. Government Officials—Local
4. Clerical and Religious Orders
5. College and University Faculty and Officials
6. Diplomats and Consular Officers
7. Military Personnel
8. Miscellaneous Professional Titles
9. Multiple Addressees

A more detailed discussion of special titles and abbreviations (*Doctor, Esquire, Honorable,* etc.) follows the Forms of Address Chart. For the use of gender-neutral salutations, see Chapter 1.

When two or more styles are shown in the Forms of Address table, the most formal appears first.

Approximately half of the entries are illustrated with a man's name and half with a woman's name. The female equivalent of *Sir* is *Madam* (or *Madame* when the addressee is foreign). The female equivalent of *Mr.* when it immediately precedes a name is *Ms.* (or *Mrs.* or *Miss* if either is known to be preferred by the addressee). The male equivalent of *Madam* standing alone is *Sir.* When *Madam* precedes another title, the male equivalent is *Mr.,* and vice versa. The male equivalent of *Ms.* is *Mr.* The terms *Her Excellency* and *His Excellency* are similarly equivalent.

Though lack of space has made it necessary to exclude lower-ranking officials, addressing such officials should present no problem. The official's title should appear in the address only if the official *heads* a department, and the salutation on letters to minor officials should consist simply of courtesy title + surname.

Mrs. Jennifer Burr, Chair   Dear Mrs. Burr
Hancock School Board

The substitution of a professional title for the courtesy title is correct only for high-ranking officials.

Dear Governor Serafino   Dear Major Stearns
Dear Judge Dvorak   Dear Sheriff [*or* Mr.] Robbins

184

Forms of Address Chart

Inside-Address Style	*Salutation Style*
Government Officials—Federal	

Attorney General
The Honorable Judith L. Smith   Madam
The Attorney General   Dear Madam Attorney General

Cabinet officer (other than Attorney General)
The Honorable Michael C. Smith   Sir
Secretary of _____   Dear Mr. Secretary
   or
The Secretary of _____   (same)

Cabinet officer, former
The Honorable Judith L. Smith   Dear Ms. Smith

Chairman of a (sub)committee, U.S. Congress (styles shown apply to both House
   of Representatives and Senate)
The Honorable Michael C. Smith   Sir
Chairman   Dear Mr. Chairman
Committee on _____   Dear Senator Smith
United States Senate

Chief justice—see SUPREME COURT, FEDERAL; STATE

Commissioner
   if appointed
The Honorable Judith L. Smith   Dear Madam Commissioner
Commissioner   Dear Ms. Smith
   if career
Ms. Judith L. Smith   Dear Commissioner Smith
Commissioner

Congressman—see REPRESENTATIVE, U.S. CONGRESS

Director (as of an independent federal agency)
The Honorable Michael C. Smith   Dear Mr. Smith
Director   Dear Director Smith
_____ Agency   Dear Director

District attorney
The Honorable Judith L. Smith   Dear Ms. Smith
District Attorney

Federal judge
The Honorable Michael C. Smith   Sir
Judge of the United States District   Dear Judge Smith
   Court of the _____ District
   of _____

Inside-Address Style	*Salutation Style*

Justice—see SUPREME COURT, FEDERAL; STATE

Librarian of Congress
| The Honorable Judith L. Smith | Madam |
| Librarian of Congress | Dear Ms. Smith |

Postmaster General
| The Honorable Michael C. Smith | Sir |
| The Postmaster General | Dear Mr. Postmaster General |

President of the United States
| The President | Mr. President |
| | Dear Mr. President |

President of the United States (former)
| The Honorable Michael C. Smith | Sir |
| | Dear Mr. Smith |

President-elect of the United States
| The Honorable Judith L. Smith | Dear Madam |
| President-elect of the United States | Dear Ms. Smith |

Representative, U.S. Congress
| The Honorable Judith L. Smith | Madam |
| United States House of Representatives | Dear Representative Smith |

Representative, U.S. Congress (former)
| The Honorable Michael C. Smith | Dear Mr. Smith |

Senator, U.S. Senate
| The Honorable Judith L. Smith | Madam |
| United States Senate | Dear Senator Smith |

Senator-elect
| The Honorable Michael C. Smith | Dear Mr. Smith |
| Senator-elect | |

Senator (former)
| The Honorable Judith L. Smith | Dear Senator Smith |

Speaker, U.S. House of Representatives
The Honorable Speaker of the House	Madam
of Representatives	
or	
The Honorable Judith L. Smith	Madam
Speaker of the House of	Dear Madam Speaker
Representatives	Dear Ms. Smith

Speaker, U.S. House of Representatives (former)
The Honorable Judith L. Smith	Madam
	Dear Madam Speaker
	Dear Ms. Smith

Inside-Address Style	Salutation Style
Special assistant to the President	
Mr. Michael C. Smith	Dear Mr. Smith
Supreme Court, associate justice	
Mr. Justice Smith	Sir
The Supreme Court of the United	Dear Mr. Justice
States	Dear Justice Smith
Supreme Court, chief justice	
The Chief Justice of the United States	Sir
or	Dear Mr. Chief Justice
The Chief Justice	(same)
Supreme Court, retired Justice	
The Honorable Judith L. Smith	Madam
	Dear Justice Smith
Territorial delegate	
The Honorable Judith L. Smith	Dear Ms. Smith
Delegate of _____	
House of Representatives	
Undersecretary of a department	
The Honorable Michael C. Smith	Dear Mr. Smith
Undersecretary of _____	
Vice President of the United States	
The Vice President of the United States	Madam
United States Senate	Dear Madam Vice President
or	
The Honorable Judith L. Smith	(same)
Vice President of the United States	

Government Officials—State

Assemblyman—see REPRESENTATIVE, STATE

Attorney general	
The Honorable Michael C. Smith	Sir
Attorney General of the State	Dear Mr. Attorney General
of _____	
Clerk of a court	
Judith L. Smith, Esq.	Dear Ms. Smith
Clerk of the Court of _____	

Delegate—see REPRESENTATIVE, STATE

Governor	
The Honorable Michael C. Smith	Sir
Governor of _____	Dear Governor Smith
or in some states	
His Excellency, the Governor	(same)
of _____	

Inside-Address Style	*Salutation Style*
Governor (acting)	
The Honorable Judith L. Smith	Madam
Acting Governor of _____	Dear Ms. Smith
Governor-elect	
The Honorable Michael C. Smith	Dear Mr. Smith
Governor-elect of _____	
Governor (former)	
The Honorable Judith L. Smith	Dear Ms. Smith
Judge, state court	
The Honorable Michael C. Smith	Sir
Judge of the _____ Court	Dear Judge Smith
Judge/justice, state supreme court—see SUPREME COURT, STATE	
Lieutenant governor	
The Honorable Lieutenant Governor of _____	Madam
or	
The Honorable Judith L. Smith	Madam
Lieutenant Governor of _____	Dear Ms. Smith
Representative, state (includes assemblyman, delegate)	
The Honorable Michael C. Smith	Sir
House of Representatives (State Assembly, House of Delegates, etc.)	Dear Mr. Smith
Secretary of state	
The Honorable Secretary of State of _____	Madam
or	
The Honorable Judith L. Smith	Madam
Secretary of State of _____	Dear Madam Secretary
Senate, state, president of	
The Honorable Michael C. Smith	Sir
President of the Senate of the State of _____ Senator	Dear Mr. Smith
Senator, state	
The Honorable Judith L. Smith	Madam
The Senate of _____	Dear Senator Smith
Speaker, state assembly (house of delegates, house of representatives)	
The Honorable Michael C. Smith	Sir
Speaker of _____	Dear Mr. Smith
State's attorney	
The Honorable Judith L. Smith (title)	Dear Ms. Smith

Inside-Address Style	*Salutation Style*

Supreme court, state, associate justice
The Honorable Judith L. Smith — Madam
Associate Justice of the Supreme Court — Dear Justice Smith
  of ———

Supreme court, state, chief justice
The Honorable Michael C. Smith — Sir
Chief Justice of the Supreme Court — Dear Mr. Chief Justice
  of ———

Supreme court, state, presiding justice
The Honorable Judith L. Smith — Madam
Presiding Justice ——— Division — Dear Madam Justice
  Supreme Court of ———

Government Officials—Local

Alderman
The Honorable Michael C. Smith — Dear Mr. Smith
— Dear Alderman Smith

  or
Alderman Michael C. Smith — (same)

City attorney (includes city counsel, corporation counsel)
The Honorable Judith L. Smith — Dear Ms. Smith

Councilman—see ALDERMAN

County clerk
The Honorable Michael C. Smith — Dear Mr. Smith
Clerk of ——— County

County treasurer—see COUNTY CLERK

Judge
The Honorable Judith L. Smith — Dear Judge Smith
Judge of the ——— Court of ———

Mayor
The Honorable Michael C. Smith — Sir
Mayor of ——— — Dear Mr. Mayor
— Dear Mayor Smith

Selectman—see ALDERMAN

Clerical and Religious Orders

Abbot
The Right Reverend Michael C. Smith, — Right Reverend and dear Father
  O.S.B. (O.F.M., etc.) — Dear Father Abbot
Abbot of ——— — Dear Father

Inside-Address Style	Salutation Style
Archbishop	
The Most Reverend Archbishop of _____	Your Excellency Most Reverend Sir
or	
The Most Reverend Michael C. Smith Archbishop of _____	Your Excellency Dear Archbishop Smith
Archdeacon	
The Venerable The Archdeacon of _____	Venerable Sir Dear Archdeacon Smith
or	
The Venerable Michael C. Smith Archdeacon of _____	(same)
Bishop, Catholic	
The Most Reverend Michael C. Smith Bishop of _____	Most Reverend Sir Your Excellency Dear Bishop Smith
Bishop, Episcopal	
The Right Reverend The Bishop of _____	Right Reverend Sir
or	
The Right Reverend Michael C. Smith Bishop _____	Right Reverend Sir Dear Bishop Smith
Bishop, Episcopal, Presiding	
The Most Reverend Michael C. Smith Presiding Bishop	Most Reverend Sir Dear Bishop Dear Bishop Smith
Bishop, Protestant (excluding Episcopal)	
The Reverend Michael C. Smith	Reverend Sir Dear Bishop Smith
Brotherhood, member of	
Brother Michael, S.J. (O.F.M., O.S.B., etc.)	Dear Brother Dear Brother John
Canon	
The Reverend Michael C. Smith Canon of _____ Cathedral	Dear Canon Smith
Cardinal	
His Eminence Michael Cardinal Smith	Your Eminence Dear Cardinal Smith
or	
His Eminence Cardinal Smith	(same)
or if also an archbishop	
His Eminence Michael Cardinal Smith Archbishop of _____	(same)
or	
His Eminence Cardinal Smith Archbishop of _____	(same)

Inside-Address Style	Salutation Style

Chaplain, college or university—see COLLEGE AND UNIVERSITY FACULTY AND OFFICIALS

Clergy, Protestant

The Reverend Judith L. Smith	Dear Ms. Smith
or with a doctorate	
The Reverend Dr. Judith L. Smith	Dear Dr. Smith

Dean (of a cathedral)

The Very Reverend Michael C. Smith	Very Reverend Sir
_____ Cathedral	Dear Dean Smith
or	
Dean Michael C. Smith	(same)
_____ Cathedral	

Monsignor, domestic prelate

The Reverend Monsignor Michael C. Smith	Reverend and dear Monsignor Smith
or	
The Rev. Msgr. Michael C. Smith	Dear Monsignor Smith

Monsignor, papal chamberlain

The Very Reverend Monsignor Michael C. Smith	Very Reverend and dear Monsignor Smith
	Dear Monsignor Smith
or	
The Very Rev. Msgr. Michael C. Smith	(same)

Mother superior (of a sisterhood)

The Reverend Mother Superior	Reverend Mother
Convent of _____	Dear Reverend Mother
or	
Reverend Mother Mary Angelica, O.S.D. (S.M., S.C., Etc.)	(same)
Convent of _____	
or	
Mother Mary Angelica, Superior	(same)
Convent of _____	

Patriarch (of an Eastern Orthodox Church)

His Beatitude the Patriarch of _____	Most Reverend Lord
	Your Beatitude

Pope

His Holiness the Pope	Your Holiness
	Most Holy Father
or	
His Holiness Pope John Paul II	(same)

President, Mormon

The President	Dear President Smith
Church of Jesus Christ of Latter-day Saints	

Inside-Address Style	*Salutation Style*

Priest, Catholic

The Reverend Father Smith	Reverend Father
	Dear Father Smith
or	Dear Father
The Reverend Michael C. Smith	(same)

Priest, president (of a college or university)—see COLLEGE AND UNIVERSITY FACULTY
AND OFFICIALS

Rabbi

Rabbi Michael C. Smith	Dear Rabbi Smith
or with a doctorate	
Rabbi Michael C. Smith, D.D.	Dear Dr. Smith

Sisterhood, member of

Sister Mary Angelica, S.C. (S.M.,	Dear Sister
O.S.D., etc.)	Dear Sister Mary Angelica

College and University Faculty and Officials

Chancellor

Dr. Judith L. Smith	Dear Dr. Smith
Chancellor	

Chaplain

The Reverend Michael C. Smith	Dear Chaplain Smith
Chaplain	Dear Father Smith
	Dear Mr. Smith

Dean

Dean Judith L. Smith	Dear Dr. Smith
	Dear Dean Smith
or	
Dr. Judith L. Smith	(same)
Dean	

Instructor

Mr. Michael C. Smith	Dear Mr. Smith
Instructor	

President

Dr. Judith L. Smith	Dear Dr. Smith
President	
or	
President Judith L. Smith	Dear President Smith

President, priest

The Very Reverend Michael C. Smith	Dear Father Smith
President	

Inside-Address Style	Salutation Style

Professor, assistant or associate

Ms. Judith L. Smith	Dear Professor Smith
Assistant/Associate Professor	Dear Ms. Smith
of _____	
or with a doctorate	
Dr. Judith L. Smith	Dear Dr. Smith
Assistant/Associate Professor of _____	

Professor, full

Professor Michael C. Smith	Dear Professor Smith
or	
Dr. Michael C. Smith	Dear Dr. Smith
Professor of _____	

Diplomats and Consular Officers

Ambassador, American

The Honorable Judith L. Smith	Madam
American Ambassador	Dear Madam Ambassador
	Dear Ambassador Smith
or if in Central or South America	
The Honorable Judith L. Smith	(same)
Ambassador of the United States of	
America	

Ambassador, foreign

His Excellency Michael C. Smith	Excellency
Ambassador of _____	Dear Mr. Ambassador

Chargé d'affaires ad interim, American

Judith L. Smith, Esq.	Madam
American Chargé d'Affaires ad Interim	Dear Ms. Smith
or if in Latin America or Canada	
Judith L. Smith, Esq.	(same)
United States Charge d'Affaires ad	
Interim	

Chargé d'affaires ad interim, foreign

Mr. Michael C. Smith	Sir
Chargé d'Affaires ad Interim	Dear Mr. Smith
of _____	

Chargé d'affaires, foreign

Ms. Judith L. Smith	Madame
Chargé d'Affaires of _____	Dear Ms. Smith

Consulate, American

The American Consulate	Ladies and Gentlemen
or if in Central or South America	

Inside-Address Style	Salutation Style
The Consulate of the United States of America	(same)

Consul, American (covers all consular grades such as *Consul, Consul General, Vice-Consul,* and *Consular Agent*)

The American Consul	Sir or Madam
or if in Central or South America	
The Consul of the United States of America	(same)
or if individual name is known	
Judith L. Smith, Esq.	Madam
American Consul	Dear Ms. Smith
or if in Central or South America	
Judith L. Smith, Esq.	(same)
Consul of the United States of America	

Consulate, foreign

The _____ Consulate	Ladies and Gentlemen
or	
The Consulate of _____	(same)

Consuls, foreign (covers all consular grades)

The _____ Consul	Sir or Madame
or	
The Consul of _____	(same)
or if individual name is known	
The Honorable Michael C. Smith	Sir
_____ Consul	Dear Mr. Smith

Minister, American

The Honorable Michael C. Smith	Sir
American Minister	Dear Mr. Minister
or if in Latin America or Canada	
Minister of the United States of America	(same)

Minister, foreign

The Honorable Judith L. Smith	Madame
Minister of _____	Dear Madame Minister

Representative to the United Nations, American

The Honorable Judith L. Smith	Madam
United States Permanent Representative to the United Nations	Dear Madam Ambassador

Representative to the United Nations, foreign

His Excellency Michael C. Smith	Excellency
Representative of _____ to the United Nations	Dear Mr. Ambassador

Inside-Address Style	*Salutation Style*

Secretary-General of the United Nations

| Her Excellency Judith L. Smith | Excellency |
| Secretary-General of the United Nations | Dear Madam (or Madame) Secretary-General |

Undersecretary of the United Nations

| The Honorable Michael C. Smith | Sir |
| Undersecretary of the United Nations | Dear Mr. Smith |

Military Personnel

The first entry below describes an appropriate form of address for any member of the armed forces. Abbreviations for each rank and the branches of service using them are shown at individual entries. In actual practice, salutations will differ according to degree of formality. The most formal will often employ the addressee's full title. The salutations shown generally represent a level of formality between the highly formal and the familiar.

For any rank

| *full or abbreviated rank + full name + comma + abbreviation of the branch of service (USA, USN, USAF, USMC, USCG)* | Dear + *full rank + surname* |

Admiral [coast guard, navy (ADM)]

Admiral Judith L. Smith, USCG (etc)	Dear Admiral Smith
or	
ADM Judith L. Smith, USCG (etc)	(same)

    —a similar pattern is used for **rear admiral** (RADM), **vice admiral** (VADM), and **fleet admiral** (FADM), with the full rank given in the salutation line.

Airman [air force (Amn)]

Airman Michael C. Smith, USAF	Dear Airman Smith
or	
Amn Michael C. Smith, USAF	(same)

    —a similar pattern is used for **airman basic** (AB) and **airman first class** (A1C), with the full rank given in the salutation line.

Cadet [U.S. Air Force Academy, U.S. Military Academy]

| Cadet Judith L. Smith | Dear Cadet Smith |

Captain [army (CPT); coast guard, navy (CAPT); air force, marine corps (Capt)]

Captain Michael C. Smith, USAF (etc)	Dear Captain Smith
or	
Capt Michael C. Smith, USAF (etc)	(same)

Chief master sergeant [air force (CMgt)]

Chief Master Sergeant Michael C. Smith, USAF	Dear Chief Smith
or	
CMSgt Michael C. Smith, USAF	(same)

    —a similar pattern is used for **chief master sergeant of the air force** [air force (CMSAF)].

Chief petty officer [coast guard, navy (CPO)]

Inside-Address Style	Salutation Style
Chief Petty Officer Judith L. Smith	Dear Chief Smith
or	
CPO Judith L. Smith, USN (etc)	(same)

Chief warrant officer [army (CW2, CW3, CW4, CW5); navy, coast guard, air force (CWO-2, CWO-3, CWO-4); marine corps (CWO2, CWO3, CWO4)]

Chief Warrant Officer Judith L. Smith, USA (etc)	Dear Ms. Smith
	Dear Chief Warrant Officer Smith
or	
CW4 Judith L. Smith, USA (etc)	(same)

Colonel [army (COL); air force, marine corps (Col)]

Colonel Judith L. Smith, USMC (etc	Dear Colonel Smith
or	
Col Judith L. Smith, USMC (etc)	(same)

—a similar pattern is used for **lieutenant colonel** [army (LTC); air force, marine corps (LtCol)], with the full rank given in the salutation line.

Commander [coast guard, navy (CDR)

Commander Michael C. Smith, USN (etc)	Dear Commander Smith
or	
CDR Michael C. Smith, USCG (etc)	(same)

—a similar pattern is used for **lieutenant commander** [coast guard, navy (LCDR)], with the full rank given in the salutation line.

Corporal [army (CPL); marine corps (Cpl)]

Corporal Judith L. Smith, USA (etc)	Dear Corporal Smith
or	
CPL Judith L. Smith, USA (etc)	(same)

—a similar pattern is used for **lance corporal** [marine corps (L/Cpl)], with the full rank given in the salutation line.

Ensign [coast guard, navy (ENS)]

Ensign Michael C. Smith, USN (etc)	Dear Ensign Smith
	Dear Mr. Smith
or	
ENS Michael C. Smith, USN (etc)	(same)

First lieutenant [army (1LT); air force, marine corps (1stLt)]

First Lieutenant Judith L. Smith, USMC (etc)	Dear Lieutenant Smith
or	
1stLt Judith L. Smith, USMC (etc)	(same)

Inside-Address Style	*Salutation Style*

General [army (GEN); air force, marine corps (Gen)]
General Judith L. Smith, USAF (etc.)   Dear General Smith
  or
Gen Judith L. Smith, USAF (etc.)   (same)

  —a similar pattern is used for **brigadier general** [army (BG); air force (BGen),
    marine corps (BrigGen)], **major general** [army (MG); air force, marine
    corps (MajGen)], and **lieutenant general** [army (LTG); air force, marine
    corps (LtGen)], with the full rank given in the salutation line.

Lieutenant [coast guard, navy (LT)]
Lieutenant Michael C. Smith, USN   Dear Lieutenant Smith
  (etc)   Dear Mr. Smith
  or
LT Michael C. Smith, USN (etc)   (same)

Lieutenant junior grade [coast guard, navy (LTJG)]
Lieutenant (j.g.) Judith L. Smith,   Dear Lieutenant Smith
  USCG (etc)   Dear Ms. Smith
  or
LTJG Judith L. Smith, USCG (etc)   (same)

Major [army (MAJ); air force, marine corps (Maj)]
Major Michael C. Smith, USAF (etc)   Dear Major Smith
  or
Maj. Michael C. Smith, USAF (etc)   (same)

Master chief petty officer [coast guard, navy (MCPO)]
Master Chief Petty Officer Judith L.   Dear Master Chief Smith
  Smith, USN (etc)
  or
MCPO Judith L. Smith, USN (etc)   (same)

Midshipman [coast guard and naval academies]
Midshipman Michael C. Smith   Dear Midshipman Smith

Petty officer first class [coast guard, navy (PO1)]
Petty Officer First Class Michael C.   Dear Petty Officer Smith
  Smith, USN (etc)
  or
PO1 Michael C. Smith, USN (etc)   (same)

  —a similar pattern is used for **petty officer second class** (PO2) and **petty
    officer third class** (PO3).

Private [army (PVT); marine corps (Pvt)]
Private Michael C. Smith, USMC (etc)   Dear Private Smith
  or
Pvt Michael C. Smith, USMC (etc)   (same)

  —a similar pattern is used for **private first class** [army, marine corps (PFC)].

Inside-Address Style	*Salutation Style*

Seaman [coast guard, navy (Seaman)]
Seaman Judith L. Smith, USCG (etc)   Dear Seaman Smith

   —a similar pattern is used for **seaman apprentice** (SA) and **seaman recruit** (SR).

Second lieutenant [army (2LT); air force, marine corps (2ndLt)]
Second Lieutenant Michael C. Smith,   Dear Lieutenant Smith
 USA (etc)
   or
2LT Michael C. Smith, USA (etc)   (same)

Senior chief petty officer [coast guard, navy (SCPO)]
Senior Chief Petty Officer Michael C.   Dear Senior Chief Smith
 Smith, USCG (etc)
   or
SCPO Michael C. Smith, USCG (etc)   (same)

Sergeant [army (SGT); air force, marine corps (Sgt)]
Sergeant Judith L. Smith, USAF (etc)]   Dear Sergeant Smith
   or
Sgt Judith L. Smith, USAF (etc)   (same)

   —a similar pattern is used for other sergeant ranks, including **first sergeant**
    [army (1SG); marine corps (1stSgt)]; **gunnery sergeant** [marine corps
    (GySgt)]; **master gunnery sergeant** [marine corps (MGySgt)]; **master
    sergeant** [army (MSG); air force, marine corps (MSgt)]; **senior master
    sergeant** [air force (SMSgt)]; **sergeant first class** [army (SFC)]; **staff sergeant**
    [army (SSG); air force, marine corps (SSgt)]; and **technical sergeant** [air
    force (TSgt)], with the full rank given in the salutation line.

Sergeant major [army (SGM); marine corps (SgtMaj)]
Sergeant Major Judith L. Smith, USMC   Dear Sergeant Major Smith
 (etc)
   or
SgtMaj Judith L. Smith, USMC (etc)   (same)

   —a similar pattern is used for **command sergeant major** [army (CSM)],
    sergeant major of the army [army (SMA)], and **sergeant major of the marine
    corps** [marine corps (SgtMaj)].

Specialist [army (SPC)]
Specialist Michael C. Smith, USA   Dear Specialist Smith
   or
SPC Michael C. Smith, USA   (same)

Warrant officer [army (WO1, WO2); navy (WO-1); air force, marine corps (WO)]
Warrant Officer Michael C. Smith, USA   Dear Warrant Officer Smith
 (etc)   Dear Mr. Smith
   or
WO1 Michael C. Smith, USA (etc)   (same)

Inside-Address Style	Salutation Style

Miscellaneous Professional Titles

Attorney
Ms. Judith L. Smith, Attorney-at-Law	Dear Ms. Smith
or	
Judith L. Smith, Esq.	(same)

Certified public accountant
Judith L. Smith, C.P.A.	Dear Ms. Smith

Dentist
Michael C. Smith, D.D.S. (D.M.D., etc.)	Dear Dr. Smith
or	
Dr. Michael C. Smith	(same)

Physician
Judith L. Smith, M.D.	Dear Dr. Smith
or	
Dr. Judith L. Smith	(same)

Veterinarian
Michael C. Smith, D.V.M.	Dear Dr. Smith
or	
Dr. Michael C. Smith	(same)

Multiple Addressees (See also following section.)

Two or more men (with same or different surnames)
Mr. Arthur W. Smith	Gentlemen
Mr. John H. Smith	
or	
Messrs. Arthur W. Smith and John H. Smith	
or	
The Messrs. Smith	Dear Messrs. Smith

Two or more women (with same or different surnames)
Ms. Barbara F. Lee	Dear Ms. Lee and Ms. Kay
Ms. Helen G. Kay	
or	
Mss. (or Mses.) Barbara F. Lee and Helen G. Kay	
or	
Mss. (or Mses.) Lee and Kay	

Special Titles, Designations, and Abbreviations

Initials representing academic degrees, religious orders, and professional ratings may appear after a name, separated from each other by commas, in the following order: (1) religious orders (such as *S.J.*); (2) theological degrees (such as *D.D.*); (3) academic degrees (such as *Ph.D.*); (4) honorary degrees (such as *Litt.D.*); (5) professional ratings (such as *C.P.A.*).

Initials that represent academic degrees (with the exception of *M.D., D.D.S.,* and other medical degrees) are not commonly used in addresses, and two or more sets of such letters appear even more rarely. Only when the initials represent achievements in different fields that are relevant to one's profession should more than one set be used. On the other hand, initials that represent earned professional achievements (such as *C.P.A., C.A.M., C.P.S.,* or *P.E.*) are often used in business addresses. When any of these sets of initials follow a name, however, the courtesy title *(Mr., Mrs., Ms., Miss, Dr.)* is omitted.

Nancy Robinson, P.L.S.	Jordan R. Dodds, J.D., C.M.C.
Mary R. Lopez, C.P.A.	The Rev. Seamus McMalley, S.J.,
John Doctorow, M.D., Ph.D.	D.D., LL.D.
Chief of Staff	Chaplain, Hancock College
Hancock Hospital	

Below are discussed, in alphabetical order by title or designation, additional issues concerning forms of address.

DOCTOR

If *Doctor* or *Dr.* is used before a person's name, academic degrees (such as *D.D.S., D.V.M., M.D.,* or *Ph.D.*) are not included after the surname. The title *Doctor* may be either typed out in full or abbreviated in a salutation, but it is usually abbreviated on an envelope and in an inside address in order to save space. When *Doctor* appears in a salutation, it must be used in conjunction with the addressee's surname.

Dear Doctor Smith   (*not* Dear Doctor)
  or
Dear Dr. Smith

If two or more doctors are associated in a joint practice, the following styles may be used:

Drs. Francis X. Sullivan and	*formal:*
Philip K. Ross	My dear Drs. Sullivan and Ross
	informal:
Francis X. Sullivan, M.D.	Dear Drs. Sullivan and Ross
Philip K. Ross, M.D.	Dear Doctors Sullivan and Ross
	Dear Dr. Sullivan and Dr. Ross
	Dear Doctor Sullivan and
	Doctor Ross

ESQUIRE

The abbreviation *Esq.* for *Esquire* is often used in the United States after the surnames of attorneys, and also of court officials such as clerks of court and justices of the peace. *Esquire* may be written in addresses and signature lines but not in salutations. It is used regardless of sex. Some people, however, object to the use of *Esquire* as a title for a woman professional, and you should follow the recipient's wishes, if they are known, using an alternative form such as "Amy Lutz, Attorney-at-Law."

In Great Britain *Esquire* is generally used after the surnames of people who have distinguished themselves in professional, diplomatic, or social circles. For example, when addressing a letter to a British surgeon or to a high corporate officer of a British firm, one should include *Esq.* after the surname, both on the envelope and in the inside address. If a courtesy title such as *Dr., Hon., Miss, Mr., Mrs.,* or *Ms.* is used before the addressee's name, *Esquire* or *Esq.* is omitted.

The plural of *Esq.* is *Esqs.,* and it is used with the surname of multiple addresses.

Carolyn B. West, Esq.	Dear Ms. West
or	
Ms. Carolyn B. West	
Attorney-at-Law	
Samuel A. Sebert, Esq.	Gentlemen
Norman D. Langfitt, Esq.	Dear Mr. Sebert and Mr. Langfitt
	Dear Messrs. Sebert and Langfitt
or	
Sebert and Langfitt, Esqs.	
or	
Messrs. Sebert and Langfitt	
Attorneys-at-Law	
Simpson, Tyler, and Williams, Esq.	Dear Ms. Tyler and Messrs. Simpson and Williams
or	
Scott A. Simpson, Esq.	
Annabelle W. Tyler, Esq.	
David I. Williams, Esq.	

HONORABLE

In the United States, *The Honorable* or its abbreviated form *Hon.*. is used as a title of distinction (but not rank) for elected or appointed (but not career) government officials such as judges, justices, congressmen, and cabinet officers. Neither the full form nor the abbreviation is ever used by its recipient in written signatures, letterhead, business or visiting cards, or typed signature blocks. While it may be used in an envelope address block and in the inside address of a letter, it is never used in the salutation. *The Honorable* should never appear before a surname standing alone: there must always be an intervening first name, an initial or initials, or a courtesy title. A courtesy title should not be added, however, when *The Honorable* is used with a full name.

The Honorable Michael C. Smith (M. C. Smith, M. Carleton Smith)
The Honorable Mr. Smith
The Honorable Dr. Smith
   not
The Honorable Smith
   and not
The Honorable Mr. Michael C. Smith

When an official and his wife are being addressed, his full name should be typed out.

The Honorable Michael C. Smith   Dear Mr. and Mrs. Smith
 and Mrs. Smith
  or
The Honorable and Mrs. Michael
 C. Smith

The styles "Hon. and Mrs. Smith" and "The Honorable and Mrs. Smith" should never be used. If a married woman holds the title and her husband does not, her name appears first on business-related correspondence addressed to both persons. However, if the couple is being addressed socially, the woman's title may be dropped unless she has retained her maiden name for use in personal as well as business correspondence.

in business correspondence:

The Honorable Harriet O. Johnson and Mr. Johnson	Dear Mrs. (*or* Governor, etc.) Johnson and Mr. Johnson
The Honorable Harriet A. Ott and Mr. Robert Y. Johnson	Dear Ms. Ott and Mr. Johnson

in social correspondence:

Mr. and Mrs. Robert Y. Johnson	Dear Mr. and Mrs. Johnson
Ms. Harriet A. Ott Mr. Roger Y. Johnson	Dear Ms. Ott and Mr. Johnson

When *The Honorable* occurs in running text, the *T* in *The* is lowercased.

A speech by the Honorable Charles H. Patterson, the American Consul in Athens

JR. AND SR.

The designations *Jr.* and *Sr.* may or may not be preceded by a comma, depending on office policy or writer preference; however, one style should be selected and adhered to for the sake of uniformity.

John K. Walker Jr. *or* John K. Walker, Jr.

Jr. and *Sr.* may be used in conjunction with courtesy titles, academic degrees abbreviations, or professional rating abbreviations.

Mr. John K. Walker, Jr.
General John K. Walker, Jr.
The Honorable John K. Walker, Jr.

John K. Walker, Jr., Esq.
John K. Walker, Jr., M.D.
John K. Walker, Jr., C.A.M.

MADAM

The title *Madam* should be used only in salutations of highly impersonal or high-level governmental and diplomatic correspondence. The title may be used to address women officials in other instances only if the writer is certain that the addressee is married.

MESSRS.

The plural abbreviation of *Mr.* is *Messrs.* (short for *Messieurs*). It is used before the surnames of two or more men associated in a professional partnership or business. *Messrs.* may appear on an envelope, in an inside address, and in a salutation, but never without the surnames.

Messrs. Archlake, Smythe, and
  Dabney
Attorneys-at-Law
	Dear Messrs. Archlake, Smythe,
	  and Dabney
	Gentlemen

(For additional usage examples, see "Multiple Addressees" in chart.)

    Messrs. should never be used before a compound corporate name formed from two surnames, such as *Lord & Taylor* or *Woodward & Lothrop*, or a corporate name such as *H. L. Jones and Sons.* For the use of *Messrs.* with *The Reverend*, see "Reverend" below.

MSS. OR MSES.

The plural form of *Ms.* is *Mss.* or *Mses.*, and either may be used before the names of two or more women who are being addressed together. It may appear on an envelope, in an inside address, and in a salutation. Like *Messrs.*, *Mss.* or *Mses.* should never stand alone but must occur in conjunction with a name or names. (For other examples in this category, see "Multiple Addressees" in chart.)

Mss. Hay and Middleton Attorneys-at-Law	Dear Mss. Hay and Middleton

PROFESSOR

If used only with a surname, *Professor* should be typed out in full; however, if used with a given name or a set of initials as well as a surname, it may be abbreviated to *Prof.* It is therefore usually abbreviated in envelope address blocks and in inside addresses, but typed out in salutations. *Professor* should not stand alone in a salutation.

Prof. Florence C. Marlowe Department of English	Dear Professor Marlowe Dear Dr. Marlowe Dear Ms. Marlowe *but not* Dear Professor

When addressing a letter to a professor and his wife, the title is usually written out in full unless the name is unusually long.

Professor and Mrs. Lee Dow	Dear Professor and Mrs. Dow
Prof. and Mrs. Henry Talbott-Smythe	Dear Professor and Mrs. Talbott-Smythe

Letters addressed to couples in which the wife is the professor and the husband is not may follow one of these patterns:

business correspondence:

Professor Diana Goode and Mr. Goode	Dear Professor Goode and Mr. Goode

business or social correspondence:

Mr. and Mrs. Lawrence F. Goode	Dear Mr. and Mrs. Goode

if wife has retained her maiden name:

Professor Diana Falls	Dear Professor (*or* Ms.) Falls and
Mr. Lawrence F. Goode	Mr. Goode

When addressing two or more professors—male or female, whether having the same or different surnames—type *Professors* and not *Profs.:*

Professors Albert L. Smith and Charlene L. Doe	Dear Professors Smith and Doe
	Dear Drs. Smith and Doe
	Dear Mr. Smith and Ms. Doe

REVEREND

In formal or official writing, *The* should precede *Reverend;* however, *The Reverend* is often abbreviated to *The Rev.* or just *Rev.*, especially in unofficial or informal writing, and particularly in business correspondence where space is a factor. The typed-out full form *The Reverend* must be used in conjunction with the full name, as in the following examples:

The Reverend Philip D. Asquith
The Reverend Dr. Philip D. Asquith

The Reverend may appear with just a surname only if another courtesy title intervenes:

The Reverend Mr. Asquith
The Reverend Professor Asquith
The Reverend Dr. Asquith

The Reverend, The Rev., or *Rev.* should not be used in the salutation, although any of these titles may be used on the envelope and in the inside address. In salutations, the following titles are acceptable: *Mr. (Ms., Miss, Mrs.), Father, Chaplain,* or *Dr.* See the Forms of Address chart under "Clerical and Religious Orders" for examples. The only exceptions are in letters addressed to high prelates (bishops, monsignors, etc.); see the Forms of Address chart. When addressing a letter to a member of the clergy and his or her spouse, follow the following style:

The Reverend (*or* Rev.) and Mrs. Philip D. Asquith	Dear Mr. (*or with a doctorate*, Dr.) and Mrs. Asquith
The Reverend (*or* Rev.) Marcia Ogden and Mr. James Ogden	Dear Mrs. (Ms., *or with a doctorate*, Dr.) and Mr. Ogden

Two members of the clergy should not be addressed in letters as "The Reverends," "The Revs.," or "Revs." They may, however, be addressed as *The Reverend* (or *The Rev.*) *Messrs.* if both are male, or *The Reverend* (or *The Rev.*) *Drs.* if both have doctorates, or the titles *The Reverend, The Rev.,* or *Rev.* may be repeated before each name.

The Rev. Simon J. Stephens and the Rev. Barbara O. Stephens Rev. Simon J. Stephens and Rev. Barbara O. Stephens	Dear Mr. and Mrs. Stephens
The Reverend (*or* Rev.) Messrs. Philip A. Francis and Lanford Beale The Rev. Philip A. Francis The Rev. Lanford Beale	Gentlemen Dear Father Francis and Father Beale

In formal lists of names, "The Reverends," "The Revs.," and "Revs." are not acceptable as collective titles. *The Reverend* (or *Rev.*) *Messrs. (Drs., Professors)* may be used if appropriate, or *The Reverend* or *The Rev.* or *Rev.* may be repeated before each name. If the term *clergyman, clergywoman,* or *the clergy* is mentioned in introducing the list, a single title *the Reverend* or *the Rev.* may be used to serve all of the names. While it is true that "The Revs." is often seen in newspapers and elsewhere, it is still not recommended for formal, official writing.

> . . . were the Reverend Messrs. Symonds, Smith, and Bennett, as well as . . .

> Prayers were offered by the Rev. J. G. Symonds, the Rev. R. R. Smith, and the Rev. Dr. L.M. Bennett.

SECOND, THIRD, FOURTH

These designations after surnames may take the form of either Roman numerals (II, III, IV) or ordinals (2nd/2d, 3rd/3d, 4th). There is usually no comma between the name and the number.

> Mr. Jason T. Cabot III (*or* 3rd *or* 3d)

Sample Letters

Fifty Business Letters

The fifty letters that form the main part of this chapter provide models for most of the types of correspondence produced in American business offices.

In many companies today, many of these letters would be written only to confirm a previous telephone call (and the call would be acknowledged in the letter itself). Many would go out initially as faxes, with the mailed letter following as confirmation. A few might even be sent as e-mail.

Many would be stored as "boilerplate" in a computer letter file and called up to be adapted for each particular occasion. And those that might be applicable to a number of recipients simultaneously—a response to a widespread consumer complaint, for example—would probably be keyboarded only once and then personalized by means of a computer "mail merge" function.

Some of these sample letters may reflect a slightly higher level of courtesy than is often observed today, especially in business-to-business dealings in high-pressure office environments. The willingness to send a letter at all is, of course, often a mark of courtesy, and will generally be appreciated as such.

Facing each letter is a set of general guidelines and a sketch of the particular situation reflected in the sample letter.

Acceptance of Invitation

GUIDELINES:

- Open by acknowledging the request and accepting the invitation.
- Repeat the details to confirm them for both parties.
- Express your appreciation and pleasurable anticipation.

SITUATION:

Kathleen Simons has been invited by a local professor to speak to his marketing class on a subject of her expertise, and she writes to accept.

Figure 5.1 Acceptance of Invitation

DATAWARE Consultants

1287 West Liberty Avenue Sacramento, CA 95833
Tel. 916-937-1212 · Fax 916-937-1232 · e-mail dwc@cap.com

January 2, 20--

Dr. John C. Thomas
Associate Professor of Marketing
Department of Business Administration
Santa Rosa State College
Santa Rosa, CA 95405

Dear Dr. Thomas:

   Thank you very much for the kind invitation to lead an upcoming session of
your senior seminar. I will be happy to do so. I understand that the seminar will be
held from 2:30 to 5:30 p.m. on March 23 in Milton Hall, Room 1289. The topic--as
you suggested in your letter--will be "Marketing the Services of the Emerging
Growth Company."

   I am enclosing a list of references to recent articles on the subject that your
students may want to acquaint themselves with beforehand.

   I appreciate your thinking of me, and I look forward to working with your
students.

Sincerely,

Kathleen Simons

Kathleen C. Simons
President

KCS/gb
Enclosure

Acknowledgment of Complaint

GUIDELINES:

- Acknowledge receipt of the letter and thank the writer.
- Explain the reason for the delay and say when a reply can be expected.
- Close the letter courteously.

SITUATION:

Frank Haverty recently ordered components of a house alarm system from Sims Security Devices and received in addition an expensive set of remote sensors. He has called Sims to complain, and a representative writes back.

Figure 5.2   Acknowledgment of Complaint

Sims Security Devices
181 Monmouth Highway   Telephone: (404) 898-7310
Atlanta, Georgia 31722   Fax: (404) 898-7725

June 7, 20--

Frank S. Haverty
33 Woodhollow Road
Albuquerque, NM 87125

Dear Mr. Haverty:

Your complaint regarding your receipt of unordered merchandise has been
forwarded to me. I am looking into the situation and hope to resolve it quickly.   I
will certainly be sharing with you the results of my investigation when it is finished.

I assure you that we are taking this matter seriously. You are a valuable
customer, and your dissatisfaction is an indication of the need for improvement on
our part.

It is possible that I may be contacting you for further information to help me
resolve this matter. In the meantime, thank you for your patience.

Sincerely,

Brandon Thomas
Account Representative

Apology for Billing Error

GUIDELINES:

- Begin by admitting your firm's error.
- Explain the situation, without overdramatizing the error.
- Tell the buyer precisely what adjustments will be made.
- Close on a positive note, again without excessive apology.

SITUATION:

Multi-Art Suppliers, a wholesale art-supply store, has been running a promotional sale on a new line of brushes. A retail-store buyer, Mr. Arnaud, has called to complain about his bill. His usual trade discount is 25%; thus, he had been expecting a 45% discount, whereas his bill reflects a discount of only 20%, the sale discount. The customer-service manager finds that the buyer has a legitimate complaint.

Figure 5.3   Apology for Billing Error

---

multi-art suppliers
1449 Palmerstown Road / Haywood TX 77011
Telephone: 409-835-1212   Fax: 409-835-1033

◆◆

June 18, 20--

Mr. David P. Arnaud
Longville Art Center
1100 Main Street
Longville, TX 77012

Dear Mr. Arnaud:

As you informed us earlier today by phone, the invoiced order you were sent is indeed incorrect. Your order should have been discounted 45% instead of 20%.

Perhaps we've done our promotional job on those brushes too well. Our billing staff is now so used to allowing the 20% discount that in your case they forgot to add on the 25% trade discount. We're in the process of recalculating your order with the correct 45% discount, and the new invoice should be processed and on its way to you by the end of this week. The new invoice replaces the original incorrect one in our files; simply disregard your copy of the original.

We do regret this slip and are happy to have the chance to set the matter straight. This month our store is featuring a promotion on a new line of high-quality acrylics; this will be offered to you at a 45% discount, which we will make sure you'll get!

Sincerely,

William T. Moore
Customer Service Manager

sgg

Apology for Damaged Goods

GUIDELINES:

- Begin by thanking the customer for notifying the company of the problem.
- Acknowledge the error, extend an apology, and offer reassurance that it will not happen again.
- Explain the reason for the error and specify the measures that will be taken to rectify it.
- Express appreciation for the customer's patronage, and close with a friendly offer of future service.

SITUATION:

Mr. and Mrs. Edwards, longtime customers of Sagarino Flowers, have called to say that a shipment of roses they recently received from Sagarino included some that were wilted. The company's president believes the Edwardses have a legitimate complaint, and uses his letter to regain his customers' goodwill and confidence.

Figure 5.4   Apology for Damaged Goods

Sagarino Flowers
♣
One Maywell Street
Beverly, MA 01915
Tel: 617-414-5252 ♣ Fax: 617-414-2296

August 15, 20--

Mr. and Mrs. James Edwards
100 Emerson Place
Beverly, MA 01915

Dear Mr. and Mrs. Edwards:

Thank you for letting us know about the roses that arrived at your house in less than perfect condition. I enclose a check refunding your full purchase price.

An unexpected delay in the repair of our loaded delivery van, coupled with an unusual rise in temperatures last Thursday, caused the deterioration of your roses. Please accept our apology and our assurance that steps will be taken to prevent this from happening again.

During the past fifteen years, it has been our pleasure to number you among our valued customers, whose satisfaction is the goal we are constantly striving to achieve. I sincerely hope you will continue to count on us for your floral and indoor plant needs.

Yours very truly,

Thomas Sagarino
President

gbb

Encl.: Check

Apology for Service Delay

GUIDELINES:

- Begin by acknowledging the product's success and explain the situation, putting the best face possible on it.
- Save a second piece of bad news, if any, for a subsequent paragraph.
- Offer possible solutions for what can be done in the meantime.
- Close by assuring the customer that he or she will be notified as soon as the new product becomes available again.

SITUATION:

Wright-Way Kitchen Products recently began carrying an unusual all-metal mixer/blender at a price comparable to its plastic models. The line sold out immediately and the store is trying to restock it; however, the factory has been unable to keep up with demand, and there will be a significant delay. Wright-Way's product manager writes a letter to the waiting customers to explain the situation.

Figure 5.5   Apology for Service Delay

Wright-Way Kitchen Products, Inc.
❖❖❖❖❖❖❖
1560 Lawton Blvd., El Yuma, CA 89110
TEL: (714) 793-4118 / *FAX:* (714) 793-4144

March 7, 20--

Mr. Hubert Johansson
15 Appleton Way
Deep Springs, CO 80213

Dear Mr. Johansson:

We're pleased to hear that you are interested in the Multi-Master 1500 food processor. This is a truly superior product with a reasonable price, and consumer demand for it has been very high. So high, in fact, that we ran out of stock a week after first offering it.

We are working with our manufacturer to help speed production of new units, but currently the factory is about three weeks behind orders.

We will be happy to hold on to your order and fill it as soon as our stock is replenished. We value our customers and are confident that we can satisfy their needs. Regrettably, we must sometimes adapt to circumstances beyond our control.

For some customers interested in the Multi-Master 1500, our smaller Mini-Master 1200, which is still in stock, may be appropriate. Please see your catalog for a complete description. If, however, you prefer to wait for us to restock the Multi-Master 1500, rest assured that we will ship your order as soon as it arrives from the factory.

Cordially,

Barney Cates

Barney Cates
Product Manager

Appointment Confirmation

GUIDELINES:

- Specify the participants, date, time, and location of the meeting.
- Provide directions or a map if appropriate.

SITUATION:

Dr. Grondahl, the head of a Norwegian publishing firm, will be in the United States for several days and has contacted Charles St. Cyr about a meeting regarding a possible joint project involving yet another firm. Since the discussion will not require much technical material, a lunch meeting seems more appropriate and relaxed than an office meeting. The correspondents have already established that midday on May 2 would be a convenient time for them both.

Figure 5.6   Appointment Confirmation

CSC BUSINESS SOFTWARE
666 Fifth Avenue, Suite 1810
New York, NY 10036
Phone • 212-876-5432
Fax • 212-876-5401
csc@hightower.com

April 17, 20--

Dr. Arne Grondahl
Internasjonalt Forlag A/S
Postboks 19--Sentrum
0101 OSLO 1

Dear Dr. Grondahl:

Charles St. Cyr has asked me to confirm your luncheon meeting with him and a representative of Third Millennium at 12:30 on Friday, May 2. The Thai Monsoon Restaurant, located in the Metropolis Hotel at 29 West 49th Street (between 5th and 6th Avenues), is convenient to numerous midtown offices and the prime shopping and entertainment districts, and you should have no trouble finding it. You will be Mr. St. Cyr's guest for lunch.

I am enclosing a map of the New York City area for your convenience.

Sincerely,

Jan Jordan

Jan Jordan
Secretary to Mr. St. Cyr

Enclosure

Claim Adjustment Refusal I

GUIDELINES:

- Remind the customer pleasantly about the stated (or unstated) policy, while acknowledging any correct assertion by the customer.
- Suggest how such a problem can be avoided in the future.
- Express regret that company policy prevents you from carrying out the customer's wishes, and conclude by soliciting the customer's understanding and acceptance.

SITUATION:

The Gem House sells high-quality jewelry through a mail-order catalog. A regular customer has returned an expensive pair of earrings because the stone's color did not match the catalog picture. Since company policy prohibits the return of earrings for pierced ears, the office manager must refuse the return—without alienating the customer.

Figure 5.7   Claim Adjustment Refusal I

THE GEM HOUSE
··

June 18, 20--

Ms. Emilia Wrightson
123 Ambler Road
Everett, WA 98807

Dear Ms. Wrightson:

We are sending back to you under separate cover the filigree tourmaline earrings ordered through the Gem House catalog last month. We are happy to explain the company's policy on returning earrings for pierced ears. Because we want our customers to be aware that for hygienic reasons--that is, for their own protection--pierced earrings cannot be returned, we include a statement to that effect at the top of each page of our catalogs. We certainly have no intention of surprising our customers with policies hidden in fine print.

Since the Gem House is a mail-order company, our catalog is, in a sense, our sales staff. Because of this, we take a great deal of care with it. The colors of the gemstones pictured in it represent as accurately as possible the colors of our gems in stock. However, colors are notoriously difficult to reproduce exactly; in addition, they vary slightly from stone to stone. Because of these factors, it is true that the tourmalines in your earrings do differ somewhat in color from those shown in our catalog.

If you are ordering jewelry to complement a specific garment and the exact shade is important, why not send us a sample of the material? Just a small swatch would be enough to allow a member of our staff to match the color precisely.

I wish it were not necessary to return these earrings to you, but unfortunately our company policy dictates that we must. I'm sure you can understand this necessity, and I hope we can serve you in a less inconvenient way in the future.

Cordially,

Lillian Ayala

Lillian Ayala
Office Manager

POWDER RIVER BOULEVARD / P. O. BOX 4439 / PRAIRIE GROVE, MT 59462
TEL 406-141-2000 / FAX 406-141-2022

Claim Adjustment Refusal II

GUIDELINES:

- Open by thanking the customer for bringing the matter to the company's attention, delaying the negative answer so as to keep the customer reading.
- Review the facts of the sale and compare them with the company's sales policy, without assigning blame.
- State that while the company is lenient in its policies, particularly for good customers, it cannot be done in this case.
- Conclude on a conciliatory note, promising that the company's intention is to treat all its customers fairly.

SITUATION:

Brandon-Rupert, a manufacturer of wall maps, holds an annual January sale. They have received a letter from the principal of Oak Hill School, a good customer of the company, who complains that the six maps he ordered were invoiced at the regular price. Since Oak Hill's order was received after the end of the sale, the school is not entitled to the sale price.

Figure 5.8   Claim Adjustment Refusal II

Brandon-Rupert Inc.
15519 Waterloo Road, Versailles, NY 11566
Tel: (516) 387-1551   Fax: (516) 387-1570

March 3, 20--

Mr. James Maloney
Oak Hill School
P. O. Box 100
Manchester, CT 06094

Dear Mr. Maloney:

We can understand your distress when the maps ordered by Oak Hill School from Brandon-Rupert Inc. arrived at the school invoiced at a price considerably higher than what you had anticipated. We appreciate your taking the time to write regarding this matter, and we welcome the opportunity to explain this company's sale policy.

Oak Hill School's order for six wall maps is dated February 13, and it was received at Brandon-Rupert on February 16. The maps were priced at $175.00 each, resulting in a total price (including tax) of $1,113.42. Oak Hill requested the January sale discount of 50%, which would have resulted in a total bill of $556.71. Instead, your school has been billed for the full price.

Our problem here has to do with the date of Oak Hill's order. As our sale brochure states, sale prices are given on orders received here before February 1. We do occasionally honor sale-price orders that reach us a few days after February 1, and we particularly try to give long-standing customers such as Oak Hill as much consideration as possible. Unfortunately, Oak Hill's order wasn't made out until February 13, and we just can't fit it into this extension period.

We hope you understand our position. If we extend our February 1 cutoff date to the middle of February or beyond, we would be shortchanging some other customers (who would by then be ordering at full price again) and creating a problematic precedent. We must abide by guidelines that allow us to be as fair as possible to as many as possible.

Sincerely yours,

Harrison Greenstreet
President

HG/ht

Collection I

GUIDELINES:

- Begin in as friendly a tone as possible, perhaps using an unusual line that will catch its reader's attention.
- Mention something positive—if possible, the customer's reliable payment history—before addressing the problem.
- Bring up the problem tactfully but firmly.
- Suggest possible reasons for the delay and express a desire to be helpful.
- Close by asking politely for a response.

SITUATION:

Donna Randall has fallen a month behind on her payments for a car purchased from Darrow Recreational Vehicles. The credit manager reminds her of the fact and urges her to attend to the overdue payments.

Figure 5.9   Collection I

DARROW RECREATIONAL VEHICLES
36 Whipple Avenue
Lynchburg, VA 24502
Telephone: 303-666-2321
Fax: 303-686-4897

November 5, 20--

Ms. Donna Randall
61 Endicott Street
Lynchburg, VA 24504

Dear Ms. Randall:

Have you ever had to write a reminder letter? We find ourselves in that position now.

You have been sending your monthly installments to us promptly for almost a year. However, we find that your payment of $260.00 for October has not yet arrived.

Perhaps your overdue payment is already on its way to us; if so, please overlook this letter. On the other hand, if some difficulty has arisen, let us know. Perhaps we can offer some helpful suggestions in order to help you maintain your good credit rating.

Won't you let us hear from you soon?

Sincerely yours,

Francine Hopkins

Francine Hopkins
Credit Manager

FH/gb

Collection II

GUIDELINES:

- Summarize the situation and express concern about it, while keeping the tone as tactful as possible, especially if the customer has been a long-standing client.
- Make a clear and simple request for immediate payment, reminding the client that the company's credit record is at risk.
- End with friendly language, making clear the desire to maintain good business relations.

SITUATION:

Quick Shop's account with the advertising agency of Douglas and Alward is now over 60 days past due, and reminders have already been sent. The agency's treasurer writes to Quick Shop to request payment once again, taking a friendly but firm tone.

Figure 5.10 Collection II

DOUGLAS AND ALWARD
❖❖❖❖❖❖❖❖❖❖❖❖❖❖❖❖❖❖❖❖❖❖❖
666 EUCLID AVENUE
NEW PEKIN, ME 04532
TEL: 207-996-1438
FAX: 207-996-2888
❖❖❖❖❖❖❖❖❖❖❖

October 6, 20--

Mr. George Sebastian
Advertising Director
Quick Shop, Inc.
7800 State Street
Portland, ME 04456

Dear Mr. Sebastian:

Our records indicate that your account with us is now more than 60 days past due.
We are very concerned that we have not yet heard from you, even though we have
already sent you a reminder about this matter.

We are requesting that you send your payment to us immediately. In this way you
can preserve your excellent credit record with us.

Quick Shop has always been one of our best clients, and we value your business
very much. If some special circumstances are preventing you from making
payment, please call us now so that we can discuss the situation with you.

Sincerely,

Carol Derwinski

Carol Derwinski
Treasurer

CD/hm

Collection III

GUIDELINES:

- State the situation and make it clear that an ultimatum (probably involving referral to a collection agency, with consequent damage to the customer's credit rating) is to come.

- Try to avoid alienating the customer any more than necessary, assuming you still hope to do business on a cash basis.

- Make one more attempt at persuasion, and end by reminding the customer what can be gained by making prompt payment.

SITUATION:

The contractor Kirchoffer & Sons' account with Tri-State Building Supply is now 120 days past due. Tri-State's credit manager has written several times to Kirchoffer requesting payment and received no reply. He has finally suspended their credit, and now writes a stern ultimatum before turning the account over to a collection agency.

Figure 5.11   Collection III

Tri-State Building Supply Company
1264 Beaver Ruin Road
West Highlands, PA 19534
717-432-1236

February 20, 20--

Mr. Andrew N. Kirchoffer
President
Kirchoffer & Sons
P.O. Box 1200
East Highlands, PA 19532

Dear Mr. Kirchoffer:

This is the third time we have called your attention to your long-overdue account. So far we have received neither your check nor the courtesy of a reply.

Credit and friendly relations are complementary efforts. We feel we have done our part and are counting on you as a fair-minded businessman to meet your obligation.

Please send your check today so that we can mark your account paid!

Sincerely,

Anthony T. Legere
Credit Manager

ATL/jm

Complaint

GUIDELINES:

- Get directly to the point without being insulting or hostile, saving the details for the second paragraph.
- Explain the sequence of events in a way that leads logically to the refund demand.
- Without exaggerating your disappointment, make clear that you consider the supplier's performance below par and hope they will try to improve their service.

SITUATION:

Helen Davison offers repair services to the guests who dock at her small marina. She recently ordered a bilge pump from her usual supplier for a docking guest. The pump was promised within seven working days but did not actually arrive until well after the guest had departed. Now she discovers in addition that it is defective. Her letter demands a full refund.

Figure 5.12   Complaint

Davison's Marina 5100 Harbor Drive, Savannah, GA 31419   (912) 333-1111

July 28, 20--

Mr. Barry Jacobs, Manager
Oceanside Supply Company
129 Fulton Boulevard
Jacksonville, FL 32217

Dear Mr. Jacobs:

You will soon be receiving via UPS the Johnson II Bilge Pump I ordered last month.
I am returning this pump both because it is defective and because it arrived too late
to be sold to its intended user.

On June 30, three weeks before the scheduled departure of the guest whose boat
required the pump, I telephoned Oceanside Supply to order the Johnson pump and
was assured that it would arrive within seven working days. It actually arrived only
on July 22, after sixteen working days, and one day after my guest's departure.

I had considered keeping the pump on hand for future use, but it arrived with bent
mounting arms that would have made installation difficult and time-consuming,
leading to a labor cost that would have had to be absorbed by me or my customer.
Under the circumstances I cannot accept this pump, and I am returning it to you
with the request that the amount of the purchase price, plus the return shipping cost
of $31.50, be removed from my account.

Davison's Marina has been a regular customer of Oceanside Supply for several
years, and I must say that we have been quite happy with your service up to now. I
hope that in the future you will pay a bit more attention both to customers' needs
and your own assurances so that we can all avoid disappointment.

Sincerely,

Helen Davison

Helen Davison

HD:gbb

Confirmation of Telephone Call

GUIDELINES:

- Restate the contents of the telephone call as you understand them, and ask politely if your understanding is correct.
- Close on a courteous and friendly note.

SITUATION:

Charlene Rice, a textbook sales representative, has called Raymond Weese, the principal of Plainville Middle School, to tell him of a sale her company is planning for the following month, which will include a new science text that the school plans to use. He understood her to say that he can begin ordering the books immediately, but wants to confirm his impression.

Figure 5.13   Confirmation of Telephone Call

Plainville Middle School
PLAINVILLE REGIONAL SCHOOL DISTRICT
1400 OLIVE STREET
PLAINVILLE, OH 44906
(614) 138-7911

November 15, 20--

Ms. Charlene Rice
Charter Oaks Publishers, Education Division
997 Hinsdale Road
Springfield, MO 65802

Dear Charlene:

This is simply to confirm some of what we discussed during our telephone conversation last Friday. You had described a sale that Charter Oaks is planning for next month, and gave me an ordering number (3507) for preferred customers. The sale is to include Levarie's *The Physical World*, a text already chosen by our science department. As I understand it, use of the number will allow us to order such textbooks at the sale price immediately, even though the sale will not officially begin until next month.

I'm about to order the science texts, but first I wanted to confirm with you that my understanding of the situation and the ordering number itself were correct.

I'm delighted to have information of this sale in advance. Buying these texts on sale will be a big help to our budget, and getting them in time for next semester will be a big help to our science department.

Sincerely yours,

Raymond Weese
Principal

Congratulation

GUIDELINES:

- Type the letter on Executive stationery if possible, omitting any secretary's initials.
- Commend your newly promoted friend on the honor, using its exact title if possible, and reflecting on its meaning.
- Close with a reiteration of personal good wishes.

SITUATION:

Herbert Duchesne, an executive at Ace Precision Tools, was recently elevated to a new position. Mary Lawrence, an executive at a firm that does business with Ace, writes to extend her congratulations.

Figure 5.14   Congratulation

·THOR BALL BEARINGS·

888 Atticus Road   **Telephone: (814) 299-9400**
Erie, Pennsylvania 16504   **Fax: (814) 299-9408**

Vice President, Personnel

January 23, 20--

Dear Herb:

   Yesterday's *Erie Recorder* announced the pleasant news of your appointment as General Manufacturing Manager at Ace Precision Tools. Congratulations!

   It's well known that great strides were made at Ace while you were Materials Manager. The recognition you're now receiving is certainly well deserved.

   Again, you have my sincere congratulations and best wishes for continued success.

                              Cordially,

                              Mary

Mr. Herbert Duchesne
General Manufacturing Manager
Ace Precision Tools
1408 Lake Avenue
Erie, PA 16509

Cover or Transmittal I

GUIDELINES:

- Open by acknowledging the recipient's interest in the materials.
- Describe the contents or promised materials.
- Offer further assistance as appropriate, and close in a friendly fashion.

SITUATION:

A professor at a nearby university has written to Fairmont Stainless Steel requesting copies of their annual report for use in his classroom. Fairmont's public-relations assistant writes to inform him that copies of the report are on the way.

Figure 5.15   Cover or Transmittal I

Fairmont Stainless Steel Corporation

1480 Hamilton Road • Milwaukee, WI 64981
Tel: 414-643-7899 • Fax: 414-643-7802

March 18, 20--

Professor James Willard
DePaul Technical College
Milwaukee, WI 64982

Dear Professor Willard:

I am pleased to enclose a dozen copies of Fairmont Stainless Steel Corp.'s Annual Report for use by the students in your research seminar.

We are always delighted to learn of interest being shown in our company by the local academic community. If there is any other means by which we can be of assistance to you and your students--by arranging a plant visit, for instance--please do not hesitate to ask.

As you may already know, Fairmont will be represented at the upcoming Capital City Regional Business Fair, May 2-4, at the Capital City Civic Center. I myself will be attending the fair, and I invite you to meet with me there and learn more about our company.

Thank you for your interest in Fairmont.

Sincerely yours,

Jean Linamen

Jean Linamen
Public Relations Assistant

Cover or Transmittal II

GUIDELINES:

- State clearly what is being delivered.
- Point out any important details.
- Add a personal note, if appropriate.
- Close with an offer of additional assistance if needed.

SITUATION:

A real-estate developer has asked the firm of Santiago & Nussbaum, an architectural firm specializing in historical restoration, to develop a proposal for restoring a building his company is thinking of buying. James Santiago writes a cover letter to accompany the initial version of the proposal.

Figure 5.16   Cover or Transmittal II

Santiago & Nussbaum

The Arcade ⌀ Hillsborough, Georgia 33209 ⌀ Telephone 912-820-3333 ⌀ Fax 912-820-3326

August 27, 20--

Mr. William Demetrius
Demetrius Bros. Inc.
1200 High Street
Hillsborough, GA 33210

Dear Mr. Demetrius:

Here is our preliminary proposal for the renovation of the McKay Building at 1300 State Street. The proposal assumes that Demetrius Bros. will be acquiring the property at 1308 State Street as well.

We have developed the proposal in such a way as to ensure that the building's conversion to a multi-use commercial space will qualify for favorable tax treatment as a historical restoration.

We think this is a very exciting project, and we look forward to hearing your reaction to this draft. If you have questions about any aspect of the proposal in the course of your review, please do not hesitate to call.

Sincerely,

James Santiago
President

JS:gic

Enclosure

Cover or Transmittal III

GUIDELINES:

- Describe the package contents precisely, mentioning any materials that will be coming later.
- Provide any instructions necessary for using the materials.

SITUATION:

Churchill Bookstores has sent a routine request for a set of trade catalogs from Hudson, a New York publisher, for the use of Churchill's buyers, and the secretary to Hudson's sales manager responds.

Figure 5.17   Cover or Transmittal III

HUDSON PUBLICATIONS, INC.

❈

97 VAN DAM STREET
NEW YORK, NY 10014
Tel: (212) 987-6543   Fax: (212) 987-8889

❈

April 2, 20--

Ms. Dana Forbush
Wholesale Accounts Dept.
Churchill Bookstores
400 Haddam Way
Chicago, IL 60641

Dear Ms. Forbush:

In response to your letter of March 28, I am sending under separate cover by UPS a complete set of our wholesale trade catalogs. The summer editions of catalogs nos. 5 and 9 will be available in one to two weeks, and I will send them as soon as they appear.

I have circled the applicable discounts on page xii of catalog no. 1.

We hope you will find our expanding list as attractive and interesting as we do.

Very truly yours,

Jeffrey Burroughs
Secretary to Mr. Lozano

Credit Application I

GUIDELINES:

- Open by explaining how you came to hear of the product (information that can be helpful to the manufacturer).

- Do an explicit calculation of the order amount, so that the manufacturer can confirm it without trouble.

- Request credit terms, giving detailed information about your business, supplying the names and addresses of credit references, as well as the name and address of a bank with which you do business.

- Close by volunteering to provide any other information the manufacturer may need.

SITUATION:

Bret Atkins owns The Pet Place, a large pet store that sells, among other things, housing and fencing for large animals. He is interested in a recent, heavily advertised fencing innovation, and writes to the manufacturer's sales manager to request commercial credit terms.

Figure 5.18   Credit Application I

The Pet Place ♥ ♥   South Carters Run Road / Fulton, MD 20814 / (410) 626-2626

June 15, 20--

Mr. Gino Russo, Sales Manager
Williams-Weeks Manufacturing, Inc.
4365 West LaSalle Street
Fairmont, WI 53522

Dear Mr. Russo:

This month's issue of *Pet Industry Bulletin* features a full-page advertisement
for your company's Unseen Fencing. I am impressed by your product and its price,
which is actually lower than the cost of conventional fencing.

According to the *Pet Industry Bulletin* ad, the Unseen Fencing kit wholesales
for $475. I would like to order 10 kits on 60-day credit terms. I understand that
there is a $200 shipping charge for orders of 10 or more, so my order totals $4,950.
I would also like to establish 60-day credit terms for the future on purchases up to
$5,000.

The Pet Place opened almost eight years ago, and it has proved to be a very
successful enterprise. The store is run in conjunction with a nearby boarding kennel
owned by my parents, so I have plenty of opportunity to talk to pet owners and
listen to their needs. The Pet Place is the only store in this area to supply a wide
variety of pet supplies, and I feel we will continue to do well. Being able to provide
quality products such as your Unseen Fencing certainly helps.

I refer you to three businesses for information on our credit reliability:

Ace Feed, 121 Amity Street, Fulton, MD 20814
Bio-Med Supplies, Inc., Winding Lane, Highland Park, MD 20833
Carter Carriers, 37 Hunter Boulevard, Everett, MD 20824

Our bank is Fulton National Bank, 49 Parker Street, Fulton, MD 28014. Our
account number is 0470-685-23.

I will be happy to fill out a formal credit application or provide you with any
further financial information you may require.

Very truly yours,

Bret Atkins

Credit Application II

GUIDELINES:

- Open with a compliment, if appropriate, before presenting your request.
- Provide any necessary supporting data.
- Close in an appreciative and courteous manner.

SITUATION:

Perretta & Sons Hardware wants to expand its variety of gardening products. Impressed by the Harkins Company line at a recent trade show, Howard Perretta writes to Harkins's credit manager to apply for a franchise to sell its products.

Figure 5.19   Credit Application II

Perretta & Sons Hardware

1510 Long Street
Kansas City, MO 68977
Phone: 913-877-3447 / Fax: 913-878-4588

October 19, 20--

Mr. David Lindberg
Credit Manager
The Harkins Company
100 Lake Street
Smithville, UT 84103

Dear Mr. Lindberg:

After inspecting your recent exhibit of fine hardware at the International Hardware Convention in San Francisco last week, we have decided that we would like to carry your line of merchandise.

Please consider this letter an application for a charge account in the $2,000-$3,000 range. Credit references will be supplied upon request.

We are delighted to have the opportunity to handle the Harkins franchise in the Kansas City area, and we look forward to building a healthy and profitable business relationship.

Very truly yours,

Howard Perretta

Howard Perretta
President

Credit Cancellation

GUIDELINES:

- Commend the customer for prompt payment in the past, if appropriate.
- Bring up the current problem as tactfully as possible.
- Suggest a solution, avoiding negative language.
- Offer special assistance if possible.
- Politely but firmly request a prompt response.

SITUATION:

Empyrean Lighting opened an account with Ellsworth Electrical Wholesalers several years ago, and initially paid its bills reliably. After several months of very late payments, however, Ellsworth has finally decided to cancel the account.

Figure 5.20   Credit Cancellation

···· Ellsworth Electrical Wholesalers ····
6802 Eastern Highway
Portland, Oregon 97229
(503) 232-4567

November 5, 20--

Mr. Howard Harris
Empyrean Lighting Co.
4628 Southern Boulevard
Portland, OR 97216

Dear Mr. Harris:

Over the past seven years we have valued your account with us and considered it one of our best. For a number of months, however, all your payments have arrived late. Your most recent payment was 90 days late, and there is still a significant outstanding balance.

It is imperative that we keep current on our accounts receivable. Therefore, regrettably, it is necessary to ask you to make future purchases on a cash-only basis until your account is cleared.

Please accept the enclosed Special Courtesy Discount card for future cash purchases. It will entitle you to a 10% cash discount to help you through this difficult period.

May we hear from you soon, Mr. Harris.

Very sincerely,

Albert Terranova
Credit Manager

AT:gbb

Enclosure

Credit Extension

GUIDELINES:

- Begin by giving the customer the good news, welcoming him or her as a new customer.
- Keep the language and content informal; the actual credit terms can be enclosed on a separate sheet in the same envelope.
- Close with friendly assurances of future service.

SITUATION:

Craft's, a luggage wholesaler, has received an order and request for commercial credit from Carry-On, a retail luggage shop now expanding its merchandise lines. Having reviewed Carry-On's credit references and found them positive, Craft's credit manager writes to Carry-On's owner to announce that his credit has been approved.

Figure 5.21   Credit Extension

Craft's
800 Thunderbird Road
Ft. Myers, FL 33801
Tel.: 813-488-9322 • Fax: 813-488-9311

September 5, 20--

Mr. Charles Gordon
Carry-On, Inc.
Silver City, VA 22304

Dear Mr. Gordon:

Welcome aboard! Craft's is pleased to have you as a credit customer. We are
sending out your order of 25 all-in-one suitcases and 10 garment bags (totaling
$2,345) by express freight service, and you should have it by the time you read this.
Our credit terms are explained in detail on the enclosed form.

We've also enclosed a brochure describing a new line of overnight bags that we feel
are an excellent buy. The bags have proved to be best-selling items in markets
similar to yours.

Congratulations on the expansion of your store. If there is any way we can be of
service to you in the future, please let us know.

Sincerely,

Martin Goodson
Credit Manager

Encl. (2)

MG/ph

Credit Refusal

GUIDELINES:

- Express appreciation for the customer's business, conveying hope for the future of the business relationship.

- State gently that the credit application has not been accepted, avoiding the word "refuse" and expressing regret for the decision.

- Avoid being specific about the customer's financial situation, and avoid criticizing or offering advice, which may seem condescending.

- Hold out hope, if appropriate, that the decision could be reversed on the basis of further information (even if such a thing is unlikely), so as to keep the letter as positive as possible.

- Offer a cheerful reminder that orders can still be filled on a cash basis, encouraging the customer not to cancel the present order.

SITUATION:

Interior Enterprises, a new interior-design firm, has placed a sizable order for office equipment with Ardmore Office, asking for 120-day credit terms. Though Interior Enterprises has been a good customer for the past year, a review of their financial statement and information supplied by credit references indicates that the firm is in financial difficulty. Ardmore decides to refuse the request but hopes to keep Interior Enterprises as a cash customer.

Figure 5.22   Credit Refusal

ardmore office

August 17, 20--

Ms. Margaret Allen
Interior Enterprises
1700 Blandford Road, Suite 101
Jackson, MS 39209

Dear Ms. Allen:

Thank you very much for the order you placed with us last week. We appreciate
your patronage, and we hope we can continue to serve you in the future.

We have carefully considered your application for 120-day credit terms. We are
sorry to say that, on the basis of the financial information we have seen so far, we
are not able to approve your request. However, if there is any added financial
information you could send us that would allow us to reconsider this decision, we
would be happy to do so.

In the meantime, we will be happy to fill this order on a cash basis, with our
customary 3% cash discount.

Sincerely,

Thomas Polani
Office Manager

TP/gbb

136 John T. Slocum Street, Jackson, MS 39218   Telephone: (601) 999-8115 Fax: (601) 999-8801

Employment Refusal

GUIDELINES:

- Thank the applicant for applying and quickly move on to the bad news.
- Inform him or her that the application is being kept on file in case there is a suitable opening in the near future.
- Politely express appreciation for his or her interest (after all, the applicant might be a potential customer).

SITUATION:

The personnel director for SportSystems Inc. has finished considering a group of applications for a sales position and has chosen a candidate. He sends a letter to the other applicants to tell them they did not get the job.

Figure 5.23   Employment Refusal

_____SportSystems Inc._____

10 Ash Grove Road   Telephone: (312) 445-5511
Webster, Illinois 60069   Fax: (312) 461-7091

October 9, 20--

Mr. Walter W. Jaffe
634 Rock River Avenue
Compton, IL 60058

Dear Mr. Jaffe:

Thank you for your letter of October 5. I am sorry to say that there is nothing open at present for someone with your credentials here at SportSystems.

We will keep your résumé on file in the event that a similar position opens up in the near future.

Thank you for thinking of us. We wish you success in finding a suitable position.

Sincerely,

Joseph J. Forester
Vice President, Personnel

Extension of Payment Deadline

GUIDELINES:

- Inform the customer that you understand and sympathize with the situation and that his or her request for an extension has been granted.
- Provide the reasons why the extension is being granted, reminding the customer of the claims and commitments that were made.
- State the terms of the extension.
- Very politely remind the customer that this extension must be regarded as an exception, and close in a friendly manner.

SITUATION:

In a recent collection letter to the owner of Modern Design Company, the credit manager of Kelley Electrical Supply indicated that Kelley Electrical was hopeful that mutually agreeable terms for payment could be worked out. Modern Design has now requested a 60-day extension, and Kelley has accepted, partly because MDC is a longtime customer who has always paid promptly in the past.

Figure 5.24   Extension of Payment Deadline

Kelley Electrical Supply
6802 Eastern Highway
Iowa City, IA 52244
Telephone: 712-841-3841

September 24, 20--

Ms. Sarah Finnegan
Modal Design Company
39 Harris Street
Marshal, SD 56759

Dear Ms. Finnegan:

I am happy to confirm that, as we discussed by phone earlier today, we have agreed to your request for a 60-day extension to pay the $1065.60 due on your account.

We understand that you are currently having problems with your own collections--and we can certainly sympathize with you on this point. We are pleased to hear that these conditions are temporary and that you feel certain you will be able to meet the extended payment deadline of November 15. We are agreed that you will settle your account in full on or before that date.

We want to emphasize that this extension constitutes an exception to our usual credit terms. We are granting it because MDC has been a good and valued customer for many years, and we want to do whatever we reasonably can to maintain that good relationship. However, you should not expect that we will be able to grant additional extensions in the future.

We thank you for your cooperation, and we wish you well.

Very sincerely,

Albert Terranova
Credit Manager

Invitation I

GUIDELINES:

- Have the cards professionally printed or engraved on heavy cream stock, approximately 4″ × 5½″.

- Double-space and center the lines.

- Instead of the R.S.V.P. block, the invitation may contain a separate card (with envelope), printed in the same style as the invitation, that reads (for example):
  I will _____ will not _____ attend
  the Christmas Ball being given
  by the Friends of the Cheltenham Museum
  on Friday, December 16.
  Name_____

SITUATION:

The Friends of the Cheltenham Museum of Fine Arts invite members and honored guests to a Christmas ball with a formal printed invitation.

Figure 5.25   Invitation I

The Friends of the

Cheltenham Museum of Fine Arts

cordially invite you to their

Thirty-fourth Christmas Ball

on Friday, the fifteenth of December

Two thousand

at seven o'clock

at the Bradford Inn

Cheltenham, New Hampshire

R.S.V.P. by December 1

Roland Frasier

(603) 756-3342

Invitation II

- Open with an attention-getting line.
- Provide details of the event's date, time, and location.
- Describe and "sell" the event.
- Include directions and other helpful information.
- Close with the hope that the recipient will attend.

SITUATION:

Global Chemical Associates, a sales-promotion organization, is hosting an exhibition of new industrial chemical applications and inviting retail and wholesale vendors to the show.

Figure 5.26   Invitation II

Global Chemical Associates
87 Highland Drive
Chicago, IL 60147
Tel: 312-120-0444 Fax: 312-120-0445 E-mail: gca@chemnet.com

June 12, 20--

Mr. William Mann
Chem-Ex National, Inc.
14 Bank Street
Bartlett, IL 60432

YOU'RE CORDIALLY INVITED

to our annual Chemical Manufacturing Technology show, to be held on August 10-11 at the North Building, McCormick Place Complex, Chicago, from 9 a.m. to 6 p.m each day.

The newest chemical manufacturing technology will be on display. Representatives from leading firms will be on hand to answer your questions. The accompanying brochures list the participating vendors as well as special presentations and other scheduled events.

Won't you join your business associates on August 10 for an exciting and rewarding day at what we expect to be the largest and most successful Chemical Manufacturing Technology show ever.

Wayne D. Thoren

Wayne D. Thoren
Sales Manager

Enclosures (3)

Invitation III

GUIDELINES:

- Type the invitation, but otherwise observe the form of a personal letter—that is, use personal stationery, omit the inside address, use first names for friends, follow the salutation with a comma, and omit a typed signature.
- Provide the date and time and a brief description of the event, including the level of formality, along with any other pertinent details such as directions.
- Specify whether a response is necessary (the sample letter asks for "regrets only"), providing a home phone number.

SITUATION:

Sandra Wilhelm, president of Wilhelm & Cook, has recently hired Jeffrey Nirenberg as the company's new finance director and is giving a dinner party to introduce the Nirenbergs to other company executives and a few important clients—about ten couples in all. The wording for each invitation may vary somewhat, but the basic text remains the same.

Figure 5.27 Invitation III

❧ Sandra B. Wilhelm ❧
47 Bridgewater Road
Oxmoor, MN 55116

May 26, 20--

Dear Sheila and Michael,

Sam and I would like to invite you to a dinner party on Wednesday, June 13, at 7:00. The party is an informal one to help welcome Jeffrey Nirenberg, our new Finance Director, and his wife, Christine, to the area.

We are hoping all company officers and their spouses will attend. In addition, we're inviting a few other friends of Wilhelm & Cook to join us. We know that Jeffrey and Christine would be delighted to see you here.

Since it's been some time since you last visited us, I'm enclosing a hand-drawn map that should get you here safely.

Please let us know only if you can't come. Our home number is 987-8613. If we don't hear from you, we'll be expecting you.

Best regards,

Sandra

Job Application

GUIDELINES:

- Specify where you learned about the opening, and why you are interested in it.
- Briefly raise any points that either don't appear on the accompanying résumé or that you think should be emphasized, particularly if the résumé was not redone especially for this application.
- Mention that you are available for an interview.

SITUATION:

Caroline Elkin, secretary to a retiring attorney in a solo-practitioner office, responds to a classified ad in the local newspaper.

Figure 5.28 Job Application

Caroline C. Elkin
123 Yurok Lane
Lynwood, CA 98765
(310) 123-4567

June 1, 20--

Ms. Anna Stone-Calvert
Director, Personnel
Brown, Black, Green & Gray, P.L.C.
Suite 112
81 Esquire Towers
Los Angeles, CA 90663

Dear Ms. Stone-Calvert:

The Brown, Black, Green & Gray employment ad in the May 30 edition of the
Sunday *Times-Republican* has attracted my interest. Because I believe that I am
qualified for the legal secretary position in your office, I enclose a copy of my
résumé.

My keyboarding rate is 70 wpm. I am experienced in the use of machine
dictation and transcription equipment. I have been commissioned a Notary Public.
I am also proficient in Spanish.

I am currently employed as secretary to Selma S. Addington, who is retiring
from her law practice at the end of July. I believe that the experience gained in this
position would be useful in your law office.

I look forward to a personal interview at your convenience. Brown, Black,
Green & Gray is a fine law firm--one for which I know I would enjoy working.

Sincerely yours,

Caroline C. Elkin

Caroline C. Elkin

Job Interview Follow-Up

GUIDELINES:

- Thank your interviewer for inviting you, and convey any favorable impressions you came away with.
- Mention anything that led you to believe you would fit the position particularly well.
- Express as much honest enthusiasm as you can for the position.

SITUATION:

On the day after the interview, Caroline Elkin writes to thank her interviewer and express her positive feelings about the position.

Figure 5.29   Job Interview Follow-Up

Caroline C. Elkin
123 Yurok Lane
Lynwood, CA 98765
(310) 123-4567

June 15, 20--

Ms. Anna Stone-Calvert
Director, Personnel
Brown, Black, Green & Gray, P.L.C.
Suite 112
81 Esquire Towers
Los Angeles, CA 90663

Dear Ms. Stone-Calvert:

It was a pleasure talking with you yesterday about the secretarial position at Brown, Black, Green & Gray. I was very impressed with the job as you described it and with the professionalism of the staff.

I hope you will give me the opportunity to put my skills and enthusiasm to work for you. I think my transcription experience and general secretarial skills would serve the firm well as it looks to expand. I am excited about the challenges I see ahead with Brown, Black, Green & Gray and look forward to having the chance to make a major contribution to its efforts.

Sincerely yours,

Caroline Elkin

Caroline C. Elkin

Job Offer

- Restate the job offer, giving the job's exact title.
- Review the terms of employment.
- Specify the starting date.
- Review the documents the new employee will have to bring on the first day.
- Request a formal acceptance of the offer, preferably a countersigned copy of the letter itself.

SITUATION:

Brandon Kiley of Communications Media Corporation has recently offered a job to Donna Reeve and has called to give her the news. This letter confirms the offer and provides various details about the position.

Figure 5.30   Job Offer

Communications Media Corp. Hawthorne Building / Pierce and Fremont Streets / Houston, TX 77001

CMC

Phone: (713) 898-7643
Fax: (713) 898-2746

July 15, 20--

Ms. Donna A. Reeve
4527 Van Dam Boulevard
Fairfield, CT 06142

Dear Ms. Reeve:

This letter constitutes our formal offer to you of the position of Assistant Director of Administration at Communications Media Corporation. Your duties will consist of assisting the Director of Administration in all areas of corporate administration and in carrying out special projects that relate to corporate communications and staff development, as assigned by the Director of Administration.

This is a full-time position, paying a salary of $40,500 a year. You will receive a salary review after three months and annually thereafter. Increases will depend on the company's general policy and on your contributions to the office. Fringe benefits and other details regarding employment are explained in the employee manual that is being sent to you separately.

We have agreed that you will begin work on August 8. Please bring with you proof of your U.S. citizenship or resident-alien status. A driver's license with photo (or a state-issued identification card with photo) and a Social Security card will suffice; if one of these is not available, you may bring alternative documents as explained on the enclosed information sheet.

If this offer is acceptable to you, please sign and date one copy of this letter and return it to us for our files.

Sincerely,

Brandon W. Kiley
Director of Administration

Signed: _____
Date: _____

BWK/hva
enclosures (2)

Meeting Notification

GUIDELINES:

- Specify the place, date, and time of the meeting.
- Mention special agenda items and, if appropriate, any necessary preparation.
- Refer to any enclosed materials.
- Request confirmation of attendance.

SITUATION:

The upcoming meeting of the Coastal Arts Center's board of trustees is three weeks away, and the trustees must be notified. Unless the director desires to send any personal messages or greetings, the secretary will probably generate a set of basically identical letters from a single letter on the computer.

Figure 5.31   Meeting Notification

♈

COASTAL ARTS CENTER

781 Santa Maria Blvd. Los Angeles, California 90027 • Tel (213) 455-5222 • Fax (213) 455-5009

January 12, 20--

Ms. Alessandra Castelnuovo
Director
Secolo Nuovo Galleries, Ocean Walk
Newport Beach, CA 92663

Dear Ms. Castelnuovo:

The regular winter meeting of the board of trustees will be held in the Arts Center boardroom at 10:00 a.m., Tuesday, February 1.

The tentative agenda and our proposed budget for FY 20-- are enclosed. Note that the principal topic will be the new tax laws, on which our legal counsel will be making a presentation.

Would you notify me before January 20 as to whether you will be able to attend.

Yours very truly,

Jasper L. Cozzens
Director

JLC:gbb

Enclosures (2)

Order

GUIDELINES:

- Express the need for the order, providing the shipping address that will best facilitate delivery.
- List clearly the quantity, description, and price of the ordered items, preferably in tabular form.
- Close by reiterating the urgency of the order, if appropriate.

SITUATION:

Paul Thomas, the purchasing agent of Rodriguez Manufacturing, a large furniture maker, has just been informed that the factory has run out of two types of hardware. He writes to order more stock from his supplier.

Figure 5.32   Order

RODRIGUEZ MANUFACTURERS, INC.

•

333 West 145th Street
New York, NY 10031
Telephone: 212-598-1534
Fax: 212-596-1444

November 13, 20--

Mr. George Holmes, Manager
Baxter and Halloway, Inc.
44 Hudson Drive
Elizabeth, NJ 07202

Dear Mr. Holmes:

    Please accept this order for immediate shipment to:
        Rodriguez Manufacturers, Inc.
        Wood Products Division
        2255 West 189th Street
        New York, NY 10032
and charge to our account no. 8189.

Quantity	Description	Unit Price	Total
1800	No. 202 T Hinges, Brass Plate	$2.15 pr.	$3,870
600	No. 78 Corner Braces, Brass Plate	$2.30 ea.	$1,380
		Total:	$5,250

    An unexpected flurry of orders has depleted our stock. We would therefore be grateful if this order could be handled as quickly as possible.

Yours truly,

Paul Thomas

Paul Thomas
Purchasing Agent

PT:gbb

Price Quotation

GUIDELINES:

- Supply the requested information in a complete and detailed manner.
- Specify the terms of sale.
- Close with an offer of additional information.

SITUATION:

Waterville Typesetting has received a request for a price quotation for typesetting a new book from Hampden Press. Their sales representative responds with an itemized estimate.

Figure 5.33   Price Quotation

WATERVILLE TYPESETTING, INC.
❖
2965 JAMES STREET, WATERVILLE, SC 29270
PHONE (303) 444-3131 FAX (303) 444-3003

December 30, 20--

Ms. Nancy L. Baines, Managing Editor
Hampden Press
44 Lincoln Street
Canton, NY 14523

Dear Ms. Baines:

Waterville Typesetting is pleased to submit the following quotation for *The Homeowner's Encyclopedia:*

COMPOSITION: Baskerville, 40 x 50 text area, 8" x 10" trim.

Quantity	Description	Unit Price	Total
10 pages	Front matter	$24.50	$245.00
354 pages	Text	28.95	10,248.30
118 pages	Space allowance for art	6.00	708.00
30 pages	Index	26.00	780.00
200 pieces	Line art to shoot and strip	4.50	900.00
512 pages	Page proofs	.75	384.00
512 pages	Negatives	3.00	536.00
		Total:	$13,801.30

The terms of sale are net 30 days, with a progress billing at the end of the galley stage. Pricing is subject to review upon receipt of the fully edited manuscript, final specifications, and scheduling requirements. Author's alterations will be billed at the rate of $1.50 per line. Shipping fees and extra sets of galley proofs will be charged separately. This estimate is valid for 90 days.

Thank you for the opportunity to provide this quotation. If you have any further questions, please do not hesitate to call me.

Sincerely,

Barry Zabroski
Sales Representative

Reference or Recommendation

GUIDELINES:

- Start immediately with the introduction.
- Provide relevant professional information.
- Give your evaluation and recommendation.
- Close with an offer of further information.

SITUATION:

After several years as children's librarian at her town library, Anita Rothstein is moving to a large city where her husband has accepted a job, and applying for a position at the city library. She has asked her employer for a letter of recommendation to accompany her job application.

Figure 5.34   Reference or Recommendation

Carnegie Library of Munstead

510 10th Avenue
Munstead, IN 45301

(219) 461-0007

May 23, 20--

Ms. Ruth Owens
Personnel Director
Atkins Memorial Library
47 Cooper Road
Montgomery, AL 36106

Dear Ms. Owens:

This is a letter of introduction and recommendation for Anita N. Rothstein, who has ably served as Children's Librarian here for eight years.

Anita's main duties have been the reorganization of the children's section, which was in a seriously neglected state when she arrived, and the day-to-day running of the section, which has included the acquisition of new books and periodicals. In addition to her regular duties, she took on the added task of arranging special programs for area children, and raised money for a wide variety of special speakers and performers. During her time here, our children benefited greatly from her efforts. Because she so efficiently took over a multitude of duties here (while simultaneously rearing her own two small children and earning her MLS degree!), I don't feel that moving from a small establishment to a much larger one will overwhelm her. She has been very quick to learn, ready to improvise when necessary, and eager to accept responsibility.

In short, I'm sorry to be losing Anita, but I do feel that our loss will be your gain. If I can help you further, feel free to give me a call.

Very truly yours,

Diana Green

Diana T. Green
Head Librarian

Refusal of Invitation

GUIDELINES:

- Express thanks for the invitation and regret at not being able to attend.
- Offer the reason for your being unavailable, which can be kept vague if necessary.
- Compliment the organization, if appropriate, and close on a friendly note.

SITUATION:

Patricia Meacam, a lawyer, has recently been in the news for negotiating an important downtown development project, and has been invited to speak at the annual banquet of a volunteer organization. She writes to convey her regrets at being unable to accept the invitation.

Figure 5.35   Refusal of Invitation

Jenkins & Danforth
Attorneys-at-Law

One Court Street, Suite H
Louisville, KY 40220

Telephone: 502-507-1440
Fax: 502-507-1476

Partners:
   Samuel T. Jenkins
   Loring P. Danforth
   Patricia J. Meacam

Associates:
   Pamela D. McGuire
   Arnaldo S. Zeeman

November 12, 20--

Ms. Estelle Sheridan
Louisville Cares
3700 Main Street
Louisville, KY 40220

Dear Ms. Sheridan:

Thank you very much for your invitation to speak at your annual awards banquet. Unfortunately, an unusually heavy workload at present prevents me from accepting any outside speaking engagements anytime in the near future.

I regret having to decline, since I have always been a great admirer of the work done by Louisville Cares, and I am honored to have been asked to speak to your group. I wish you well with what is sure to be a splendid evening.

Sincerely,

Patricia Meacam

Patricia J. Meacam, Esq.

lol

Reminder I

- Tactfully remind the recipient of precisely what is needed and of any deadlines.
- Refer to any relevant supporting materials (including any that might actually be sent with the letter).

SITUATION:

The November executive meeting of Highsmith Laboratories was partly devoted to planning for the coming two years. Tentative goals were proposed, but hard figures were not then available. The executive vice president has asked his secretary to send a reminder letter to each participant.

Figure 5.36   Reminder I

R. J. Highsmith Laboratories Inc.

1698 Massachusetts Avenue
Cambridge, MA 02138

Telephone 617-488-2848
Fax 617-488-2858
highsmith@techsite.com

November 25, 20--

Mr. Joseph Sonnenschein
R. J. Highsmith Laboratories Inc.
4860 South Beach Drive
Palo Alto, CA 94303

Dear Mr. Sonnenschein:

In the wake of the November 18 executive meeting, this letter is merely intended to remind you that we require some information from each participant within the next two weeks in order to complete our near-term prospectus: (1) proposed new personnel (and salary) requirements and/or reductions for each separate branch over the next two years; and (2) expected equipment purchases over the same period. (You will recall that guidelines and materials for estimating equipment costs were distributed at the meeting.)

I know how pleased Mr. Coe was with the meeting and the role of each of you in making it so productive. I hope to hear from you soon.

With best wishes for the holidays,

Charlene Daitz

Charlene Daitz
Administrative Assistant to Mr. Coe

cc: Mr. Lynes
    Mrs. Caswell
    Mr. Kumar

Reminder II

GUIDELINES:

- State all the relevant details—precise product name, number, cost, date, etc.—of the original order.
- Summarize the situation and express your concern.
- Request notification if there will be a further delay.

SITUATION:

The office manager for Holliston & Beem ordered the newsletter *Monthly Management Records* eight weeks ago. She has received her canceled check but no issues to date.

Figure 5.37   Reminder II

Δ *Holliston & Beem Associates* Δ

Faunce Building, Fourth Floor
2 Market Street
Tacoma Heights, WA 92614
Phone (206) 484-0411 / Fax (206) 484-0421

June 30, 20--

Jenkins Press
Subscription Dept.
95 High Ridge Road
Park City, MD 20633

To whom it may concern:

On May 2 we sent you a purchase order for a one-year subscription to *Monthly Management Records*, along with a check for $73.50. A copy of the purchase order is enclosed.

To date, we have not received our first issue of the magazine, although we *have* received our canceled check. We are concerned that the order may somehow have gone astray. Would you please check your files and let us know the status of our subscription.

Sincerely,

Claire T. Odom

Claire T. Odom
Office Manager

enclosure

Request for Information

GUIDELINES:

- Get to the point immediately.
- Compliment the manufacturer on its product, if appropriate.
- Specify as precisely as possible what you require.

SITUATION:

Acme Equipment, a company that does most of its business through its catalog, plans to add a line of tractors to the equipment it leases out, and has chosen Laprade Industries' Titan line. Acme's marketing manager needs product specifications for the upcoming catalog and writes to Laprade to request them.

Figure 5.38   Request for Information

Acme Equipment Company
42 Grove Street
Rockford, IL 61107
815-327-0605

September 17, 20--

Sales Manager
Laprade Industries
1525 State Street
Cleveland, OH 44140

Dear Sir or Madam:

We are currently planning to add yard and garden tractors to our line of leased equipment. It is my pleasure to announce that we shall feature your line of Titan tractors.

Would you please send us a catalog containing a complete list of models and specifications for Titan tractors. In particular, we require the following data on each model:

1. Horsepower
2. Range of job function
3. Commercial or homeowner equipment (specify one)
4. Contract samples and sales terms

We need this information no later than September 30 in order to include it in our November catalog.

We are delighted to have found such an excellent line of products, and we look forward to a pleasant and profitable business relationship.

Sincerely yours,

Thomas Domizio

Thomas Domizio
Marketing Manager

TD:gbb

Request for Price Quotation

GUIDELINES:

- Describe in detail the specifications of the service you are requesting.
- Specify schedule requirements.
- Ask to receive the quotation by a given date.
- Close with an offer to answer any further questions that may arise.

SITUATION:

Hampden Press is ready to begin production of a new book, and the managing editor is soliciting price quotations from several typesetters, including Waterville Typesetting.

Figure 5.39   Request for Price Quotation

Hampden Press
44 Lincoln Street
Canton, NY 14523

Tel: 607-555-6926
Fax: 607-555-6977

December 20, 20--

Mr. Barry Zubroski
Waterville Typesetting, Inc.
2965 James Street
Waterville, SC 29270

Dear Mr. Zubroski:

SUBJECT: *The Homeowner's Encyclopedia*

We are writing to request a quotation for typesetting services for the above new title.

The book will be approximately 512 pages long, composed of about 10 pages of front matter, 474 pages of main text, and 30 pages of index. The text will include approximately 200 pieces of line art (equaling approximately 25% of the text space), which we will ask you to scan in. The trim size will be 8" x 10". The text will be set double-column in 10/11 Baskerville in a total text block of 40 x 50 picas. A diskette containing the text for the letters A-C is enclosed.

We will require one set of galleys, one set of page proofs, and final repro.

The copy will be in the form of computer diskettes, which we expect to send over a period of about 6 weeks, with the last arriving by April 30. We would like to receive final negatives by August 1.

Could you return your quotation to us within two weeks? If you have any questions, please do not hesitate to call.

Sincerely,

Nancy L. Bains

Nancy L. Bains
Managing Editor

NLB/rg

Request for Speaker

GUIDELINES:

- Begin by complimenting the speaker and describing the occasion.
- Specify the date, time, and location.
- Suggest a possible topic or topics, leaving the final choice and specifics to the speaker, as a courtesy and a compliment to the speaker's judgment.
- Either specify a fee or let the speaker suggest one.
- Close with a courteous reminder that you are waiting to hear from the speaker.

SITUATION:

The Altamont Conservation Club needs a speaker for the annual banquet, which they hope will be a memorable one despite their limited budget. The club president writes to their first choice for speaker.

Figure 5.40   Request for Speaker

Altamont Conservation Club

P.O. Box 20 / Altamont, MS 39211 • (601) 444-5535

February 14, 20--

Prof. Susan Compton
29 Fairfax Lane
Jackson, MS 39209

Dear Professor Compton:

The upcoming Altamont Conservation Club spring banquet will be held this year at the Marriott Hotel in downtown Jackson on Thursday evening, May 30. When the subject of an outside speaker for the occasion was recently raised, several members eagerly suggested your name. I am writing to ask whether you would be interested in joining us.

Our spring banquet is an annual event that caps our year's calendar of activities. Our theme this year is "Ecology and Human History in the Delta," which is broad enough to allow you considerable leeway in choosing a specific subject for your talk. A speech of 35-40 minutes, followed by a 10-minute question-and-answer period, would be ideal for us.

Could you let us know by the first of next month whether you are available and what your fee would be. If the idea appeals to you and we can agree on an honorarium, I'm sure our members will have a noteworthy evening in store for them.

I look forward to hearing from you.

Sincerely,

Elaine Goodrich

Elaine Goodrich
General Secretary

Reservation

GUIDELINES:

- Restate precisely the event's dates and the rooms and room arrangements that will be needed.
- Request written confirmation as soon as possible.

SITUATION:

After surveying a number of sites, Pineland Paper has decided on a site for its annual branch managers' conference, and its C.O.O. is writing to reserve facilities for the meeting.

Figure 5.41 Reservation

▼ **PINELAND PAPER COMPANY, INC.** ▼
▼
608 SOUTH STREET
SHREVEPORT, LA 71118
TELEPHONE (318) 123-4567
FAX (318) 123-4588

March 20, 20--

Mr. Philip Keane, Reservations Manager
Willoughby Hotel
674 Dennis Drive
Kansas City, MO 64128

Dear Mr. Keane:

We would like to confirm that we have chosen the Willoughby Hotel as this year's site for our branch managers' conference.

As we discussed by letter earlier this month, we want to reserve the Pioneer Suite, your principal three-room conference suite, for June 16 and 17. (You already have our business credit-card number.) We shall need conference tables arranged in a U for 20 people in one room, space for large product displays in another, and an informal social meeting area in the third. Further arrangements will be worked out as the conference date approaches.

We would appreciate confirmation of this reservation as soon as possible.

Yours sincerely,

ROBERT ANDERSON -- C.O.O.

RA:gbb

Resignation

GUIDELINES:

- State the basic facts simply at the outset.
- Reflect on aspects of your present position that have given you honest satisfaction, including personal relationships.
- Express good wishes for the company's future if possible.

SITUATION:

Stan Williams is leaving a senior position at Blaine-Butler to take a new job. His tenure at Blaine-Butler has not always been easy, and he has frequently found the job disappointing. He masks his unhappiness, however, by focusing on the colleagues he has enjoyed and on aspects of the job that he found genuinely satisfying.

Figure 5.42   Resignation

Blaine-Butler Distributors

July 6, 20--

Dear Howard:

This is to inform you that I am resigning my position as Regional Sales Manager with Blaine-Butler Distributors as of July 30 to take the post of Mid-Atlantic Sales Manager with the software marketing firm of Aaron A. Davis Associates in Dallas.

This has not been an easy decision for me. I hold great affection for the people of Blaine-Butler and the corporate culture we have developed. I have been generally pleased with the changes that have recently taken place, and in particular I have been gratified by the overall success of my own efforts to streamline our field operations and by your recognition of my achievements in this area. I see only continued growth and success for you and the company in the future, and I regret that I will not be here to share in it with you.

I appreciate the support and encouragement you have given me over the past five years and wish you all the best for the future.

Very truly yours,

Stanley J. Williams

Montrose Building, 500 Lone Star Avenue, Austin, TX 77004
Tel: (512) 789-7897 Fax: (512) 789-7898

Sales I

GUIDELINES:

- Address the store manager by name if possible to lessen the possibility that the letter will be treated as junk mail.
- Try a unique opening that will catch the reader's attention.
- List the advantages of the product and describe your company's services.
- Offer the reader the opportunity to review the product, if possible, in order to convey your own confidence in its quality and convince the reader as well.
- Close with encouragement to the recipient to take action immediately.

SITUATION:

Parsons Office Management Services publishes a monthly newsletter that digests information on new office equipment. Hoping to increase the newsletter's circulation, Daniel Parsons has drawn up a list of office-supply stores that are not currently subscribing, and writes to describe his company's product.

Figure 5.43   Sales I

Parsons Office Management Services
15 Evergreen Street / Jonesville, NC 35886
Phone: 919-935-0246 / Fax: 919-935-0852

October 12, 20--

Mr. James Huntwell
Morris Office Supply
250 Maple Street
Belchertown, MA 01043

WHAT'S *NEW* FOR THE OFFICE?

Today's office manager is continually faced with the challenge this question poses.
    Parsons Office Management Services, a widely recognized authority on the
    subject, can provide all the answers--every month!

Each month, **Office Products Update**, our 8-page newsletter, reviews new entries
    in the office supply and equipment arena to aid the beleaguered office manager
    in making educated and money-saving decisions fast. Our testers track the
    product lines, ask the right questions, and report their findings to many of
    America's largest corporations.

Gain a competitive edge by joining us and obtaining the latest office-products
    information in summary form each month. It won't be long before your
    customers recognize Morris Office Supply as a discriminating leading-edge
    supplier of office equipment.

This month's edition, featuring comparative ratings of the newest portable
    photocopiers and labeling systems, is enclosed. Please accept it with our
    compliments.

Office Products Update may be yours each month at the new-subscriber rate of
    only $66.00 for the entire year--a 25% discount from the normal subscription
    rate of $88.00. And, Mr. Huntwell, if you make use of the enclosed special
    subscriber's card before the end of this month, you will receive two extra
    issues at no extra cost. May we hear from you soon?

Daniel B Parsons

DANIEL B. PARSONS
Vice President

Sales II

- Briefly review the customer's past history with the company, leading up to the question of why the customer is now inactive.
- Ask straightforwardly why the customer is no longer ordering from the company.
- Mention an enclosed questionnaire, if applicable.
- Bring up items that may interest the customer, if appropriate, in order to take advantage of having the reader's attention to use the letter as a selling opportunity.

SITUATION:

The sales manager of the Hanson Company, an optical-supply wholesaler, has recently noticed an overall fall-off in orders, and writes to each inactive customer.

Figure 5.44   Sales II

:: Hanson Phototech

50 Front Street
P. O. Box 1435
Wyanchochee, MI 48121
Phone: (313) 543-6660
Fax: (313) 543-6503

October 14, 20--

Mr. Ralph Chauncey
The Camera Shop
1397 Rosemont Avenue
La Crosse, WI 54601

Dear Mr. Chauncey:

Every year for the past seven years, our company has been pleased to fill at least one order from The Camera Shop. Recently, however, I had the opportunity to go over our sales list, and I've made the somewhat disquieting discovery that we haven't received an order from you in 14 months.

Is it possible that this may indicate a failure at our end? Have you experienced delay or been dissatisfied with an order? Since I can't find any evidence of a complaint in our files, I'd very much like to know if you've encountered any problems that you haven't told us about.

Although you probably don't have time to sit down and write us a letter, we'd still like to hear from you. I've therefore taken the liberty of enclosing a brief postage-paid questionnaire, and I do hope you'll take a moment to check off your answers on it.

I'm also sending along something else that may be of interest to you. We're currently offering the entire Monatrex line of cameras at one third off our usual price. This is one of our best-selling lines, and we think you'll spot some excellent buys in the enclosed brochure, which includes an order form.

Sincerely,

Daniel McMillan
Daniel McMillan
Sales Manager

lvt
Encl. (2)

Sales III

GUIDELINES:

- Open by reminding the client that you have met before.
- Mention one of the company's products that may interest him.
- State a desire to meet with the client and suggest a date and time.
- Say you'll call to confirm the appointment; a call will allow you to get a better idea of the client's needs and to presell the product, and will allow the client to suggest an alternative time or to decline entirely.

SITUATION:

Grace Diaz, a sales representative for Grayson Paper, writes to confirm an appointment with Brian Watson, purchasing agent for the Pikeville School District. She has done business with him in the past and is aware of at least one product need that her company can now supply.

Figure 5.45   Sales III

Grayson Paper Company
12555 Berea Road, Fayette, AL 35910
Telephone: (205) 349-6200 ■ Fax: (205) 349-6440

March 3, 20--

Mr. Brian Wilson, Purchasing Agent
Pikeville Township School District
Pikeville, TN 37022

Dear Mr. Watson:

Last year when I visited Pikeville, you found some essay paper in the Grayson line that you felt would suit several different needs within the district. At that time, you and I also discussed the problem you were having in finding multicolor file folders large enough to accommodate your oversize record forms. Grayson was then in the midst of production planning for a new line of file folders, but manufacturing had not yet begun. Now I have samples of our new file folders, which I believe fulfill all your requirements.

I would like to call on you at your office later this month to show you samples of these folders and some other new products that may be of interest to you. Perhaps the morning of Wednesday the 24th would be convenient for you. I will call early in the week of March 15 to confirm this date or perhaps set up an alternative time.

If you need to reach me before then, please feel free to call me at 205-349-6222.

I look forward to meeting with you and talking about the current needs of the Pikeville School District.

Sincerely,

Grace Diaz

Grace Diaz
Sales Representative

Sales Follow-Up

GUIDELINES:

- Express personal appreciation for the order.
- Offer further services, if appropriate.
- Close in a friendly but not effusive manner.

SITUATION:

After being chosen by the Sullivans as the sole lumber supplier for their new house, the president of Cheney Lumber writes to express his gratitude.

Figure 5.46   Sales Follow-Up

CHENEY LUMBER COMPANY
650 MAIN STREET
BRATTLEBORO, VT 05302
TELEPHONE (802) 643-2101
FAX (802) 643-2102

August 6, 20--

Mr. and Mrs. Gerald Sullivan
68 Cottage Street
Essex Junction, VT 05452

Dear Mr. and Mrs. Sullivan:

Congratulations on your decision to become new homeowners! And thank you for
the confidence you have shown in us through opening an account and placing your
order at Cheney Lumber.

It will be a pleasure to supply the lumber and millwork for the beautiful home you
have designed. You can build with confidence knowing that only the highest-
quality materials and supplies are being used.

Ralph Fuchs, our customer service officer, will be glad to help you at any time with
the choice of materials for your new house. Please let us know throughout the
course of the project if there is ever any way in which we may be of further
assistance.

Sincerely,

Larry Cheney
President

gbb

Sympathy or Condolence I

GUIDELINES:

- Handwrite the letter on personal stationery.
- Offer your condolences at the outset. Avoid being maudlin, and take care to choose the appropriate words for your feelings.
- Recall pleasant circumstances under which you met the deceased, if possible.
- Offer something specific you can do, if possible; otherwise, a vaguer offer of assistance is adequate.
- Close on a mildly cheerful note or a more somber one, as appropriate.

SITUATION:

James Artandi, the buyer for a furniture store, deals regularly with Steve O'Donnell, a manufacturer's representative, whom he regards as an acquaintance rather than a close friend. O'Donnell's wife has recently died after a long illness.

Figure 5.47   Sympathy or Condolence I

Galen Furnishings

June 8

Dear Steve,

I was very sorry to hear of Eileen's death. I extend to you my heartfelt sympathy.

I well remember meeting Eileen the evening you and she hosted a swimming party for local furniture buyers. I was new to the area at that time, and felt more than a little like an outsider. Eileen took the time to perform introductions and make me feel at home (she even provided me with a towel when George Harkness's four children and the basset hound were discovered playing tug-of-war with my own). I've never forgotten her way of making a stranger feel welcome.

You probably haven't made any definite plans yet, but if you should decide that you would like to get away for a while, I would be happy to keep an eye on the house for you. It would be no trouble at all to stop by each day, and I'd welcome the chance to come admire your garden.

Best personal regards,

Jim

Sympathy or Condolence II

GUIDELINES:

- Type the letter on Executive stationery.
- Begin by offering sympathy simply and straightforwardly on behalf of you and your staff as well, if appropriate.
- Offer business-related assistance, if appropriate.

SITUATION:

Randolph Parker, president of a textile mill, has heard that Gunnar Caroleen, president of a company that does business with Parker's firm, was recently widowed. The two men have met on business occasions, but not socially.

Figure 5.48   Sympathy or Condolence II

PARKER MILLS
2605 Commerce Boulevard
Omaha, NE 68124
Telephone: 402·241·7425
Fax: 402·241·7366

Office of the President

September 9, 20--

Dear Gunnar:

My staff and I wish to extend our heartfelt sympathy to
you during this period of your bereavement since the
passing of your wife, Helen.

Your many friends here at Parker Mills join me in
offering assistance with special scheduling of your
orders at this time. Please do not hesitate to let us know
how we may help.

It must be a comfort to have your family so near. May
the memories of your years together sustain you all and
bring you strength and peace.

Sincerely,

Mr. Gunnar Caroleen
President
Sunrise Home Furnishings
North Platte, NE 69103

Thanks for Hospitality

GUIDELINES:

- Type the letter on company stationery, addressing the recipient by first name if appropriate (but retaining the colon after the salutation) and omitting the typed signature.
- Express appreciation for the hospitality, mentioning specifically the occasions on which you were entertained.
- Further convey good feelings and thanks as appropriate.

SITUATION:

The plant manager for Fairfield Textiles recently attended an out-of-town convention and trade show, during which he was entertained by Fairfield's local sales representative and her husband. On his return, he writes a thank-you note to express his appreciation.

Figure 5.49   Thanks for Hospitality

Fairlane Textiles

2900 Northrup Way, Tulsa, Oklahoma 74136
TELEPHONE: 305-555-9318 / FAX: 305-555-8344

December 1, 20--

Ms. Barbara Raycroft
Fairlane Textiles Company
2100 Broadway, Suite 901
Tampa, FL 66250

Dear Barbara:

Thank you very much for all the kind hospitality that you and Bill showed to me during my stay in Tampa. I thoroughly enjoyed my tour of the city and the wonderful meal that you and Bill managed to put together on such short notice.

I certainly hope to see you again at this year's sales meeting. And again, many thanks to you both for making my trip such a pleasant one.

Best regards,

Mark

Thanks for Information or Service

GUIDELINES:

- Thank the recipient for what he or she provided, recalling specifically what it consisted of.
- Describe the benefit derived from the interview.
- Close with a compliment and further thanks or pleasantries, as appropriate.

SITUATION:

A freelance writer specializing in local history has been granted an interview with a librarian who oversees a collection of historical papers, and writes to thank her for the interview.

Figure 5.50   Thanks for Information or Service

CHRISTOPHER SOULE

EDITORIAL RESEARCH RESOURCES

September 27, 20--

Mrs. Barbara Chase
New Lancaster Public Library
New Lancaster, RI 10621

Dear Mrs. Chase:

   Thank you very much for giving me the chance to learn about your impressive collection of books, periodicals, and papers relating to the history of New Lancaster. Not only have you helped me with my current research project, but you have also introduced me to a valuable resource that I hope to be able to draw upon in the future. I certainly appreciate the time you spent with me, and I applaud the work that you and your staff are doing to preserve and make available these valuable materials.

Sincerely,

Christopher Soule

1292 PARK STREET
PROVIDENCE, RI 10623
TEL 401-468-0246   FAX 401-468-2332

Correspondence with Government Agencies

The extensive dealings between government and private industry have made it necessary for civilian contractors to be familiar with government agencies' special correspondence and security procedures. While letter format and security precautions vary with the policies of each government contracting agency and the nature of each contract, the following overview should serve as a general orientation for anyone dealing with government correspondence for the first time.

The two basic aims are to ensure that (1) all material, regardless of its classification, be quickly delivered to its intended addressee and copies of it be readily retrievable, and (2) all classified material be safeguarded according to government guidelines so that unauthorized persons cannot gain access to it.

CORRESPONDENCE FORMAT

Letters to government agencies should conform to the guidelines of the agency with which your firm is working. Letters incorrectly formatted and addressed may be delayed, lost, or even rejected and returned—any of which can result in costly delays or even the loss of a contract, especially when bidding under a deadline is involved.

Nonmilitary agencies Correspondence with a nonmilitary government agency may be formatted in any of the generally accepted business-letter styles discussed earlier. A subject line and a reference line are always included, since they are necessary for proper intra-agency routing of the letter. The correct forms of address for elected and appointed officials can be found in the Forms of Address chart.

Department of Defense The following general principles are applicable to correspondence directed to the Department of Defense. Most are illustrated in Fig. 5.51.

1. The Modified Block Letter style with numbered paragraphs is recommended.

2. If any section of the letter is classified, the highest classification category for any material therein must be stamped at the top and the bottom of each page. This stamp appears above the printed letterhead and below the last line of the message on the first sheet, and above the heading and below the last notation on all continuation sheets. The CLASSIFIED BY _____ and NATIONAL SECURITY INFORMATION stamps must appear at the bottom of the letterhead sheet.

3. Any special mailing notation is typically typed in capital letters or stamped on the upper left corner of the letterhead sheet and any continuation sheets.

4. The writer's courtesy title and surname, the typist's initials, and the writer's telephone extension (if not already included in the printed letterhead) may be typed in the upper right corner of the first sheet, separated by slashes.

5. The dateline appears flush left about three lines below the letterhead. The date may be styled in either of two ways: "1 January 2000" or "1 Jan 00," for example. The style chosen should be used consistently throughout the letter. For the second style, each of the twelve months may be abbreviated to its first three letters, with no period following.

6. Companies contracting with the government for a specific project usually assign a control number to files and correspondence related to the project. This reference number should appear on the line below the dateline.

7. The next element of the letter—the SUBJECT block or the TO block, depending on the agency—is typed flush left about three lines below the reference number. The SUBJECT block, shown first in the following facsimile, consists of three lines: (1) the contract number, (2) the name of the program or project, and (3) the subject of the letter, followed by the appropriate security classification—(C) = Confidential, (S) = Secret, or (TS) = Top Secret.

8. The TO block, which is really the inside address, is typed about three lines below the date block or the SUBJECT block. It consists of four lines: (1) the initials or name of the office, (2) the name of the administrator (addressee), (3) the name of the organization, and (4) the geographical address.

9. The THROUGH or VIA block (the caption varies depending on the agency) is typed about three lines below any other blocks that precede it. This block is used in letters that must be sent through designated channels before reaching the addressee. Each agency, office, or individual should be named and addressed as in the TO block.

10. The REFERENCE block is typed about three lines below the last block. It contains a list of material or previous correspondence that the addressee must consult before acting on the letter. The items are numbered or lettered sequentially.

11. The captions SUBJECT, TO, THROUGH, and REFERENCE should not be visible in the window area of a window envelope (which can only be used for nonclassified material); only the address in the TO block should be visible. The style of these captions varies: they may be entirely in capitals, they may be in capitals and lowercase, or they may be abbreviated (SUBJ, THRU, etc.). Use the style recommended by the individual agency.

Figure 5.51   Letter Styling for Department of Defense Correspondence

CONFIDENTIAL

Merriam Webster

CERTIFIED MAIL   Mr. _____/tp/413-734-4444

1 January 20--
97TRANS123

SUBJECT: Contract AF 45(100)-1147
                Foreign Technology Program
                Life Sciences Translation QC (C)

TO: Initials or Name of Office
                Name of Applicable Administrator
                Organization
                Address

THROUGH: Applicable Channels
                and Addresses
                Listed and Blocked

REFERENCE:(a) WXYZ letter ABCD/EF dated 1 December 20--
          (b) EFGH letter IJKL/MN dated 1 November 20--

1.   This is a typical format for letters directed to the Department of Defense. Styling varies with the
       agency or department one is writing to; thus, a format consensus is shown here.

2.   In letters containing classified information, the highest classification category of any included
       information must be noted at the top and bottom of each page.

       a. Since the letter is supposed to be CONFIDENTIAL, it is so stamped above the
       letterhead and at the bottom of the page, and the abbreviation (C) for CONFIDENTIAL is
       typed at the end of the subject line.

       b. Appropriate classification stamps are affixed at the bottom of the first page.

3.   Special mailing notations, if required, are typically typed in the upper left corner of the page.

4.   If the writer's name and telephone number are not on the printed letterhead, they may be
       typed with the typist's initials in the upper right corner of the first age.

CONFIDENTIAL

CLASSIFIED BY:
EXEMPT FROM GENERAL DECLASSIFICATION
SCHEDULE OF EXECUTIVE ORDER 11652
EXEMPTION CATEGORY _____
DECLASSIFY ON _____

NATIONAL SECURITY INFORMATION
Unauthorized disclosure subject to
criminal sanctions.

Merriam-Webster Inc.

47 Federal Street • P.O. Box 281 • Springfield, MA 01102 • Telephone (413) 734-3134 • Facsimile (413) 731-5979

Figure 5.51 *(continued)*

CONFIDENTIAL

CERTIFIED MAIL

Contract AF 45(100)-1147   1 January 20--
Foreign Technology Program   76TRANS123
Life Sciences QC (C)   Page 2

5. The dateline, with the date in inverted form, and the company control number are aligned
    flush left, with the dateline three lines below the letterhead.

6. The SUBJECT block, sometimes placed after the TO and/or THROUGH blocks
    depending on agency preference, contains the contract number, project name, and subject
    of the letter.

7. The TO block is really the inside address. The THROUGH or VIA block lists the
    designated channels through which the letter must pass before it reaches the addressee.

8. The REFERENCE block lists related material or previous correspondence that must be referred
    to before action can be taken.

9. The SUBJECT, TO, THROUGH, and REFERENCE blocks are separated by triple-spacing, and
    are internally single-spaced.

10. There is no salutation. The message, comprising numbered paragraphs and alphabetized
    subparagraphs, begins two lines below the REFERENCE block.

11. Continuation-sheet headings begin six lines from the top edge of the page and contain subject
    data, date, page number, and control or reference number. The classification category must be
    stamped at the top and bottom of each continuation sheet.

12. There is no complimentary close. The company name is typed all in capitals two lines below the
    last message line, followed four lines down by the writer's name, title, and department, if
    necessary, in capitals and lowercase.

13. The keyboarder's initials, if not shown at the top of the first page, may appear two lines below
    the signature block. Enclosures should be listed numerically and identified, as should carbon-
    copy recipients. Only external distribution lists appear on the original.

MERRIAM-WEBSTER INC.

Executive Signature

Executive Signature
Project Manager

Enclosures   (1)   (C) 3 copies of Translation
                                 Printout dated 30 December 20--
                 (2)   1 copy of Contract AF 44(100)-1147

                                                                              CONFIDENTIAL

12. There is no salutation.

13. The message begins flush left, two lines below the last line of the REFER-ENCE block. Paragraphs are numbered consecutively and single-spaced, with a blank line after each paragraph. Subparagraphs are alphabetized and single-spaced, with a blank line after each subparagraph. As in a standard outline, if there is a paragraph 1, there must be a 2; if there is a subparagraph *a*, there must be a *b;* and so on.

14. There is no complimentary close.

15. The company name is typed flush left in capital letters two lines beneath the last line of the message. The writer's name is typed in capitals and lowercase at least four lines below the company name, also flush left. The writer's title and department name, if not already on the letterhead, may be included beneath his or her name in capitals and lowercase, also flush left.

16. The typist's initials, if not already included in the top right corner of the first sheet, may be typed flush left two lines below the last element of the signature block.

17. Enclosures are listed and identified two lines below the typist's initials or the signature block. The numeral styles 1. or (1) may be used. The appropriate headings are *Enclosure(s), Encl.,* or *Enc.* for the Air Force and Navy, and *Inclosure(s)* or *Inc.* for the Army. Classification categories should be noted at the beginning of each applicable enclosure description, as shown in enclosure (3) below. Even if enclosures are to be mailed under separate cover, they must be listed on the letter and their classification categories must be noted.
    Enc.(1) 3 copies of Test Procedure Report
        WXYzz dated 1 January 20—
    Enc.(2) 1 copy of Contract AF 45(100)-1147
    Enc.(3) (C) 2/c ea. specifications mentioned in paragraph 7
Some government agencies require that enclosures be noted in a block two or three spaces below the REFERENCE block.

18. The copy notation *cc:* or *Copy to* is typed flush left two lines below any other notations. It includes an alphabetical listing of all individuals not associated with the company who will receive copies. Their addresses should be included. Internal copies should contain a complete list of both the external and internal copy recipients.
    cc: COL John K. Walker
        Fort Bragg, NC 28307
        (w/enc. (1)-2 copies)

19. Continuation-sheet headings are typed six lines from the top edge of the page, and the message continues four lines beneath the heading.

Continuation-sheet headings should include the SUBJECT block data as well as the reference number, the date, and the page number (see facsimile).

20. If the contracting agency must approve the material and return it to the contractor, an approval line must be the last typed item on the page. In this case, two copies of the letter must be enclosed in the envelope.

    APPROVED

    _____
    [addressee's title]
    [date]

    This material may be typed two to four lines beneath the last notation and blocked with the left margin.

CLASSIFIED MATERIAL

Both the U.S. government and its civilian contractors are responsible for the security of sensitive material passing between them—responsibility that specifically means the safeguarding of classified material against unlawful or unauthorized dissemination, duplication, or observation. Each employee of a firm that handles or has knowledge of classified material shares responsibility for protecting it while it is in use, in storage, or in transit. The security regulations of the Department of Defense are outlined in DoD publication 5200.1-R, *Information Security Program Regulation,* for sale through the National Technical Information Service, U.S. Department of Commerce, Springfield, VA 22161 (703–487–4650).

Classification in industrial operations is based on government security guidance. Private-sector management must implement the decisions of the government contracting agency with respect to classified information and material developed, produced, or handled in the course of a project. Management also must designate persons within the firm who will be responsible for assuring that government regulations are followed. Each system and program involving research, development, testing, and evaluation of technical information is supported by its own program security guide.

Terminology   The following short glossary, adapted from Department of Defense definitions, will introduce the basic concepts of security classification.

Classified information   Official information that requires, in the interest of national security, protection against unauthorized disclosure and has been so designated.

Declassify   To determine that certain classified information no longer requires protection against unauthorized disclosure and to remove the classification designation.

Document   Any recorded information (including written or printed material, data-processing cards and tapes, graphics, and sound, voice, electronic, or magnetic recordings in any form), regardless of its physical form or characteristics.

Downgrade To determine that certain classified information does not require as high a degree of protection against unauthorized disclosure as is currently provided, and to change the classification designation to reflect this.

Information Knowledge that can be communicated by any means.

Material Any document, product, or substance on or in which information may be recorded or embodied.

National security A term encompassing both the national defense and the foreign relations of the United States.

Official information Information owned by, produced for or by, or subject to the control of the U.S. government.

Regrade To determine that certain classified information requires a different degree of protection against unauthorized disclosure than is currently provided, and to change the classification designation to reflect this.

Upgrade To determine that certain classified information requires a higher degree of protection against unauthorized disclosure than is currently provided, and to change the classification designation to reflect this.

Classifications The following classification categories must be designated on correspondence and other matter by stamps not less than 1/4″ in height:

Unclassified (U) For information or material that requires no protection against unauthorized disclosure.

Confidential (C) For information or material requiring protection because its unauthorized disclosure could cause damage to the national security.

Secret (S) For information or material requiring a substantial degree of protection because its unauthorized disclosure could cause serious damage to the national security.

Top Secret (TS) For information or material requiring the highest degree of protection because its unauthorized disclosure could cause exceptionally grave damage to the national security.

The phrases "For official use only" and "Limited official use" should not be used to identify classified information.

Marking documents The following general marking procedures are required by the government:

1. The overall classification of a document, whether or not permanently bound, or any copy or reproduction thereof must be conspicuously marked or stamped at the top and bottom on the outside of the front cover (if any), on the title page (if any), on the first page, on the last page, and on the outside of the back cover (if any). Each inside page of the document must be marked or stamped top and bottom with the highest classification category applicable to the information appearing there.

2. Each section, paragraph, subparagraph, or part of a document must be marked with the applicable parenthetical classification abbreviation (TS), (S), (C), or (U) when there are several degrees of classified information within the document.

3. Large components of complex documents that may be used separately should be appropriately marked. These components include attachments and appendices to a memorandum or a letter, annexes or appendices to a plan or program, or a major part of a report.

4. Files, folders, or packets for classified documents should be conspicuously marked on both front and back covers with the highest category of classification occurring in documents they enclose.

5. Transmittal documents including endorsements and comments should carry the highest classification category applicable to the information attached to them.

Mailing   Basic mailing procedures for classified documents are outlined below. (For detailed information on mailing and hand-carrying such documents, see *Information Security Program Regulation.*)

1. Classified material must be enclosed in two sealed opaque envelopes or similar wrappings before it may be mailed through the U.S. Postal Service or an approved commercial carrier.

2. Both envelopes must contain the names and addresses of the sender and the receiver.

3. The inner envelope must contain the appropriate classification category stamp, which must not be visible through the outer envelope.

4. The classified information should be protected from the inner envelope by being folded inward, or by use of a blank cover sheet.

5. The inner envelope must contain an appropriate classified-material receipt.

6. Confidential material must be sent by CERTIFIED MAIL, and Secret information must be sent by REGISTERED MAIL. Top Secret documents require specialized transit procedures.

7. Classified material should be addressed to an official government agency and not to an individual.

Storage   The storage of classified material must conform to government security requirements. In general, locking steel file containers should be used and strict custodial procedures should be followed. Care must be taken to guard against unlawful access through computer networks, terminals, or disk files. Records should be retained for no more than five years. For details, see the publication *Physical Security,* available through the National Technical Information Service.

Downgrading   Classified material is downgraded and declassified when the Department of Defense determines that there is no longer any national-security reason for it to be classified. An automatic schedule of downgrading has been set up for the three categories:

1. TOP SECRET will be downgraded automatically to SECRET at the end of the second full calendar year following the year it was originated; downgraded to CONFIDENTIAL at the end of the fourth full calendar year following the year it was originated; and declassified at the end of the tenth full calendar year following the year it was originated.

2. SECRET will be downgraded automatically to CONFIDENTIAL at the end of the second full calendar year following the year it was originated, and declassified at the end of the eighth full calendar year following the year it was originated.

3. CONFIDENTIAL will be automatically declassified at the end of the sixth full calendar year following the year it was originated.

Classified documents therefore must be conspicuously marked or stamped to indicate the intended automatic downgrading schedule. This information is typed or stamped on the first or title page of a document immediately below or adjacent to the classification stamp.

Exemptions to the General Declassification Schedule will bear an exemption stamp immediately below or adjacent to the classification stamp on the first or title page (see Fig. 5.51, lower left corner).

Disposal   Authorized disposal techniques must be observed. Classified material is generally destroyed by burning, and a record of destruction should be kept for two years.

CHAPTER 6

Memos, Reports, and Other Documents

Memorandums

The intraoffice memo is the traditional means of relaying written information to an individual or to all or part of the corporate staff. Office memorandums are written for circulation only within the organization. (This is not limited to those working in a single building, but may also include branch offices in distant cities.)

Many companies still use printed or photocopied memorandum forms that can be fed through a typewriter. But today memo forms, like form letters, are commonly kept on the computer. The option of using a memo format will automatically appear on-screen when you indicate that you want to create a new document. Word-processing programs usually include predesigned memo templates or formats; however, a company can also design its own format, which will then appear as a separate option along with the predesigned templates. A computer memo form that incorporates the company logo or letterhead design can be created by electronically scanning the design onto a diskette (if the office has no scanner, this can be done at a local service bureau) and using the Insert function to save it onto the appropriate template. Your word-processing manual or the on-screen Help function will guide you.

Standard memorandum format requires four opening headings in the following order: TO, FROM, SUBJECT, and DATE. (The DATE line sometimes comes first.) The TO and FROM lines take the place of any salutation, complimentary close, and signature, though memos are often initialed by the author, either beside his or her name or at the end. No inside address is included, since the recipients are always at the company itself.

The four standard headings are usually arranged in a single column. The headings may align left, or they may align on their colons. The author name, recipient name, subject, and date should generally be aligned as well. Other arrangements—for example, with the first two headings positioned on the left and the last two directly across from them on the right—are also used.

The TO line may specify an individual, several individuals, or a section, department, or other group:

TO: Frances Rummel, Customer Services Supervisor

TO: TKL, PRW, FWD

TO: Administrative Staff, School of Business

If several managers are named, they should be listed in order of corporate rank.

A CC (courtesy-copy) line, which performs exactly the same function as in a letter, may follow either the TO line or the message itself, using approximately the form of such notations in a letter.

If the memo will be going to a large number of named individuals, they should usually not be listed under the TO heading. Instead, the word "Distribution" or a group name such as "All Employees" or "Customer Service Dept." may follow "TO," and a distribution list or routing slip, listing all the intended recipients, may be stapled to the memo. Such lists may be pre-typed listings of the members of a given department or the entire company. A single copy will then be passed through the office, with each recipient checking off his or her name and passing the memo on. This means of distribution saves paper and is therefore desirable when individuals will not have to keep their own copies. (When a memo is urgent, routed sheets left on the desks of absent employees will fail to move as quickly as they should; urgent memos should therefore be labeled as such, perhaps with the specific direction that they actually be handed to other employees.)

An optional LOCATION (floor, extension, or branch) line may follow the TO line.

The FROM line may include not only the name but also the title of the writer.

The SUBJECT line, like a title, encapsulates the memo's content for the recipient, which also makes it useful for filing purposes. It should run to no more than a single line. It is generally capitalized headline-style (that is, with all words except prepositions and articles capitalized) but sometimes is typed entirely in capital letters:

SUBJECT: April Meeting of the Advisory Council

SUBJECT: NEED FOR A NEW LASER PRINTER

SUBJECT: New Wholesale Discount Schedule

An optional PRIORITY line, indicating the memo's degree of urgency, may follow the SUBJECT line.

The message itself should be formatted exactly like a letter message. If the memo runs to a second sheet, the continuation sheet should be blank, just as it would be for a letter, though a page number, the date, and the subject line may be repeated as a header. (Computer memo templates will provide such headers automatically.)

Though memos will sometimes read just like letters, more often they will dispense with some of the courtesies of normal business letters. The opening sentence will generally begin directly with the subject at hand, for example, and any courteous language at the close will usually be brief.

If any materials accompany the memo, an "Attachment" line identifying the document attached (taking the place of an "Enclosure" line in a letter) should follow the message.

Memos may be sent in reusable manila interoffice envelopes, with the recipient's name written on the outside, or they may not require an envelope at all.

A typical memo is shown in Fig. 6.1.

Faxes

The facsimile, or fax, machine dramatically changed the way businesses exchange documents and other information when it became widely available in the 1970s. For certain kinds of material, fax machines replaced overnight couriers, first-class mail, and local messengers as the means of choice for rapid transmission. Today, even with the widespread use of e-mail, few firms can conduct routine business without a fax machine.

Fax machines work by scanning your document and creating a digitized "bit map" of it, which is then sent over telephone lines, and the receiving fax machine prints a copy of the image by reading the digitized map. (Since the fax is simply sending an image, handwritten messages and diagrams may be sent by fax just as easily as typed material.) The sending machine typically prints out a company identification (if one has been programmed into the machine), along with the time, date, and page number, and these appear as headers on each page.

Faxes are particularly useful for sending such documents as order forms, invoices, price schedules, price quotations, engineering diagrams, and tables of data of all kinds. It is very common to send a document by fax and simultaneously mail the original copy of the document to serve as a more formal record.

Many fax machines can be programmed to broadcast a single document to many recipients whose numbers have previously been entered. This capacity is often used for advertising to targeted groups; however, such "junk mail" is often not appreciated by its recipients.

Currently the market offers three basic means of printing out the transmitted images: *thermal-paper fax machines, plain-paper fax machines,* and *computer-based fax transmission.*

Figure 6.1   Memorandum

LYMAN INDUSTRIES

Memorandum

To: All Employees   **Date:**   May 2, 20--

From: T. L. Cooper _TLC_

Subject: Summer Hours

I'm pleased to announce a new summer schedule that will take
effect on May 27, 20--, and run through August 30.

The workday will increase by one half hour on Monday through
Thursday, and on Friday we will leave two hours early. You may
choose either to take a half hour off your lunch break or to add
a half hour to your total workday.

Closing times based on flexible starting times will be as
follows:

Start	Leave
7:00 a.m.	2:00 p.m.
8:00	2:30
8:30	3:00
9:00	3:30

If you plan to take vacation time on Friday, you may work regular
hours Monday through Thursday.

Vacation and sick days taken Monday-Thursday will count as
regularly scheduled workdays.

Please notify your supervisor at least one week in advance if you
choose to adjust your starting time or lunch break.

Here's to a great summer ahead!

A thermal-paper fax machine reproduces an image by means of a hot stylus that burns black dots into thermally sensitive paper. The expensive paper, clumsiness, slow speed, and low reproduction quality of thermal-paper faxes all contributed to their decline; in addition, faxes printed on thermal paper fade in a few months and become difficult, if not impossible, to read, necessitating photocopying onto plain paper if the document is to be stored. Although new models are still available, thermal-paper fax machines have been largely replaced by plain-paper machines.

Plain-paper fax machines use standard photocopier paper and offer superior reproductions of the original documents. Originally expensive, these machines can now be had for a reasonable price (the lowest-priced machines will lack certain features reviewed below). Most plain-paper faxes require *toner*—"ink" in the form of tiny dustlike particles—to create their images. Some instead use thermal printing technology; in such machines, heat supplied to a thermal transfer ribbon melts wax or resin containing ink, allowing the ink to transfer to the receiving paper, where it cools and solidifies.

By installing a fax modem (a modem capable of sending and receiving faxes, an ability most modems now have) and communications software on your computer, you can send electronic faxes directly, bypassing the need to create your own paper documents. Your fax modem will receive its own telephone number. Faxes can be sent from a computer to a fax machine or to another computer. When a fax is received by a computer, it can be displayed on-screen or printed out on the computer's printer. Ask your system administrator or local computer-service vendor about computer-based fax transmission.

CHOOSING A FAX MACHINE

Choosing a new fax machine (or a multifunction machine that may combine fax, scanning, computer printing, and photocopying capacities) requires a practical understanding of the features it offers, the kinds of consumables it uses, and the quality of its images. The list below is intended to serve as a guide to choosing a new fax machine or reviewing the capacities of your current machine.

- How much memory does it have for storing incoming documents in the event that it is depleted of toner or paper or is otherwise inoperable? Is the memory protected until someone makes the machine operational again? When memory is filled, what happens to incoming documents? How does the machine indicate that it is out of paper or toner or is having other problems?

- Does it provide for undersized or nonstandard-sized document transmission? If it accepts oversized documents, does it reduce the image sent or decrease one or both margins?

- How fast does it print incoming documents? What is the highest modem speed at which it is capable of operating?

- Does it have memory for transmitting documents? Will this memory allow users to enter a telephone number and charge code and scan in a document before transmission begins (sometimes called *walk-away capability*)? Can it store a document and send it later? If yes, how many pages of single-spaced text on standard letter-sized paper can be stored for transmission? What happens when memory is full?

- Can the machine perform more than one task at once? For example, is it possible to scan in a document for transmission while receiving and reproducing another document?

- Can its memory be increased? If it can, what do the additional memory increments cost?

- What happens if the number you enter is incorrect or for some other reason the transmission fails?

- Does it offer speed-dialing for commonly used numbers? If so, how many numbers will it store? Can you program several numbers to a specific speed-dial number for group distribution? If so, how many?

- How do you stop or remove a job? What are the consequences?

- Can it dial other fax machines to determine if a receivable document is stored, and then proceed to receive it?

- Can it receive a confidential document and store it until its intended recipient enters a personal identification number (PIN)? Does this feature work with all other fax machines with which your machine is in contact or only with similar makes and models?

- Will the machine allow you to notify someone at the other fax machine that you want him or her to pick up the handset and speak with you over the phone line (one of the principal uses of the fax phone, the other being to serve as an ordinary phone set when you want to notify the recipient of an incoming fax)?

- Does it include document stamping, so that you know when a document was sent or received?

- Does it provide a time, date, and number-dialed log or registry for all outgoing documents, or does it print a confirmation page that includes this information following each transmission?

Whether you visit an office-supply store or order a fax machine from a catalog or on-line, be sure you have all your questions answered before you make a choice. You should also find out about the various types and costs of supplies you will need (toner, paper, etc.) and how many full pages of text each supply item will support. These supplies will include the photoreactive drum or similar component that must be replaced after a specified number of copies have been made. If you have the opportunity to actually test various models, do so.

SENDING FAXES

It is good practice to send a cover sheet with fax transmissions. The sheet should include the name of the recipient and the recipient's department (especially if he or she is in a large organization) and personal phone number. It should also include your own firm's fax number and your own name and phone number, and should state the number of pages being sent (the cover sheet itself should be specifically included in the total).

Many fax machines can be programmed to generate one or more individualized styles of cover sheet automatically; if yours does not, your word-processing program can provide fax cover-sheet templates. You can choose to use one of these templates or to modify it as desired, or you can create an original form. The company logo may be imported to become part of a cover-sheet template. If your company has already created a company cover-sheet template, it should be available on your own computer.

Number the pages you are sending, especially if they are part of a larger document or need to be referred to by a numbering other than that provided by the fax machine. This will make it easier for the recipient to make sure all the pages have been received. Also, since some fax machines just drop received pages on a table or in a bin, numbering the pages will help the recipient put the received document in the correct order.

If a document contains small type or pictures or graphics, test the transmittal quality by using the machine's copy function. If the copy is not clear, try using the "Fine" mode. This will increase the transmittal time but should add to the document's clarity. Alternatively, you can enlarge the document on a photocopier before sending it.

When receiving a fax, check to see that all the pages have been sent and that they are readable. If pages are missing or some are unreadable, notify the sender. Always make sure received faxes are delivered quickly to their intended recipient; faxes should be handled with the same urgency as telephone messages.

SECURITY AND MISDIRECTED FAXES

When the information being sent is confidential, you must use your judgment about whether to fax it at all, since many fax machines are shared. If you are concerned, you should either call the recipient first or ask your employer. An alternative means of delivery, such as overnight courier, may be better. Some firms have "executive" fax machines or other fax machines that are monitored to ensure secure private delivery.

You may occasionally come across a misdirected fax document, just as you will occasionally receive misdirected mail or phone calls. Misdirected incoming faxes should be treated with confidentiality, in accordance with strict ethical standards, and be immediately returned to the sender with a cover letter stating that you have taken care to preserve the document's confidentiality (including not having read it yourself).

When sending any fax, take extreme care in verifying the recipient's number, including checking the digital display after punching in the number. Any number that is regularly used should be entered in the auto-dialing list.

COMMERCIAL FAX SERVICES

If you anticipate sending many copies of the same document to a specified group, you should consider using a commercial fax-distribution service. Such services allow you to send one copy to a central receiving computer from which it will be sent to a list of recipients that you maintain with the service provider. This type of service will save wear and tear on your fax machine and keep it open for incoming documents. For information, check the Yellow Pages under "Fax Transmission Service."

Meeting Minutes

Transcribing meeting minutes may present several special issues of style and format.

Meetings may be conducted formally or informally. At informal meetings, the presiding officer joins in the discussion and many of the formalities of parliamentary procedure are waived. Formal meetings (such as stockholders' meetings), by contrast, call for strict adherence to parliamentary rules and bylaws. Following proper procedures for minutes transcription is naturally most critical for the most formal meetings.

It is generally essential to record the following basic facts about a meeting:

1. Date, time, and location
2. Name of the presiding officer
3. Kind of meeting (regular, special, executive, committee, board, etc.)
4. Names of officers and members present and absent (for groups of under 20 persons)
5. Agenda
6. Motions made, motions' originators (and seconders if specifically required), mode of voting, adoption or rejection

Minutes style should be factual, brief, and devoid of editorial comment. Good minutes capture the gist of the meeting and follow the agenda closely. A verbatim record is required only for main motions and resolutions. It is normally unnecessary to record details of discussion; minutes should concentrate primarily on actions taken rather than topics discussed.

Since meeting minutes serve as the official record of a meeting, accuracy is essential. A tape recorder can be very helpful for checking the precise wording of motions.

Minutes should be typed while the meeting is still fresh in your mind. Before beginning, you should assemble at least the following items:

The agenda (if any)

Attendance information

Previous minutes

Copies of any reports and materials distributed

Copies of any motions or resolutions

A copy of the organization's constitution or bylaws (if the meeting was conducted formally)

The precise format for corporate minutes is usually dictated by the organization itself; thus, previous minutes will be your best guide. Some organizations provide printed forms for the first page of their minutes and special continuation sheets. If special paper is not provided, high-quality plain bond paper should be used.

Standard elements of minutes include the following:

Name and address of the organization

Type of meeting

Call to order: time, date, presiding officer

Attendance information: names of individuals, or a statement that a quorum was present

Reading and correction of previous minutes

Reports submitted: by whom, title, subject

Unfinished business: motions, by whom, votes

Program, including speakers' names and titles

Announcements, including time and place of next meeting

Adjournment, time

Reports from officers and committee chairs are frequently attached to the minutes as appendixes. These can be referred to by a notation such as "Mr. Hedley read the Finance Committee report, a copy of which is appended to these Minutes." Lengthy resolutions, and any resolutions recorded on printed forms, may be handled in the same way.

As mentioned above, minutes should normally follow the format of previous minutes precisely. If you are free to adopt your own format, the following guidelines are recommended:

1. Type the title in capital letters and center it.
2. Center the date two lines beneath the title, and allow two blank lines to the main text.
3. Type headings for each separate piece of business or agenda item. These may be side headings, arranged in their own column on the left, or they may be typed within the text block just as in a report.

4. Single-space the text paragraphs.
5. Number all pages at the bottom.
6. Provide underlines for your signature and the chairperson's.

Corporate titles and the names of specific corporate entities are tradition-ally capitalized in minutes; for example, "the Chairman," "the Board," "the Company," "Common Stock," "the Annual Meeting of the Corporation." However, some companies prefer that they be lowercased.

All sums of money mentioned in motions and resolutions should be speci-fied in both words and figures.

Depending on the organization's preferred style, the text of all motions may be typed entirely in capital letters to facilitate reference to them; for example, "Roger Clark moved THAT THE ORGANIZATION DONATE THE SUM OF TWO HUNDRED DOLLARS ($200.00) to . . . ." Alternatively, they may simply be enclosed in quotation marks like ordinary quotations.

Resolutions are formal expressions of the opinion, will, or intent of the body. Resolutions as usually recorded follow certain special style conventions, illustrated in the following example:

> *Whereas*, It has become necessary . . . ; therefore, be it
>
> *Resolved*, That . . . ; and
>
> *Resolved*, That . . . .

An informal resolution might be phrased more simply:

> *Resolved*, That . . . .

The presiding officer will frequently need to approve a draft of the min-utes before the final copy is typed.

An example of corporate minutes is shown in Fig. 6.2.

Minutes are normally filed in a notebook, either a regulation locking type or an ordinary loose-leaf notebook. There may be an index to facilitate reference to important decisions.

Corrections made at the next meeting should be written in ink above the affected line or in the margin. Major corrections and additions may be typed on a separate page and attached, with a note in the margin of the original page directing the reader to the attachment. Never discard the origi-nal minutes, no matter how many mistakes they may hold. If you retype a page, it must be attached to the original, uncorrected page.

A less formal way of recording the business transacted at a meeting is a *meeting summary*. Such a summary generally follows the format of normal minutes, with certain exceptions. The word "SUMMARY" appears at the top of the page, and the signature lines are omitted. Since meetings covered by a meeting summary are not conducted according to parliamentary procedure, there is usually no requirement for verbatim transcription of motions or resolutions, and no need to record votes or the various formalities observed in strictly run meetings.

Figure 6.2   Minutes of a Meeting

The Hooper Trust   **Board of Trustees Meeting**   **May 11, 20--**

The regular monthly meeting of the Board of Trustees was held on Tuesday, May 11, 20--

Present: Dr. Fitzpatrick, President   Ms. Simon, Director
       Mrs. Ulrich, Vice President   Mr. Arangio, Secretary
       Mr. Jorge   Mrs. Nizzi, Treasurer
       Mr. Reddy   Ms. Jordan, Clerk
Absent: Ms. Hendrix, Judge Brown, Ms. Bennett

Call to Order
Dr. Fitzpatrick called the meeting to order at 6:30 p.m.

Approval of the Minutes
On a motion by Mr. Reddy, the minutes of the last meeting were read and approved as corrected.

Treasurer's Report
The Treasurer reported $184,344 in the EAB money market account, $22,229 in the checking account, and $28,000 in a CD (due 10/21/04 @ 2.90%), for total funds of $234,573.

Reports of Standing Committees
The Special Services and Personnel reports were distributed before the meeting and were accepted for filing on a motion by Mr. Arangio.

    On a motion by Mr. Reddy, the Board approved the following change order for the annex: "Substitute Terne-coated stainless-steel roofing material for the zinc material originally specified."

    Yes: Mrs. Ulrich   *No:* Mr. Reddy
          Mr. Arangio
          Mr. Jorge

Reports of Special Committees
The special committee appointed to investigate the situation with Summit Roofing reported that after we notified Summit of our intention to place them in default, they returned to work last week.

Unfinished Business
After amendment and further debate, the following resolution was adopted: "*Resolved,* That the Trust hire Stuart DeRosa at a sum of $1,500 to appraise the 56 Main St. property."

New Business
The Board agreed that a special meeting should be held on May 18 at 4:00 p.m. to discuss the company's goals.

Adjournment
The meeting was adjourned at 10:00 p.m.

Clara Jordan
Clara Jordan, Clerk

Press Releases

Press releases are news stories submitted by the company itself to the news media for publication. Many companies submit such releases from time to time in order to keep the public abreast of newsworthy company events—product launches or successes, promotions, changes in management, and the like. Press releases should be as interesting, factual, informative, and concise as possible. Look in the newspaper for comparable articles to serve as models for your own style, bearing in mind that such articles can often be improved upon.

Press releases should be written in "inverted pyramidal form"; that is, the main idea should be set forth first, followed by the major details relating to that idea, followed in turn by inessential minor details or supplementary ideas. Such an article can be cut from the bottom by an editor (as must often be done for space reasons) without deleting important information. An acceptable release thus contains all the vital information at the beginning: the five *W*'s—*Who, What, When, Where,* and *Why*—as well as an important *H—How.*

Since accuracy is essential, the article must be carefully proofread. All details, especially numbers and the spelling of names, must be checked and verified. Press releases must almost always be approved by senior management before being submitted for publication.

A press release may be typed on plain $8\frac{1}{2}'' \times 11''$ paper or on the company's own press-release form. Double-spacing is preferred, as it facilitates further editing. Allow top and side margins of about 1"; the bottom margin may be wider to allow for editorial comments. If a preprinted form is not used, the words P R E S S   R E L E A S E are usually typed in spaced capital letters at the top of the page. See the example shown in Fig. 6.3.

The heading contains what are called *source data:* the name, address, and telephone number of the individual and/or company issuing the release, and specific release instructions: for example, "For Release June 26, 20—," or "IMMEDIATE RELEASE."

The title line, centered on the page and typed in capital letters, tells the reader at first glance what the article is about. (The newspaper or magazine editors may choose to substitute their own headline.)

The article itself starts with an indented dateline consisting of the city and the date. The city name appears in capital letters; the date appears in capital and lowercase letters and is followed by a dash. The name of the state is needed only if the city has a very common name or is not well known.

If there is more than one page, the word "MORE" is typed in capital letters at the bottom of the first sheet either in the center or on the right. Continuation sheets should be numbered and should include a brief header (e.g., "PROFIT INCREASE") flush left at the top of the page.

Figure 6.3   Press Release

PRESS RELEASE

LARRIMORE
NATIONAL

Contact: Alicia DeSalvo
Phone: (816) 756-8834
Fax: (816) 756-7009
E-mail: amdesalvo@aol.com

49 Quadrangle North, St. Albans, MO 96007

IMMEDIATE RELEASE

LARRIMORE NATIONAL LAUNCHES WEB SITE

ST.ALBANS, MO--June 7, 20-- Larrimore National, Inc., has joined
the ranks of Internet entrepreneurs with the opening of a World
Wide Web site for its Lance and Integral lines of athletic
equipment.

Linda Kitsworth-James, newly appointed vice president for
development at Larrimore, said "This new cyberspace outpost is part
of our strategy to use technology to market our products in a broad
range of distribution pathways and emerging markets."

Like the lines themselves, the site will be geared to consumers in
their teens and twenties. It will initially offer access to
visually exciting previews of upcoming product designs and lines as
well as the entire range of existing products. Visitors will be
able to order any item on-line by credit card. The site, which
will be updated daily, will also offer a range of professional
sports news, including the scores for all of the week's
professional games, color photographs from selected events, and
further features in the months to come. The site address is
http://www.lni.com.

-30-

One of the following devices, centered on the page, signals the end of the release:

-30-

###

-end-

(END)

If appropriate, a photograph should be submitted along with the release itself. The company's name, along with the identity of the person or persons in the photo or a description of the event pictured, should be written lightly on the back.

Reports

Business reports—including product analyses, trip reports, inventory reports, project summaries, feasibility studies, and sales analyses, among many other types—are an essential form of corporate communication, and a report writer will usually be expected to observe one of a few conventional report styles or formats.

FORMATS OF BUSINESS REPORTS

The formats of business reports vary widely, and will often bear a direct relationship to their contents. Some company manuals offer guidelines for report styling; however, the writer is normally given wide latitude in selecting a format that will best suit the report's purpose. Guidelines concerning four basic kinds of reports—distinguished according to the degree of formality required and the amount of information covered—are presented in this section in ascending order of formality: (1) the memorandum report, (2) the letter report, (3) the short report, and (4) the formal report.

The memorandum report The memorandum report is an in-house communication that is generally routine and informal, and employs the memorandum format (see "Memorandums" above). A weekly sales report or a report from an assistant manager to a manager would be a typical example. Since the memorandum report is an internal document, it can be objective and impersonal in tone. Introductory comment is normally very brief. Simple headings, positioned flush left in bold or italic type, may be used for quick reference and to highlight certain aspects of the report.

Use matching plain bond paper for continuation sheets. The header style for continuation sheets should be similar to that for standard memos. Some writers may wish to sign their reports above a typed signature line four lines below the end of the report; others will prefer to initial it next to their name at the opening. Often the memorandum report is not signed at all.

The letter report   A report in letter format is known as a letter report. The letter-report format is useful for informal reports running to several pages. Letter reports are usually directed to persons or groups outside a company. They are typically used by outside consultants to present analyses and recommendations, and an organization's board of directors often will use a letter report to describe recent changes and developments to its membership. Such reports may contain tables or illustrations that an ordinary letter would not have. The first page is typed on letterhead stationery; matching plain bond paper is used for continuation sheets. The headings on the continuation sheets should resemble those on regular letters. The letter should open with a subject line, which takes the place of a title. The report body should employ simple headings (in the same style as those in memorandum reports) for emphasis, clarity, and ease of reference.

The short report   Short business reports differ from memorandum and letter reports in scope and format. The short report may include the following elements: title page; preliminary summary (with emphasis on conclusions and recommendations); authorization information; statement of the problem; findings; conclusions; and recommendations. Tables and graphics may be added if needed. The short business report may be single-spaced or may employ wider line spacing, depending on the company's style or the writer's preference. Headings such as those described for formal reports below may be used.

The formal report   The formal report is distinguished from other types of report by its sophisticated style of presentation, the complexity of its scope and content, and its greater length. A formal report may contain all the following elements, each of which will be illustrated and discussed in detail:

Cover	List of figures or illustrations
Flyleaf	Synopsis
Title fly	Text
Title page	Endnotes (or Footnotes)
Letter of authorization	Appendixes
Letter of transmittal	Glossary
Foreword or Preface (optional)	Bibliography
Acknowledgments	Index
Table of contents	

Some of these elements may be omitted and others may be combined; for example, the letter of transmittal may be conflated with the synopsis.

Side-bound reports should have wide left-hand margins ($1\frac{1}{2}''$-$2''$), and their page numbers should never be positioned at the left of the page.

The report should be on good-quality bond paper. It may be single-spaced or it may use wider line spacing; company style may require one or the other. The opening material of a formal report (excluding the title page) is usually paginated with lowercase Roman numerals, while the rest of the report, including all appendixes, is paginated with Arabic numerals.

Headings and subheadings must adhere to a uniform editorial and typographical style throughout the report. Formal reports often employ the decimal style of subdividing report topics, but the writer may prefer the traditional outline listings of alternating numbers and letters instead. A third alternative is to dispense with such numbers and letters altogether. The decimal system is handled as in the left-hand example below; the outline system employing numbers and letters alternately should follow the style of the right-hand example.

1. Main heading	I. Main heading
1.1 Subheading	A. Subheading
1.2 Subheading	B. Subheading
1.21 Sub-subheading	1. Sub-subheading
1.22 Sub-subheading	2. Sub-subheading
1.3 Subheading	C. Subheading
2. Main heading	II. Main heading
2.1 Subheading	A. Subheading
2.2 Subheading	B. Subheading
3. Main heading	III. Main heading

A uniform heading style requires attention to the logic of dividing topics into subtopics. No subheading should appear by itself; that is, there should never be a part 1 without a following part 2, or a section A without a corresponding section B.

Unacceptable

A. Dictation procedures
  1. Pre-dictation guidelines
B. Transcription procedures

Acceptable

A. Pre-dictation guidelines
B. Dictation procedures
C. Transcription procedures

or

A. Guidelines for better dictation
B. Transcription procedures

or

A. Dictation
  1. Pre-dictation guidelines
  2. Procedures for effective dictation
B. Transcription

Similarly, headings and subheadings at a given level should be grammatically similar, or parallel.

Nonparallel	*Parallel*
1. Selecting a topic	1. Selecting a topic
2. The outline	2. Writing the outline
3. How to gather information	3. Gathering information
a. Primary research	a. Primary research
b. Doing secondary research	b. Secondary research

The relative importance of each level of heading should be reflected in its typographical style, with the most important headings shown in the most prominent style. For example, the highest-level headings (sometimes called *A-heads*) could use boldface 13-point type with an underline extending across the entire page, with ample space left above and below to normal text. The medium-level headings (or *B-heads*) could be in underlined 9-point bold capitals, with space above but no space below. The lower-level headings (*C-heads*) could be in 10-point boldface type with only the very first letter capitalized, with space above but with the following normal text continuing on the same line as the heading, separated from it only by a short space. All headings should generally be positioned flush left. (The heading style that was standard before the era of word processors, when boldface and different type sizes were unavailable or at least less convenient, achieved this hierarchical effect by other means. In this traditional style, A-heads are generally all-capitalized, B-heads are capitalized headline-style and underlined, and C-heads have only their very first letter capitalized and are underlined and run in on the same line with the following text.)

The following pages discuss in order each item in the preceding list of report elements.

Cover　Report covers are available in a great variety of materials. The cover should display the title and the author's name, which may be typed in capital letters either directly on the cover or on a gummed label that is then affixed to it. (If a transparent cover is used, the title fly or title page will itself serve as the cover title.) An informal report without a cover may be stapled; if a single staple is used, it should be placed diagonally in the upper left corner. Long report titles are typed as several centered lines on the upper third of the cover, the title fly, and the title page. Extremely brief report titles may be spread—that is, typed with a space after each letter and with three or more spaces after each word.

Flyleaf　A flyleaf is a blank sheet of paper. Formal reports generally have two flyleaves, one at the beginning and the other at the end, which dress up the report and and provide space for written comments.

Title fly　The title fly, if used, contains only the report title in capital letters on the upper third of the page.

Title page　This page typically contains the report's title and subtitle, if any; the name, corporate title, and department and/or address of the writer; the name, title, department, firm name, and address of the recipient; and the report's completion date. If a report does not have a cover and title fly, the title page should be on stock heavy enough to serve as the cover. If the report is being copyrighted, the copyright notice should appear on the reverse of the title page.

Letter of authorization If the writer has received written authorization for the investigation, that memorandum or letter may be included in the report. If the writer has only received oral authorization, this should be cited in the letter of transmittal or the introduction.

Letter of transmittal A letter of transmittal often accompanies a report and may also serve as its preface. Here the writer conveys to the recipient (often the person who assigned the report) the purpose, scope, and limitations of the report, its authorization, and the research methods employed. The letter usually ends with expressions of appreciation for having received the assignment and willingness to provide additional information or answer any questions concerning the report. The letter of transmittal is typed on letterhead stationery and is signed. A typical letter of transmittal is illustrated in Fig. 6.4.

Foreword or preface Another individual—a department head, for example—will sometimes contribute a foreword to a report.

Acknowledgments It is proper to acknowledge any individuals, companies, and institutions that assisted in the preparation of the report. Acknowledgments may be made either in the letter of transmittal or in the introduction; however, if there are many acknowledgments, a special page should be included, which should observe the style used in acknowledgment pages of published books.

Table of contents The table of contents is essentially an outline of the report showing its pagination. All headings down to a particular level (perhaps omitting C-heads) should be reproduced precisely. The example in Fig. 6.5 comes from a report that did not number or letter its various sections, but any such numbers or letters that are used should be reproduced.

List of illustrations If the number of illustrations is small, a list may be appended to the table of contents; if there are numerous illustrations, the list may appear on a separate page. The illustration numbers as well as the page numbers should be included. The styling of the list should follow that of the table of contents.

Synopsis The synopsis (also called the *abstract, summary, digest, highlights,* or *introduction)* is a condensation of the report that provides a quick overview of its significant findings. Most readers prefer that a long report include such a summary. The synopsis usually appears on a page by itself, and it may either be single-spaced or have wider line spacing. In some

Figure 6.4   Letter of Transmittal

Arcturus Consultants
678 Darnton Drive
Bryceville, GA 30062

phone: (404) 452-7899
fax: (404) 456-7890
email: info@arcturus.com

May 29, 20--

Ms. Sarah Leland
Lincoln Reference, Inc.
678 Dow Parkway
Atlanta, GA 30327

Dear Ms. Leland:

This letter accompanies the completed report *Online Professional Reference Products,* commissioned by Lincoln Reference in June 20-- in the attached letter of authorization.

Every topic specified in that letter has been dealt with in the report, which is based on extensive library and internet research and numerous field trips and interviews with specialists.

I would like to acknowledge the assistance of Jan C. Thomas, who supplied most of the report's graphics.

Thank you for the opportunity to prepare this report, which I hope addresses every relevant question about its subject. I am naturally available to discuss any aspect of it at your convenience.

Respectfully submitted,

Catherine St. James

Catherine St. James

gbb

Figure 6.5 Table of Contents

offices, additional copies of the synopsis are distributed separately from the report itself.

Report body   The body of the report usually comprises three parts: a brief introduction, the main body of the text, and a final section reporting its conclusions and recommendations.

The introduction presents the purpose of the study, a clear definition of the issues to be considered, the scope of the study, any limitations imposed on it, and any pertinent background information. It should provide a somewhat broader overview than the synopsis.

The main body provides the prime discussion of the issue. A sample page is shown in Fig. 6.6.

The conclusions should be strictly derived from the findings of the study. They are often numbered.

The recommendations, which should result from the conclusions, are usually numbered. In some formal reports, they appear in the introductory matter and are only summarized at the end.

Appendixes   Supplementary material is often placed at the end of the report in a separate appendix section.

Glossary   Technical terms that might be unfamiliar to the reader should be defined in a glossary. Abbreviations should also be included in the glossary, even if they are spelled out the first time they appear in the text, as they should be.

Bibliography   The bibliography lists all the sources of information used to compile the report. (See the following "Bibliographies" section for a fuller discussion.)

Index   Though an index can safely be omitted from shorter reports, a major report may require one.

The computer may be helpful in creating an index. However, even with the help of a computer, proper indexing is a fairly time-consuming process, since it requires highlighting separately each term you desire to appear in the index and copying it individually to an index file. Check your user manual or the on-screen Help function.

Two common index styles are the *run-in* and the *indented*. (Either can be chosen as an option when preparing an index on the computer.) The former requires less space, but the latter is easier for a reader to scan. See the following examples:

Run-in	*Indented*
Inside address: abbreviations in, 33; page placement of, 27-28; Simplified Letter, 27; street address styling in, 32-34; zip codes in, 33. *See also* Letters.	Inside address. *See also* Letters. 　abbreviations in, 33 　page placement of, 27-28 　Simplified Letter, 27 　street address styling 　　in, 32-34 　zip codes in, 33

Figure 6.6   Page from Body of Report

COMPUTER OPERATING SYSTEM

It is critically important to understand each of the target industry's computer buying habits, typical installation, and wants and needs in order to achieve predictable products sales growth.

In some vertical industries DOS-based applications set the industry standard. For example, in the legal industry the DOS operating system accounts for the majority of system use. The same operating system use pattern can be found in the medical industry. While DOS seems to "own" the medical and legal PC marketplace, the Windows operating system is most prevalent in general offices and in the insurance industry. The following chart illustrates the preference/usage of DOS vs. Windows by vertical industry.

Figure 7. Operating System Usage by Vertical Industry

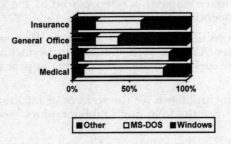

To successfully plan and market products specifically designed to fit into the named industries, it will be necessary to build products on operating platforms that match the target industry usage pattern:

- Products for the General Office and Print & Broadcast Media industries should be Windows-based.
- Products for the Legal and Medical industries should be both DOS-based and Windows-based.
- Products for the Education industry should be built to run on Apple II machines.

The basic elements of an index are as follows:

1. *Entry*   Each principal entry is typed flush left. The first letter of each entry is usually capitalized; all other words are lowercased unless they are proper nouns. In the preceding examples, "Inside address" is a principal entry.

2. *Subentry*   A subentry is a subheading listed (alphabetically with any other subentries) beneath an entry, typically either indented one or two spaces or run in as in the example on the left above. It enables the reader to locate specific points that fall within the larger subject encompassed by the entry. Subentries are lowercased unless they are capitalized in the text.

3. *Sub-subentry*   A sub-subentry is subordinate to a subentry and is indented further. Though sub-subentries are sometimes employed in book indexes, they can produce an excessively complex index and should usually be avoided in report indexes by reconceiving the main entry and subentries.

4. *Cross-references*   Cross-references direct the reader elsewhere in the index. The two most common types are the *See* and the *See also* cross-references. A *See* cross-reference directs the reader to the entry where the desired information can be found.

> Stationery, quality of. *See* Paper.

A *See also* cross-reference directs the reader from one entry with page references to a related entry that may also be useful.

> Shorthand, 88-92. *See also*
> Stenographic notebook.

Cross-references are always followed by a period. Multiple cross-references for a single entry are separated by semicolons.

> Salutation, 37-40. *See also* Courtesy titles; Letters.

Punctuation should be kept to a minimum in indexes. Periods are used only before and after *See* and *See also* cross-references. Commas are used between an entry or subentry and any word or words modifying it, and before page references:

> Computers, use of,
> in correspondence, 25

Though indexing is a specialized area that cannot be covered in detail here (see instead a style manual for editors and writers), you can create a very acceptable report index by using care and common sense and by studying actual indexes in books such as this one.

DOCUMENTING SOURCES

The writer of a report may use any of several different methods to indicate the source of quotations or pieces of information borrowed from other works. This crediting of sources, known as *documentation,* is necessary for several reasons: (1) to acknowledge the work of another writer rather than appear to take credit for it oneself; (2) to allow the reader to judge the likely quality of the information in light of what he or she might know about the quality of the source; and (3) to enable the reader to find the source and verify the information or read further on the subject.

Style of documentation has traditionally differed depending on the subject area. Scientific writing generally uses parenthetical references primarily; writing intended for a more general public—which includes most business writing—has tended to use footnotes or endnotes, but parenthetical references are becoming more common. Within the citations themselves, scientific style also differs from nonscientific style.

In a carefully documented report, an alphabetical bibliography or list of sources may be provided at the end of the entire text (and after any endnotes). Since a bibliography largely repeats information already given in the notes, it may seem unnecessary; however, its alphabetical arrangement makes it useful to readers interested in finding bibliographic information quickly.

The following guidelines describe a careful style of documentation appropriate for published books. Some firms will have their own rules or preferences, which may be detailed in a company style manual. If your company has such a manual, the rules in the manual should be followed, as they may conflict with the styles shown here.

Footnotes and endnotes   The most familiar method of documentation and reference is the use of footnotes or endnotes, along with a bibliography. In this system, superscript numbers in the text refer the reader to short notes either set at the bottom of the page (footnotes) or gathered at the end of the section or the entire report (endnotes). These notes contain full bibliographical information about the works cited, and sometimes also include brief comments about the works or brief discussions of subjects related to the report but not tied to any specific cited work.

Footnotes and endnotes take exactly the same form; they differ only in where they are placed.

Word processors now make the inclusion of both footnotes and endnotes in keyboarded documents simple and convenient. Each note reference and its text can be entered easily by using the Footnotes option on the Insert menu; this function will automatically number (and if necessary renumber) the notes each time a new one is added, and will place the notes in order either at the bottom of successive pages or at the end of the report, as desired.

Footnote and endnote numbering will generally be consecutive throughout a report; in a long report divided into chapters, the numbering may start over at the beginning of each chapter.

Fig. 6.7 shows how footnotes (and their numerical references) appear on a report page. Each footnote is single-spaced internally. A short underline, flush left, separates them from the text. Fig. 6.8 shows a page of endnotes.

The basic rules of footnote and endnote form are as follows:

A simple citation of a book, article, or report begins with the author's name (given exactly as it appears on the title page), followed by a comma

Figure 6.7   Report Page with Footnotes

---

42 • U S E R   N E E D S

accessed, dBTool called up the entire database, making the program cumbersome, slow, and frustrating to users, since the same process had to be matched for each simultaneous user.[6] Apollo, on the other hand, follows a successful client/server model, calling up from the server only portions of the database requested by the client PC.[7]

THE PROFESSIONAL MARKET: A PRELIMINARY SURVEY
Software products fitting the client/server architecture model are much more prevalent now than they were as recently as 19--. Note the growth of this class of product in each of the industries listed, as shown in the table on page 43.[8] Of all software applications installed in each industry, the prevalence of client/server applications has increased in all cases by at least 50%.[9] This may be true in part because of the widespread availability of network-ready PCs.

Another critical issue for client/server software applications is the application's dependence on a network operating system, which carries data back and forth between client and server. Choosing a network operating system is obviously an important issue for the software application developer, since it is the developer's responsibility to make sure the application works with the appropriate network protocols.

Lincoln Reference can meet the needs of the majority of customers by providing a client/server application that will work with the most widely used local area network. As Figure 10 shows, the market leader controls about two thirds of the total U.S. market, while none of its competitors retains more than 8% of the market.[10]

---

[6] K. Lyman Burns, "Does dBTool Stack Up?" *Net Galaxy,* Aug. 2000: 42-44.
[7] Ben Knowlton, "Two New Systems: A Feature-by-Feature Comparison," *Network Guide,* June 2000: 16-17.
[8] "The Month in Figures," *OfficeNet,* Jan. 2001: 25.
[9] James Ling and Carl Fortnum, "The Widening Net: Surveying the Office Landscape," *Network News,* Aug. 10, 2000: 35.
[10] C. B. DeLatta, "Who's on First?" *OfficeNet,* Dec. 2000: 11-13.

Figure 6.8   Endnotes

1. Robert L. Cranston, review of *The ORB Revolution*, by Jay Astor Carteret, *PC Now*, Oct. 2000: 56-58.
2. Lance Bordman et al., *Client/Server Hardware: An Integrated Course*, 2nd ed. (New York: Irving Place Press, 2001), 351.
3. R. R. Loring, "The Office 'Intranet': A Look into the Near Future," *Cambridge Business Review* 17, no. 3 (Dec. 2000): 450-73.
4. P. K. Norawanda, "The Complete Electronic Suite," *The Wired Office*, ed. Cynthia J. Charles (San Francisco: Online Press, 2000), 156-59.
5. "History," *The Ultimate Network Encyclopedia* (New York: John Wiley, 2001), 2: 297.
6. K. Lyman Burns, "Does dBTool Stack Up?" *Net Galaxy*, Aug. 2000: 42-44.
7. Ben Knowlton, "Two New Systems: A Feature-by-Feature Comparison," *Network Guide*, June 2000: 16-17.
8. "The Month in Figures," *OfficeNet*, Jan. 2001: 25.
9. James Ling and Carl Fortnum, "The Widening Net: Surveying the Office Landscape," *Network News*, Aug. 10, 2000: 34-35.
10. C. B. DeLatta, "Who's on First?" *OfficeNet*, Dec. 2000: 11-13, 45-48.
11. Jane D. Sanders, Paul Kliban, and Mark Ryman, *Electronic Research in the Professional Office* (New York: Business First, 1999), 357.
12. Ricardo Rubio, *Intranetworking: The Shape of Things to Come* (New York: Millennium3, 1999), 75.
13. Ling and Fortnum, 43.

and the item's full title. Titles of books are italicized (or underlined); titles of articles and unpublished works are enclosed in quotation marks but not italicized. Both the title's and the subtitle's first and last words are normally capitalized, as are all other words except prepositions, conjunctions, and articles *(a, an,* and *the).*

A book title is followed by its edition number, if any, and its publication data: the city where published, the publisher, and the year of publication, all enclosed in parentheses. The city name is followed by a colon, and the publisher's name is followed by a comma. The publication data are followed by the number of the page or pages where the cited information can be found, usually preceded by a comma and followed by a period. (The abbreviations *p.* and *pp.*, for *page* and *pages,* may be omitted.)

An article title is followed by a comma (placed within the closing quotation marks) and the italicized or underlined title of the magazine, journal, or book in which the article appeared. A journal or magazine citation does not include its publisher or place of publication. However, the issue of the journal must be identified either by volume or by date or both. Scholarly journals are almost always cited by volume number. (A volume corresponds to a year's worth of issues; thus, volume 12 of a given magazine may run from April 1995 through March 1996, volume 13 from April 1996 through March 1997, etc.) This will sometimes be followed by an issue number within that volume. (The issue number is often unnecessary, since serious journals are usually paginated continuously throughout the annual volume, and thus the page number alone will suffice to lead the reader to the cited information.) This will be followed by the date, usually consisting of the month (or season) and year, enclosed in parentheses.

Since popular magazines are not paginated continuously throughout an annual volume, the precise date of the issue must be given. Though popular magazines usually have a volume and issue number printed somewhere inside, these are usually omitted from the citation; the full date is provided instead, set off by commas rather than parentheses. Newspapers are generally treated similarly to popular magazines.

The title of an unpublished report is enclosed in quotation marks but not italicized. It is followed by an acknowledgment of the organization that commissioned it, its date, and any other relevant information.

When the name of a book's editor or translator appears on the title page, the name should usually be included in the footnote or endnote. If a book has an editor but no author, the editor's name takes the place of the author's in the citation.

If a work is in more than one volume, that fact should appear in the note. If the volumes are paginated separately, the number of the volume should immediately precede the page number, followed by a colon.

If a book is part of a series, the series name should be included, capitalized like a title but not italicized or underlined.

When citing major reference works, the name of the editor will often be omitted.

If an organization rather than a person is credited as the author on the title page, it should be treated as the author and alphabetized by its first word (excluding *The*). Government publications are usually alphabetized by the name of the government (e.g., "United States," "Delaware," "San Francisco"). Most U.S. government publications are published by the Government Printing Office, which can be abbreviated "GPO."

When referring to a work for the second (third, fourth, etc.) time, the note should include only the author's last name, a shortened version of the title (which may be omitted if it is the only work by the author being cited in the report), and the page reference.

In the sciences, footnotes and endnotes are used far less. When they are used, they observe the style differences listed in the "Bibliographies" section below. However, most science reports will instead employ parenthetical references of the author-date type (see below).

Parenthetical references The chief alternative system of reference employs highly abbreviated bibliographical citations enclosed in parentheses within the text, use of which can save time, effort, and space. These parenthetical references direct any reader who needs more information about a source to the bibliography, which is similar in most respects to one that would be used with footnotes or endnotes.

If necessary, footnotes or endnotes may be used in addition to parenthetical references, particularly when the writer wants to discuss a peripheral subject briefly, in which case they should be numbered sequentially by themselves.

There are two basic styles for parenthetical references. The *author-date style*, generally used in the sciences, provides the author's last name, the year of publication, and sometimes the page number. The *author-page style*, used in most other areas, provides the author's last name and the page number. In the author-date style, if more than one work by a given author is cited, lowercase letters may be used after the dates (1999a, 1999b, etc.). In the author-page style, if more than one work by a given author is cited in the report, the shortened title of the particular work may be included after the author's name. Fig. 6.9 shows the same report passage as Fig. 6.7 but with the footnotes converted to parenthetical references.

Bibliographies A bibliography is frequently simply a list of the works cited in the report's notes or parenthetical references. It may also include other works used in the course of research that were not actually cited. An *annotated bibliography* includes brief comments on each work.

Bibliographies are ordered alphabetically by author's name. If no author or editor is cited, the book's title is listed alphabetically as if it were an author's surname.

Bibliography entries are generally identical to initial footnote citations except in the following respects: (1) The author's surname comes first, (2) periods rather than commas separate the elements of the entry, (3) the publication data are not enclosed by parentheses, and (4) page references are used only to locate a complete article (not just the pages cited in a note or reference) within a journal or book. Scientific bibliographies observe their own set of rules, which differ in several respects from the general style described above: (1) The author's first name is shortened to an initial, (2) all words in titles are lowercased except the first word (and the first word of any subtitle) and proper nouns and adjectives, and (3) article titles are not set off by quotation marks. In addition, in scientific bibliographies the year of publication always immediately follows the author's name. (In this way, the bibliography's entries are similar to the author-date parenthetical references.)

Study Figs. 6.10 and 6.11 to see how to deal with a variety of bibliographical problems.

Figure 6.9   Report Page with Parenthetical References

42   •   U S E R   N E E D S

accessed, dBTool called up the entire database, making the program cumbersome, slow, and frustrating to users, since the same process had to be matched for each simultaneous user (Burns, 42). Apollo, on the other hand, follows a successful client/server model, calling up from the server only portions of the database requested by the client PC (Knowlton, 16-17).

THE PROFESSIONAL MARKET: A PRELIMINARY SURVEY
Software products fitting the client/server architecture model are much more prevalent now than they were as recently as 19--. Note the growth of this class of product in each of the industries listed, as shown in the table on page 43 ("Month," 25) Of all software applications installed in each industry, the prevalence of client/server applications has increased in all cases by at least 50% (Ling & Fortnum, 35). This may be true in part because of the widespread availability of network-ready PCs.

Another critical issue for client/server software applications is the application's dependence on a network operating system, which carries data back and forth between client and server. Choosing a network operating system becomes an important issue for the software application developer, since it is the developer's responsibility to make sure the application works with the appropriate network protocols.

Lincoln Reference can meet the needs of the majority of customers by providing a client/server application that will work with the most widely used local area network. As Figure 10 shows, the market leader controls about two thirds of the total U.S. market, while none of its competitors retains more than 8% of the market (DeLatta, 45).

Despite the current dominance of a given operating system within an industry, we must bear in mind that the field remains in a state of flux,

Figure 6.10   Report Bibliography

Bibliography

Bordman, Lance, et al. *Client/Server Hardware: An Integrated Course.* 2nd ed. New York: Irving Place Press, 2001.

Burns, K. Lyman. "Does dBTool Stack Up?" *Net Galaxy,* August 2000: 40-47.

Cranston, Robert L. Review of *The ORB Revolution,* by Jay Astor Carteret. *PC Now,* October 2000: 56-58.

DeLatta, C. B. "Who's on First?" *OfficeNet,* December 2000: 11-13, 45-48.

Knowlton, Ben. "Two New Systems: A Feature-by-Feature Comparison." *Network Guide,* June 2000: 12-17.

Ling, James, and Carl Fortnum. "The Widening Net: Surveying the Office Landscape." *Network News,* August 10, 2000: 34-45.

Loring, R. R. "The Office 'Intranet': A Look into the Near Future." *Cambridge Business Review* 17, no. 3 (December 2000): 450-73.

"The Month in Figures." *OfficeNet,* January 2001: 25.

Norawanda, P. K. "The Complete Electronic Suite." *The Wired Office.* Ed. Cynthia J. Charles. San Francisco: Online Press, 2000.

Rubio, Ricardo. *Intranetworking: The Shape of Things to Come.* New York: Millennium3, 1999.

Sanders, Jane D., Paul Kliban, and Mark Ryman. *Electronic Research in the Professional Office.* New York: Business First, 1999.

The Ultimate Network Encyclopedia. 2 vols. New York: John Wiley, 2001.

Figure 6.11   Report Bibliography in Scientific Style

Bibliography

Bordman, L., et al. 2001. *Client/server hardware: An integrated course.* 2nd ed. New York: Irving Place Press.

Burns, K. L. 2000. Does dBTool stack up? *Net Galaxy,* Aug.:40-47.

Cranston, R. L. 2000. Review of *The ORB revolution,* by J. A. Carteret. *PC Now,* Oct.:56-58.

DeLatta, C. B. 2000. Who's on first? *OfficeNet,* Dec.:11-13, 45-48.

Knowlton, B. 2000. Two new systems: A feature-by-feature comparison. *Network Guide,* June:12-17.

Ling, J., and C. Fortnum. 2000. The widening net: Surveying the office landscape. *Network News,* 10 Aug.:34-45.

Loring, R. R. 2000. The office 'intranet': A look into the near future. *Cambridge Business Review* 17:450-73.

The month in figures. 2001. *OfficeNet,* Jan.:25.

Norawanda, P. K. 2000. The complete electronic suite. *The wired office.* Ed. C. J. Charles. San Francisco: Online Press.

Rubio, R. 1999. *Intranetworking: The shape of things to come.* New York: Millennium3.

Sanders, J. D., P. Kliban, and M. Ryman. 1999. *Electronic research in the professional office.* New York: Business First.

The ultimate network encyclopedia. 2001. 2 vols. New York: John Wiley.

CHAPTER 7

E-mail

Invented in 1971, electronic mail, or e-mail, expanded gradually over two decades, then grew explosively in the 1990s to become the most widely used function of the Internet, producing perhaps the greatest revolution in personal communications since the invention of the telephone.

E-mail permits communication without having to interrupt a colleague with a phone call or by walking into an office. Within a large company, e-mail can eliminate the need for many meetings by permitting ongoing "conversations" in which any number of individuals may participate, each broadcasting his or her responses to as many colleagues as desired. With e-mail, a memo can be sent to each desk in a high-rise building almost instantaneously, without wasting a single sheet of paper. Communications with employees at other sites, especially those scattered widely geographically, have been greatly facilitated. A single message can be sent simultaneously to 25 branch offices, to a 50-person national sales force, or to 500 customers on four continents.

Unlike telephone communication, e-mail is completely unintrusive, and it permits recipients to answer at their convenience. Once the system is set up, it costs virtually nothing to send a message. It is so efficient that a brief message can be sent in 30 seconds. Saved or printed-out messages can serve as a valuable permanent record of an exchange for all parties. Extensive electronic files (e.g., 10-page contracts or 30-page reports) can be attached and sent by e-mail with ease, avoiding the expense of ordinary mail or courier services. E-mail can enable communication to countries where telephone and mail service is unreliable, and it can speed the transmission of documents past borders where they might otherwise be held up for many days. The gentle urgency of e-mail often succeeds in extracting answers from correspondents where other means have proven less effective.

E-mail Basics

SETUP

E-mail programs are now available from hundreds of sources, many of which offer their software free of charge. Widely used programs include Eudora, Pegasus, Pine, Elm, and Microsoft Outlook Express.

The home user can acquire e-mail capacity by going to the provider's Web site and downloading the necessary software. Some companies offer free e-mail programs that provide only limited capacities, requiring that customers pay for full-capacity service. Some free e-mail services will append advertisements for their service at the end of every message you send; you may wish to choose one that does not. Visit the Web sites of several e-mail providers to learn about the variety of capacities they offer before choosing your own service.

Once you have chosen and downloaded an e-mail program, read the tutorial material carefully, testing the program's various capacities when necessary by sending messages to your own address.

For a discussion of connection issues, see "Internet Connections," page 363.

ADDRESSES AND ADDRESS BOOKS

When specifying one's own e-mail address, it is best to include a recognizable version of one's own name in what will appear on the recipient's screen (for example, "Alicia Gomez" rather than "ag2@brierwood.edu"). This can easily be done by specifying a name in your general settings. However, if your company has a standard style, you may not have the option of changing it.

Most e-mail users keep their correspondents' addresses in a so-called *address book,* a directory on one's e-mail system into which the user types the addresses of frequent correspondents. Along with the person's address (e.g., lduberman@uscoax.com), the user enters a familiar short version of the person's name called a *nickname, alias,* or something similar (e.g., "Lou"). When writing to the person, the user merely types the nickname in the *To:* box, and the mail is automatically sent to the proper address. This feature offers speed and convenience, makes memorizing addresses unnecessary, and prevents mail from being sent by accident to a very similar address (or a nonexistent address) typed in by mistake.

One can send a message to several recipients simultaneously by typing all their addresses or nicknames (see below) in the address box, separated by commas. Address books also permit the use of electronic *distribution lists.* If a user frequently sends messages to a certain group of people, all the individual addresses of the group's members can be collected under a single nickname, thus making it just as easy to broadcast an e-mail as to send one to a single person. By entering "office" in the *To:* box, an office manager could distribute a message to all 90 members of an office staff, and by typing in "reps," a sales manager could send a message to all 25 sales representatives working under her, for example. The traditional alternatives to such mailings—sending around a memo attached to a distribution sheet (or a separate copy of the memo for each employee), and making 25 separate phone calls to the sales force—would obviously take far longer and, in the case of the phone calls, cost much more.

Using a short nickname such as "office" to broadcast a message will suppress the addresses of those receiving the message so that they won't appear at the top of your message for all to read, which may be thought desirable in some cases, either because the list is annoyingly long to scroll through or because the sender may prefer that some recipients not know the others' identities. However, the user may instead choose to leave visible the complete list of addresses of a message's recipients.

SUBJECT LINES

The subject line provides the message's recipient with a quick identification of its general contents. An e-mail user who receives 25 e-mails a day may find that subject lines are valuable in organizing his or her responses. Perhaps more important, subject lines can become essential when the e-mail has been archived. Some users' files may consist of several thousand e-mails, and even if these are divided into numerous folders, subject lines may be of considerable value when the user is seeking information buried in a given folder. (Some e-mail programs even permit the user to arrange for all messages with particular keywords in the subject line to be automatically filed in particular folders.)

Subject lines should generally run no longer than five or six words, since that is usually as much as will be visible in the subject column when they are listed in a new-mail or saved-mail index.

CC'S (CARBON OR COURTESY COPIES)

Anyone who should be kept apprised of a correspondence should be listed in the message's *cc* box. (Whenever someone is included in the message's salutation, his or her address should naturally be included as one of the principal addresses to which the message is sent rather than in the *cc* box.) Just as in the principal address box, multiple addresses can be listed in a *cc* box, separated by commas.

Blind cc's are desirable when the sender prefers not to announce to the principal recipient that a copy is being sent to another person as well. The option of sending blind cc's may not be available in all e-mail systems; the alternative is to forward a copy of the e-mail to the other recipient after it has been sent to its primary addressee. (This assumes that the user has chosen the very important option of saving a copy of every e-mail sent.)

For most business purposes, it is desirable to automatically retain a copy of every message one sends—the equivalent of keeping carbon copies for a traditional correspondence file. If a save option is selected, all mail sent will be automatically saved, in a special copies-to-self folder. From there, the saved copies can subsequently be moved to their appropriate project or client folders, usually by highlighting the item on the copy list, clicking on a Move button, and double-clicking the project folder. You may be given the alternative option of choosing whether to save each message individually—by having a dialog box appear after each new piece of mail has been read—and specifying where you want each to be filed.

SIGNATURE BLOCKS

Many e-mail users choose to close their messages with a signature block that prints automatically on all messages. Businesses often set up signatures on all employees' messages, generally consisting of the user's name, business title, business street address, and telephone and fax numbers—essentially, the contents of a business card—and may add a line of advertisement as well.

Signatures may also be customized by the user. Most commonly, a user will add a pithy or witty quotation (which may be changed weekly or monthly) at the end of the signature. Your signature can be checked or edited by clicking on a menu option.

See also "Electronic Signatures," page 355.

REPLYING, FORWARDING, COMMENTING-OUT

An essential e-mail feature is the one that permits replying to a message open on the screen by merely clicking a button.

Using the Reply feature automatically places the address of your correspondent in the *To:* box. The original message is retained in the reply (unless the user has chosen the option of not including it), so the recipient of your reply can refer to the original while reading the response and thereby check to see, for example, whether you have answered all the questions asked in the original message.

Any number of previous messages from both parties can be preserved. Thus, if both employ the Reply feature, an exchange on a particular topic running to 10–20 e-mails can all be read sequentially in the last e-mail of the exchange. Some users find it very helpful to be able to review a correspondence on a particular subject in this way. Thus, it is generally advisable to try to maintain any such subject "thread" by continuous use of the Reply feature by both correspondents until the exchange is finished.

Replies should normally be typed in *above* the message they are responding to, so that the recipient won't have to scroll down through the original message to locate the response.

When replying to long e-mails that deal with several topics, you will probably find it convenient to respond to each subject individually at the point where it is raised in the original message. When you choose the Reply option, the original message is highlighted in some distinctive way (often by having a > symbol inserted at the beginning of each of its lines, or changing the color of its type, or both) and you can insert comments (which show up without the distinctive symbol or marking) at various points in the message. Thus, a response might be inserted following a message's first paragraph, another following its second paragraph, another after the first sentence of the third paragraph (if it raised a separate issue by itself) and another following the paragraph's last sentence; a final paragraph consisting only of pleasantries could be deleted.

A Forward button enables the user to send on a message received from someone else by merely typing in the new address.

ATTACHMENTS

Though text can be imported into the body of an e-mail message by copying it from a word-processing program and pasting it directly into an open e-mail, using the standard copy-and-paste function, the text will generally lose its formatting—that is, its margins and layout, distinctive typefaces and styles, the structure of any tables, its art, and so on—and new, undesired elements will replace those deleted, rendering many documents useless in their new form.

One of the most valuable features of e-mail is the Attachment function, with which virtually any kind of electronic file can be "attached" to a message (as if it were being paperclipped to a cover letter and enclosed in an envelope). Attached documents preserve all their original formatting; thus, documents of all kinds can be sent intact, with all their formatting preserved. (However, when unusual types of files are sent, the recipient may have to have the proper software in order to open them.)

The variety of document types that can be sent as attachments is enormous. A map to one's office, a five-page memo, a photograph, a spreadsheet, a database, computer software, a 30-page report with graphs and tables, a draft of an edited document with the editing (strikethroughs, substituted text, annotations, etc.) visible for review, audio and video files—all can be sent as attachments.

Virtually any file residing on the user's computer can become an attachment. Before sending a very large attachment, however, the user should verify that it will not overload the capacity of your recipient's system. Inordinately large files, such as audio and video files, tend to clog a company's system, and some companies discourage sending them at all.

A basic test of whether an attachment will transmit properly is to send it to yourself (by typing your own address in the address box) and try to open it.

FILE COMPRESSION

Large files that must travel as e-mail attachments or are available for downloading from the Internet are generally compressed. Compression reduces the amount of storage space a file requires and makes it easier to transfer and open. Compression is accomplished by means of mathematical equations that scan the file looking for repeating data patterns and replace each pattern with a space-saving code. Special software is required to compress files, and also to decompress them at the receiving end.

Ordinary text requires relatively small amounts of data and rarely requires compression except when a file consists of a particularly large quantity of text. The efficient transfer of graphics, audio, and video files, however, usually requires compression.

Compressed files can be identified from the extensions on their file names. The extensions .zip and .sit are the extensions for two very common compression formats. The most popular graphics compression standards use the extensions .jpg, .gif, and .tif.

Common audio file extensions include .mp3, .au, .wav, and .ra; video extensions include .avi, .mpg, .mov, and .qt. Since both audio and video files are generally very large, however, most companies discourage or prohibit using e-mail to send and receive them.

Most decompression software is distributed as "shareware"—that is, software that can be downloaded from the Internet and tried out free of charge but requires a modest fee for regular use. All the software companies maintain Web sites from which their software can be obtained. Since such software is regularly upgraded, the user may have to return from time to time to obtain the newest version.

PRINTING

Any e-mail can be printed out by clicking on a Print button. Recipients generally print out e-mails that run to more than about two pages of text, since most people find long e-mails hard to absorb on-screen. Attachments may have to be saved as ordinary computer files before being printed out.

E-mails are sometimes printed out to preserve a paper record of an exchange. However, although printing may sometimes be desirable as a way of backing up important electronic files, printed-out e-mails are rarely necessary for formally documenting correspondence, since e-mails saved on one's computer generally represent a reliable record. In fact, for legal purposes the original electronic version may be necessary, since evidence of tampering with a saved message can generally be detected.

SAVING E-MAIL

Though e-mail can readily be deleted as soon as (or even before) it has been read, business e-mails are often saved indefinitely to serve as the equivalent of the traditional correspondence file. Just like traditional correspondence, e-mail can be organized in its own (electronic) folders, each labeled with the name of a project or client, and those folders can usually be divided into subdirectories in order to further organize a given subject area.

The archiving process could hardly be simpler. The user clicks on the folder icon, then chooses the option of creating and naming a new folder. Once the folder exists, any e-mail received can be moved to its appropriate folder by clicking on a button or icon, either when the message is open or after its name on a new-mail list has been selected. Thereafter, the message can be called up by again clicking on the folder icon, the proper folder within the archive file, and the appropriate item on the folder's list.

Folders can easily be added, renamed, and deleted. Moving misfiled messages from one folder to another is generally a matter of merely dragging and dropping the highlighted item.

All saved e-mail in a given folder can additionally be organized according to such criteria as subject, sender, date, and size (in kilobytes) by merely selecting one or another of these as sorting options (perhaps by clicking on the appropriate column heading). However, the subject and sender sorting options can be problematic, since the program simply organizes subjects or senders alphabetically according to the precise wording of the subject lines or the way a correspondent's address appears in the address box. Thus, if the subject lines for several messages on a given subject read "Xmas promotions," "Christmas promotions," "Seasonal promotions," etc., alphabetical ordering will be of no help. Likewise, if a given sender's name appears variously as "woh@compuserve.com," "W. Olin Hargroves," "olin," and "syncope@northern.com" on the mail he sends and the replies sent back, alphabetical ordering may be problematic. Thus, traditional chronological ordering may generally prove most useful.

An important advantage that e-mail files have over traditional paper files is that they can be readily searched. The search function available on e-mail systems, much like standard word-processing search functions, permits searches for words in subject lines only or full-text searches of message content. Thus, for example, a full-text search for "Quark" in a folder containing 250 messages might quickly produce a list of seven messages that could be opened sequentially to review the entire discussion of Quark's page-layout capacities.

CHECKING E-MAIL

E-mail should be checked at least twice a day (morning and afternoon), but many users check their e-mail dozens of times a day. One's e-mail program can be kept open throughout the working day by minimizing the e-mail screen (using the minimizing button at the upper right) to an icon on the status bar at the bottom, from which it can be accessed instantaneously. By selecting an option, you may be alerted that a new message has arrived by means of an icon, a sound alarm, or a dialog box.

Options

FORMATTING AND FONTS

E-mail systems offer a variety of formatting choices for one's messages, and all the fonts available to a user's word-processing program are now generally available on his or her e-mail system as well. Boldface, italic, and underlined type can be specified just as in word processing, and text may be set right-justified or centered or in various indention formats. Most systems offer the option of colored type as well.

Unfortunately, such fancy formatting options often do not transmit well between different e-mail systems. Transmission generally requires the use of *rich text format* (RTF) or the markup language HTML, and the recipient of a formatted message may have to specifically enable the receipt of messages employing such formats or markup languages by selecting an option offered among the user preferences. Messages without special formatting can generally be sent in the plaint-text mode, however.

For normal business messages, the usefulness of such options is obviously limited, and unusual formatting, which can easily come across as frivolous, should generally be avoided even if transmission poses no problems.

Users may specify the maximum width of their message blocks—that is, the maximum length to which a line of type may run—usually in terms of number of characters. If line length is not limited, lines may run to inordinate length when opened on some recipients' screens, and may even be cut off and unrecoverable by the recipient. A permanent setting of 65 characters should keep your messages easily readable by all recipients.

E-MAIL AND WORD PROCESSING

Most documents prepared in word-processing programs will be sent as attachments rather than pasted into the body of an e-mail message. However, text may be copied back and forth from a word-processing program and an e-mail message without difficulty, as long as formatting has been kept to a minimum. When composing a long and complex e-mail message, for example, a user may prefer to work in a standard word-processing program and only transfer the letter to e-mail when it is in final form. Once transferred to e-mail, the message's line length, typeface, spacing, and so on can be reformatted exactly like any other e-mail message; the same holds true for any text copied from e-mail and pasted into a word-processing program.

Now that spell-checking and various formatting options are available within e-mail programs, the need for importing text prepared in a word-processing program into an e-mail has become rare.

BOILERPLATE

When a user frequently employs a particular passage of standard text—"boilerplate" or "canned" text—in correspondence, it can be far more efficient to insert it automatically than to retype it each time it is needed.

A common way of doing this in e-mail programs is by using the same feature that serves for spelling out abbreviations. If a user frequently uses the name of an organization, for example, and desires that its full name appear in her messages but wishes to avoid typing it out at every reference, she can use this feature. Once she has typed both an abbreviation and the complete name into a dialog box, she can thereafter type the abbreviation into her e-mails and then hit a certain combination of keys that will expand the abbreviation into the complete name.

Inserting boilerplate language works in exactly the same way. One simply chooses a code word for the passage of boilerplate (which may range in length from a few words to many pages of text) and pastes the language into the proper frame in the dialog box, and thenceforth it is available to be inserted in any future e-mail with a few keystrokes.

Some systems may provide an alternative mode of pasting standard text into a message. Such text may be placed in an electronic "notepad," from which it can rapidly be accessed and manually pasted into a message.

CONFIRMING DELIVERY AND READING

Confirmation that one's e-mail message has been delivered to a correspondent's computer (the confirmation itself arrives as a message) can be requested as an option. Even when requested, however, confirmation may not be provided for all addresses to which e-mail is sent.

You may also ask for confirmation that an e-mail has actually been opened and displayed on the screen of the person to whom it was sent. However, if you yourself object to letting all your correspondents know when you have opened and read your mail, the option of blocking such confirmation for all incoming mail is available to the recipient. When that option has been chosen, notification that you do not permit such confirmation will appear on the screen of any sender who has asked for confirmation as soon as the latter has sent you a message. (Such notification will naturally appear on your own screen when the situation is reversed.)

ANNOTATIONS

E-mail programs usually let the user add annotations (for the user's own purposes) to messages that have been received. Adding an annotation is analogous to scrawling a note to yourself on a letter in a traditional correspondence file, and annotations are thus not intended to be read by the person who sent the message. In some programs, when the recipient clicks on a menu option, a box opens and the user types in the annotation; when the box is closed, a symbol appears next to the message name in its list to indicate that it has been annotated. In other programs, the user may enter the annotation directly into the body of the e-mail. Annotations can be added immediately on receiving a message, or added months later to a saved message.

AUTOMATIC FORWARDING AND REPLY

Auto-forwarding can be set up at the server level—generally by the system administrator—to forward mail sent to one address to an alternative address before it is opened.

Many e-mail systems permit the sending of automatic replies to correspondents who write when you are away from your desk for a period of days.

The reply may specify when you will return, how you can be reached, or who can respond to questions in your absence. Your system administrator may be asked instead to arrange for messages to be forwarded to a designated person while you're away.

CIRCULATION MESSAGES

Since messages or memos sometimes need to be circulated for comment to a series of people in succession, some e-mail systems make it easy by permitting the original sender to list in the address box the recipients' addresses, in order of preferred viewing. Each person who receives the message is instructed to review and comment on it in the comment box provided.

SPECIAL CHARACTERS

The basic ASCII character set includes a variety of special characters, including the most common European accents and diacritics, and these will thus generally transmit well. On most computers they can be inserted into a message by holding down the Alt key and typing the appropriate three-digit ASCII code on the numeric keypad at the right of the keyboard (not the number keys at the top of the keyboard). The complete ASCII character set can be found at various Web sites, and a short list of frequently used characters can be kept near your computer.

ELECTRONIC SIGNATURES

Electronic signatures, which in 2000 were given the same legal weight as signatures on paper, are a means of authenticating identity over the Internet. *Digital signatures* are the most commonly discussed method. Creation of a digital signature requires a trusted certification authority. People or organizations wishing to obtain a digital signature (or *digital certificate*) supply the certification authority (CA) with proof that they are who they claim to be; when satisfied with the proof, the CA issues a certificate. The certificate, a unique digital code, can be attached to e-mails or documents. Because storing the certificate on your computer's hard drive leaves it vulnerable to security breaches, some manufacturers offer methods of storing it elsewhere—on a special card, for example, that can be slid through a reader on your computer when you want to attach your signature to something. Public-key cryptology (see page 359) also plays a role: your signature goes out encrypted, and to validate it, recipients of your message must go to the CA's system, where they can retrieve a public key that will let them decrypt and validate your signature.

Biometrics technologies make use of biological characteristics that are unique to each person, such as fingerprints or iris patterns. One manufacturer allows users to create a "signature stamp" that can be based on a fingerprint scan.

Image recognition can also be used to digitally record a user's actual signature. The user signs on a pressure-sensitive tablet that stores the signature digitally as a three-dimensional shape, with the third dimension representing the pressure used to write the signature.

Style and Etiquette

A standard rule for e-mail message content is that messages should address a single subject and should be kept as short as possible (generally shorter than a standard page of text). Limiting an e-mail to a single subject permits the subject line to reflect the message's entire contents. This makes it easy for its recipient to file and retrieve the message later for reference. It also helps guard against the recipient's too-hasty deletion of a message that actually goes on to discuss other important matters that aren't mentioned in the subject line.

Because of its ease and speed, use of e-mail has led to a considerable decline in formality in business correspondence in a surprisingly short time. Correspondents who would once have been addressed as "Mr." and "Ms." for some time are frequently being addressed by their first names (often preceded by "Hi") immediately after the initial message. And the same informality has tended to extend to e-mail prose as well.

Nevertheless, when making initial contact with a new correspondent, the writer should maintain about the same level of formality as he or she would when writing a letter.

Since rapid e-mail exchanges may resemble slow-motion conversations, e-mail communication may easily come to resemble casual conversation. The user must therefore remember how much of the meaning of face-to-face conversation resides in facial expression and vocal inflection, which are lost in e-mail communication. Messages intended as humorous should be read over carefully before sending to ensure that they won't be misread by the recipient as sarcastic criticism or in some other way. The little typed face symbols known as "smileys" or "emoticons," which often indicate the spirit in which a preceding sentence should be taken, may be used when the correspondents are on very casual terms. Lists of standard symbols can be found at various Web sites.

As in a letter, boldface or italic type may be used to set off or emphasize individual words. However, since such type styles may fail to transmit, the use of asterisks ("I actually meant the *second* version," "This is what the Houston office calls *circuit management*") may be more reliable. Capitalizing complete words for emphasis ("This is the THIRD time I've had to correct that reference") is regarded as rude. Underlining may similarly fail to transmit, so it is often indicated by a single underline character at the beginning and end of the title or other text (e.g., "in _Encyclopaedia Britannica_").

A number of initialisms or acronyms that have become standard in non-business e-mail communication are sometimes used in casual business communications, along with such pre-e-mail abbreviations as ASAP and FYI:

BTW	By the way
FWIW	For what it's worth
IMHO	In my humble opinion

IOW	In other words
OTOH	On the other hand
TIA	Thanks in advance

Even these will strike many recipients as too breezy for business use, however, and various other common initialisms (lists of which can be found on a number of Web sites) are still less appropriate in office correspondence.

Keep your paragraphs short. Long paragraphs are harder to read and absorb on-screen than on paper.

Just as when writing a letter, always check the spelling, grammar, and punctuation of your finished message before sending it. Except when you are on very friendly terms with the recipient, pretend that all your messages will be disseminated and printed out and that people you don't know will be examining them critically.

If a message you receive will take some time to reflect on and respond to, or if a response may require consultation with others, it is polite to acknowledge receipt quickly and let the writer know when to expect a response. If a recipient of one of your own messages doesn't respond after a reasonable interval, it can often be helpful to drop a gentle reminder.

It cannot be overemphasized that it is essential to be professional and careful about what you discuss in office e-mail, and especially about what you say about others. Never send intimate, revealing, or potentially embarrassing messages from your office. E-mail exchanges accessed by third parties—sometimes long after they have been deleted from the correspondents' own computers—have led to disastrous consequences for the correspondents. (See section on "Privacy and Security," below.)

Never under any circumstances send insulting or intemperately angry e-mails. Such "flaming" has become an e-mail issue chiefly because of the speed with which e-mails are written and sent. Unlike letter writing, which requires considerably more effort and time (during which a temper can cool down) and in which the writer realizes that his response will not reach its intended recipient for days, e-mail makes it easy (and momentarily gratifying) for a user to send a response in the heat of the moment.

Though it may be temptingly easy to do so, never use e-mail to breach a normal chain of command. Trying to circumvent the corporate hierarchy by sending messages over the head of your boss can have unpleasant consequences.

Privacy and Security

Whether you have just accepted your first office job or have just been hired as a new senior manager, you will have to deal with the intertwined issues of e-mail privacy and security. Broadly, issues of security divide into internal breaches (as when employees reveal confidential company information, either unintentionally or intentionally) and external ones (as when hackers break into a company network to read messages going through the network and extract information). The privacy issue generally pits employees against employers. Employees feel oppressed at the thought that personal e-mails sent from their desks may be monitored. Employers feel threatened by their vulnerability in lawsuits if it turns out that their employees have been sending threatening or offensive e-mails, and also feel the need to balance creating a pleasant working atmosphere with preventing productivity losses due to inordinate personal e-mail activity.

PRIVACY EXPECTATIONS AND REALITIES

Although the status of employees' rights to privacy with regard to e-mail has not yet been thoroughly clarified, currently employers have the stronger position; that is, there is in fact little or no actual right to e-mail privacy in the workplace. If companies have clear policies stating to what degree they monitor e-mail and what level and nature of personal e-mail use is permitted, then employees usually are in no position to argue privacy infringement in court if they are disciplined or fired for inappropriate e-mail use. If a company lacks such policies, employees may be able to claim that they have an expectation of privacy, and suits brought against the company have a greater chance for success. Even then, and even if a company's policy promises privacy, employees should still be careful about what they write in e-mails. In an important case involving the Pillsbury Company (1996), the courts found in favor of the company even when it had violated its own stated policy guaranteeing e-mail confidentiality, holding that the company's need to prevent inappropriate, unprofessional, or illegal e-mail activity overrode its need to be faithful to its privacy policy.

When you begin a new job, you should ask about company policy regarding personal e-mails and adhere to it, always remembering the rule of thumb that your e-mail messages are no more private than messages written on a postcard.

If you are in a position to create an e-mail policy, keep your company's priorities in mind and be realistic. Aside from forbidding e-mails that could create a hostile work environment for others (such as messages containing sexually explicit jokes or racist remarks), you may want to explicitly forbid unauthorized discussion of company business with outsiders. Permitting a modicum of personal e-mail use is probably reasonable, however, and no more damaging to productivity than permitting personal telephone use. If you plan to monitor e-mail (and by 2000 about half of large U.S. companies admitted to monitoring their employees' electronic communications, which also include communications by voice mail and fax), make that fact known. Explaining your method and your reason for the monitoring can reduce employee resentment. You should also explain clearly how unauthorized e-mail use will be punished, and you should be consistent in your application of discipline.

SECURITY

There are several measures that companies or (in some cases) individual employees can take to make electronic exchanges more secure. Firewalls protect a company's internal computer network (intranet) from outside intrusion. Virus-protection software prevents known types of e-mail viruses from being accepted by a network. Encryption systems make it possible to send and receive sensitive information that is indecipherable to all but those who have a key to the encrypted message. Filters screen out unsolicited commercial e-mail ("spam").

Firewalls   Firewalls are software barriers that protect an intranet or sometimes an individual computer from unwanted intrusion from the Internet. Unless you are working in your company's information technology department, you will probably not have to concern yourself with the company firewall; it is enough to know that the company has (or lacks) one. Occasionally, especially when a firewall is newly installed, legitimate contact from the outside world can be refused or there can be delays in e-mail delivery; that is usually the extent to which the firewall affects the ordinary employee.

Viruses   E-mail viruses generally ride along on attached files rather than in the e-mail itself; when the recipient opens the attachment, the virus launches. The least damaging of this sort of virus merely replicate themselves by raiding the recipient's e-mail directory and sending themselves to all the addresses listed there. More damaging ones can overwrite files or steal confidential information. Antivirus programs (well-known ones include the various Norton and McAfee packages) combat viruses by scanning attached files on incoming e-mails. The programs can isolate infected files before recipients open their e-mail, and can destroy the infected files, repair them, or quarantine them for further examination. Antivirus programs are intended to be capable of identifying even hitherto unknown viruses, but virus creators are often one step ahead of them. Consequently, antivirus software must be updated frequently, and e-mail users should never open suspicious attachments, even if they purport to be from friends or coworkers, and should make sure their e-mail systems are not set to open attachments automatically.

Encryption   Encryption is the most aggressive form of e-mail security. Ordinary e-mail messages can easily be read in transit at any of the various computer systems they pass through (a message may travel around the world before arriving at its destination in the next state), if the snooper employs a packet sniffer, a software tool that "sniffs" and extracts interesting content from the stream of information flowing (in units called packets) through the system. Encryption converts a message into unintelligible gibberish that can only be read with a special key.

There are two types of encryption system. In the symmetric type, the sender and the recipient share the same key; in the asymmetric type, the message is encoded using one key (the public key) and read using another (the private key). The advantage of the symmetric type is that it is simple and quick; the drawback is that one must find a secure method of sending the key to the recipient (courier services are often used). With asymmetric encryption, a person or company makes known its public key; people wishing to send messages to the person or company encrypt them using that key, and the recipient then decodes them using a private key. The advantage of this system is that it avoids the problem of how to transmit a secret key, since the public key can be shared freely without compromising the encryption. The drawback is that it is more cumbersome to run.

The Data Encryption Standard (DES) is a well-known symmetric encryption algorithm; RSA (Rivest-Shamir-Adleman) is a widely used asymmetric algorithm. Encryption programs that use DES now often use "triple" DES (a group of three 56-bit DES algorithms), whose encryption key claims to be 168 bits long. With RSA, keys as long as 512 bits are common, and longer ones are also used. The best-known encryption program is probably PGP (Pretty Good Privacy), available free to individuals and for a fee to companies. Its encryption is so powerful that when its creator first made it available on the Internet, he was investigated for possibly compromising U.S. security.

Spam Spam, the electronic equivalent of junk mail, is more of a nuisance than a security risk. It can waste employees' time, however, and can cause temporary e-mail shutdowns when it comes in too thick and fast. Several e-mail programs allow the individual user to filter out spam by targeting words that are likely to appear in the subject line of an e-mail (for example, "get rich quick!") and either not accepting the e-mail or segregating it from genuine correspondence. The programs also let you refuse further e-mail from a spammer who has victimized you once. There are also filters that can do the same thing at a companywide level when installed on the company's server.

The best way to cut down on spam is to limit how often you reveal your e-mail address while surfing the Web, since spammers use automated programs called *spam bots* to collect valid e-mail addresses from places such as newsgroups, bulletin-board services, chat rooms, or company Web sites. When you visit a Web site that asks for your e-mail address, check its confidentiality statement to be sure that it won't sell your address and other private information. While such an assurance won't prevent a spam bot from gleaning your e-mail address, it will at least mean that your address will not be actively disseminated. Finally, if you receive spam, ignore it; answering it will only generate more.

On-line Group Participation

Most probably, on-line group participation will not be among the activities required of you at your office; instead, it will be something you are tempted to by your workplace e-mail and Internet access. If so, remember that the same cautions that apply to workplace e-mail privacy and personal e-mail use apply to workplace Internet use. Assume that the sites you visit may become known to your employer, and that improper Internet use could be grounds for disciplining or even dismissal. Before you venture to surf the Net during work hours, check your company's policy on the matter.

There may, however, be instances when you may be called on to do on-line research for work—whether for material for an article or newsletter, or to survey competitors' products, or to discover the general level of awareness of a given topic. Whether for work-related research or your own investigations, any or all of the following may be helpful. Keep in mind that the terminology is somewhat amorphous (see headings below).

BULLETIN-BOARD SYSTEMS AND MESSAGE BOARDS

Like their cork-and-wood counterparts, electronic bulletin boards are places where people can leave messages for one another. In the early days of personal computing, people with a personal computer, a modem, and some special software could create what was called a bulletin-board service (BBS) to share their hobbies or skills with others. People dialed up the modem, thereby connecting to the host's computer, from which they then could download computer programs, games, and text files. Visitors could also leave files on the computer for the host or other visitors to access; on some, people could also receive and post e-mail. Some early bulletin-board services became Internet service providers (e.g., America Online). Today, the term "electronic bulletin board" is used to mean a place, often on a Web site, where people can read and post messages on a given topic. A Web site on multiple sclerosis, for example, might have a bulletin board where sufferers can share their experiences and offer one another support. Within a company, an intranet may have an electronic bulletin board for general notices.

USENET NEWSGROUPS (DISCUSSION GROUPS, FORUMS, CONFERENCES)

In 1979, two graduate students linked computers for the exchange of news on—or, more accurately, for the discussion of—various topics. Those discussions were called newsgroups, and *Usenet* became the term for newsgroups taken as a whole. In the 1980s, the number of newsgroups exploded. One way early Internet service providers attracted customers was by acting as news servers; that is, by hosting newsgroups, either directly or through links to hosting computer systems or networks. Modern e-mail software usually has a newsreading capability. You can search through old postings on the Web at DejaNews (www.deja.com), and if you find a newsgroup whose postings particularly interest you, you can subscribe to it. On moderated newsgroups (newsgroups whose postings are vetted before they appear), there are fewer advertising messages (spam) and fewer violently acrimonious postings (flames).

MAILING LISTS (LISTSERVS)

E-mail mailing lists, like newsgroups, are discussions on a topic of interest to the subscribers. Some are discussion lists, in which an e-mail sent in by one person will go out to all subscribers; others are newsletters sent out to subscribers. Hundreds of thousands of lists can be found by typing in "mailing list" on a Web search engine or by going to such sites as Topica (www.topica.com) and eGroups (www.egroups.com). Once you find a mailing list you wish to subscribe to, you can sign up to receive—in the form of ordinary e-mail—either a newsletter or all the comments sent to the mailing list or a digest of the day's postings.

SYNCHRONOUS COMMUNICATION

Synchronous communication allows a number of people to talk at the same time electronically. *Groupware,* software that allows groups to work together, is put out by such software manufacturers as Lotus, Microsoft, and Novell. It is installed on a company's intranet and allows a number of in-house users to communicate with one another simultaneously. It will also allow multiple users to work on a document at the same time. Other company-oriented products are Web-based and allow people to meet in a virtual project room, where they can work on documents and participate in discussions.

Internet Relay Chat (IRC), developed in the late 1980s, allows people anywhere on the Internet to join in live discussions. There is special software available for Mac users, Windows users, and UNIX users that makes it possible to connect to an IRC server (one of the various networks of IRC users). Once connected, you can join one of thousands of *channels,* or particular discussions, or set up your own channel or channels.

MUDs (Multi-User Dimension) and *MOOs* (MUD, Object-Oriented) are outgrowths of on-line interactive role-playing games; participants come together in the on-line "world" and interact with each other and with creatures or people generated by the program. MUDs and MOOs have become popular with teachers both for the innovations they make possible in teaching and as sites for meeting far-flung colleagues. MUDs and MOOs also exist purely for socializing. Text-based MUDs and MOOs are accessible over the Internet using telnet, a program that will connect your computer to distant servers; extremely elaborate and large (including tens and even hundreds of thousands of players) commercial MUDs are available through subscriptions and the purchase of necessary software.

INSTANT MESSAGING

Instant messaging is an alternative to e-mail that lets you send a message that will appear instantly on the recipient's computer screen. ICQ ("I seek you"), created in 1996, was one of the first instant-messaging systems; its software is available free. In 1998 it was acquired by America Online, the creator of another popular instant-messaging system, the AOL "Instant Messenger" (AIM). With both systems, users list certain other users with whom they wish to be able to exchange messages. The user is informed whenever those people are on-line, and can then send them an instant message. AOL serves most of those engaged in instant messaging. Other on-line providers (such as Microsoft Network) and Web portals (such as Yahoo) offer similar services, as do smaller Web-based companies.

Instant-messaging systems are extremely vulnerable to viruses and hacker attacks, so if your company uses one, or if you are self-employed and choose to use one, exercise caution when downloading files (save them to a hard disk and scan them with antivirus software) and keep the personal information you reveal to an absolute minimum. Instant-messaging systems also exist for company intranets, which give a company the convenience of instant messaging among its employees without the risks involved in on-line instant messaging (some do make available outside messaging, however). Because e-mail is less intrusive than instant messaging and poses less of a security risk, you should use e-mail for work-related messages unless your company explicitly prefers instant messaging.

Internet Connections

Unless your company maintains e-mail purely for internal communications, your e-mail will travel across the Internet to reach its destination. Most employees need not concern themselves with their companies' connections, since specialists will maintain the link. If you are self-employed or are working remotely, however, you may need to decide which form of connection best suits your needs.

SIMPLE MODEMS

Modem is short for *modulator-demodulator,* which describes a modem's function: it modulates digital data so that the data can be sent out as analog information over a phone line, and demodulates the signal it receives over the phone line back into digital data. Although the telephone system has largely converted to digital signal transmission, modems are still necessary because the final portion of the journey, the portion from the local relay point (called the "central office") to an individual residence or office building, is still analog. Modem speeds have steadily increased, and by 1998 the standard modem speed was 56 kbps (kilobits per second). Internet service providers now usually require a modem speed of at least 28 kbps.

ISDN

Through the installation of special switches, the final portion of a regular phone line can be made to carry data digitally. Customers desiring an ISDN (Integrated Services Digital Network) connection also need special terminal adapters and ISDN routers to communicate with the ISDN switches. The two types of service available are Basic Rate Interface, which provides users with two 64-kbps channels for data, voice, and other services ("B" channels), and one 16-kbps channel for control and signaling information. ("D" channel), and Primary Rate Interface, which provides 23 64-kbps B channels and one 64-kbps D channel. Multiple devices can use the ISDN connection at once, so extra phone lines are unnecessary. Because the signal degrades with distance, you must live within 18,000 feet of the central office to receive the service. Despite the speed of the ISDN connection, ISDN has been hampered by high fees, lack of standardization, and the development of cheaper connection methods.

DSL

Whereas even the fastest of the simple modems transmit all their data on the 3-kilohertz (kHz) bandwidth (the bandwidth used for speaking over the telephone), DSL (Digital Subscriber Line) modems transmit their data between 24 kHz and 1.1 megahertz (MHz). The signal still travels over the phone line. One common form of DSL for home use and small businesses is ADSL (Asymmetric Digital Subscriber Line); the line is asymmetric because it allows users to receive information from the Internet at much faster speeds than they can send it. Large businesses are more likely to use HDSL (High-bit-rate DSL); the line is symmetric, allowing data to be transmitted at the same speed at which it can be received. Both ADSL and HDSL have downstream (to-the-user) speeds of 1.5 mbps (1.5 million bps); the upstream (from-the-user) speed for ADSL averages a slower 64–640 kbps. DSL service is not available in areas where fiber-optic cables are used for phone service; other phone-service technicalities may also disqualify you from DSL eligibility. Transmissions can be received at optimum speed only if the distance from your modem to the central office is 18,000 feet or less.

CABLE MODEMS

Cable modems use the television cable connection to connect users to the Internet. Data travels downstream on a 6-MHz channel that is equivalent to a television channel, and travels upstream on a 2-MHz channel. Internet access via cable modem does not degrade with distance the way DSL service does, but the service does degrade as more and more users share a given channel. Under optimal conditions, cable modems transmit data at 3–50 mbps.

SATELLITE TRANSMISSION

It is possible to access the Internet by satellite, although there are some serious limitations. Currently only downstream transmissions can come by satellite; upstream transmissions require an ordinary modem or some other system. Satellite access also requires a satellite dish and an unobstructed line of sight to the south. The maximum transmission speed from the satellite, although quick (400 kbps), is not as fast as the transmission speed available with DSL and cable modems, and the speed goes down as the number of people sharing the satellite transponder goes up. Finally, satellite service costs more than DSL and cable-modem service.

PHONE LINES

The technologies discussed above work with or supersede ordinary phone lines, but the phone lines themselves allow for differing levels of traffic. Which sort your company will have depends on your company's size and how intensive its Internet use is. *DS0 lines* are ordinary digital phone lines, with a maximum speed of 56 kbps, the speed of the fastest ordinary modems. *T1 lines,* which are leased, can carry 24 digitized voice channels; having one T1 line is the equivalent of having 24 DS0 lines. A T1 line can carry data at a theoretical maximum rate of 1.544 mbps. T1 lines can be dedicated, which means that one organization or entity commands the entire bandwidth of the line at all times, or they can be fractional, which means that a number of organizations or entities share the line's bandwidth. A *T3 line* is the equivalent of 28 T1 lines, and carries data at a theoretical maximum rate of 43.232 mbps. Even faster lines exist for very large organizations and Internet service providers: an *OC3* line is equivalent to 100 T1 lines, an *OC12* line is equivalent to 4 OC3 lines, and so on.

Office Mail

Even with the increasing use of e-mail, fax machines, and other electronic means of communication, the services offered by the U.S. Postal Service (USPS) and commercial delivery services such as United Parcel Service and Federal Express continue to be indispensable for business communications.

Outgoing Mail

Responsibility for processing outgoing mail in a business office is usually related to the size of the business. While a large office may have a special mailing department, including a messenger service, the mail must still be prepared for the mail room. In a smaller office, one person may have total responsibility for mailing.

GENERAL POINTERS

Sorting the mail   For faster service, the Postal Service recommends that outgoing mail be handled as follows:

1. Presort your mail into categories such as Local, Out-of-Town, State, and Precanceled. Each bundle should have a label identifying its category.
2. Use a postage meter (see "Metered Mail" below). When five or more pieces of metered mail are mailed together, they must be faced (arranged so that the address sides all face the same direction) and bundled. The post office will provide the needed printed bands. For large amounts of metered or permit mail, it will also provide trays; trayed mail should be faced as well.
3. Presort your mail by zip code. Large mailings can be further expedited by ordering the zip codes from lowest to highest. Mail can be bundled by zip code if there are 10 or more pieces destined for a single zone.

See Chapter 1 for more on addressing envelopes for maximum speed of delivery.

When to mail   The Postal Service suggests early mailings to alleviate the usual congestion at the close of the business day, and thereby speed your mail's delivery. If possible, mailings should be made throughout the day; a single large mailing at the end of the day should be avoided.

Zip codes   To handle mail efficiently, the Postal Service relies on the zip code—both the standard five-digit number and the more precise number known as zip + 4, which consists of the standard zip code followed by a hyphen and four digits (for example, 03060-1234). A mailpiece lacking a zip code can be delayed for a day or more. Companies in particular are encouraged to use the zip + 4 in large mailings in order to save money and speed delivery through the automated processing that the nine-digit code permits. You can refer to the following sources for zip-code information:

1. Your telephone directory should have a map indicating local postal zones and a complete listing of area zip-code numbers.

2. The Postal Service will willingly answer questions concerning zip codes. Post offices in many cities have a special telephone listing for zip-code information, found under "United States Government, United States Postal Service" in the telephone directory. The USPS Web site (www. usps. gov) will also automatically provide you with zip codes for your mailings, as will various off-the-shelf software packages. Regardless of which method you use, you simply need to enter a street address or post-office box number along with the city and state in order to be provided the full zip + 4 code.

3. The *National Five-Digit ZIP Code and Post Office Directory* lists all the five-digit numbers in use in the United States. The directory is available at many post offices for purchase, and may also be obtained by writing to: U.S. Postal Service, National Five-Digit ZIP Code Directory Order, National Customer Support Center, 6060 Primacy Parkway, Ste. 101, Memphis, TN 38188-0001. The *ZIP + 4 Code State Directory* is available for purchase from: U.S. Postal Service, ZIP + 4 Code State Directory Orders, at the same address. (You must specify which state directories you desire; many include more than one state.) Order forms are available at most post offices. For more information, call 800-238-3150

There are rate incentives for companies to use barcodes corresponding to the five- or nine-digit codes. The Postal Service also uses optical character readers (OCRs) that can "read" a zip code and apply a barcode. These barcodes allow fast sorting of mail on automated equipment throughout the delivery process. Check with your local USPS business office for details. The better dial-up services and software packages will generate barcodes that can be printed directly onto the envelope by most laser or impact printers.

METERED MAIL

Mail that bears an imprinted meter stamp is called *metered mail.* A postage meter is a useful convenience for many mailers. The postmark, date, and cancellation are imprinted by the meter either directly onto the envelope or onto an adhesive strip that is then affixed to large envelopes or packages.

The meter may also seal and stack envelopes. Sophisticated electronic mailing machines can even compute the most efficient way to send a particular piece of mail. Meters are leased or rented from the manufacturer, and the mailer must obtain a meter permit from the post office. Payment for a given amount of postage is made in a lump sum to the post office, and the meter is then limited to that amount in advance. For a fee, a Postal Service representative will set the postage meter at your office. Some of the advantages of metered mail are (1) accurate postage accounting that eliminates the theft of stamps, (2) speedier processing of mail in the office, (3) speedier processing of mail at the post office, since envelopes will already be faced and stamps do not have to be canceled, (4) the option of using personalized meter ads, and (5) reduction in the number of trips to the post office.

REPLY MAIL

Businesses that use direct marketing (direct mail) techniques to solicit customer orders frequently make use of *business reply mail* (BRM), which typically consists of postage-paid customer response cards or similar mailpieces included within an initial mailing and intended to be returned for order processing. The business must first establish an account with the post office and make an initial deposit to guarantee payment of first-class postage and handling charges for all reply pieces. Many specialized formatting, addressing, and barcoding standards apply in the case of BRM; ask your post-office business center for a copy of Publication 353, *Designing Reply Mail,* also available at the USPS Web site. Other useful information can be found in the *Domestic Mail Manual* (available both at the Web site and at most post offices).

Some businesses, such as billing firms or departments, may want to include preprinted return cards or envelopes in their outgoing mail but leave responsibility for paying the return postage to the customer. This is called *courtesy reply mail* (CRM) and, like BRM, requires the business to work with the post office in meeting various requirements.

Postal Services and Classes of Mail

MAIL CLASSIFICATION

If your office does not have a mail room, responsibility for the mail may be left to other office personnel. Since postal rates change frequently, you will need to write or call the post office for brochures or posters showing the various classes of mail, special services, and rates for each class or service. These are offered at no charge and contain a wealth of information on mail preparation, wrapping instructions, weights, and zones. Other useful references are the *Mailer's Companion* and the *Domestic Mail Manual* (DMM), mentioned earlier. The DMM provides detailed information on every aspect of domestic mail and special postal services, some of which are discussed below.

Express Mail   This category is for next-day or second-day delivery to most destinations. All packages must use an Express Mail label, and weight and size limitations apply. Flat-rate envelopes are available for letter packages up to two pounds. Posters summarizing current prices, time schedules, weight limits, and any restrictions are often available at your local post office. As with commercial carriers, packages can be tracked, and you can track your own package on-line.

Priority Mail   This category is for two-day service to most domestic destinations. Items that fit into a special flat-rate envelope can travel for the two-pound rate, regardless of their actual weight. For other items, the cost goes up with weight to a maximum weight of 70 lbs. The maximum allowable size is 108″ in length and girth combined.

First-Class Mail   This category is for ordinary correspondence, bills and statements of account, postcards and postal cards (postal cards are the ones printed by the USPS), canceled and uncanceled checks, and business reply mail. First-class mail is normally sealed and may not be opened for postal inspection. Large envelopes or packages sent as first-class mail should be stamped "FIRST CLASS" just below the postage area to avoid confusion with Standard Mail (A) at the post office. Envelopes with green diamond edging will immediately identify the contents as first-class mail.

Periodicals   This category, used primarily by publishers, includes magazines and newspapers issued at least four times a year. A permit is required to mail material at the periodicals rate.

Standard Mail (A)   This category includes circulars, booklets, catalogs, and similar printed materials commonly referred to as "advertising mail" or "direct mail." A minimum volume of 200 pieces or 50 pounds per mailing is required to qualify for Standard Mail (A) rates. Standard Mail (A) has a weight limit of 16 oz. Any item sent as Standard Mail (A) but exceeding 16 oz. will be reclassified by the USPS as Standard Mail (B). Standard Mail (A) is usually left unsealed so that it can be opened easily for postal inspection. It is generally slower than other types of mail, including Standard Mail (B).

Standard Mail (B)   This category consists mainly of domestic parcel post, but it may also include special catalog and library ("book rate") mailings. There is no minimum volume required. It is used to send packages weighing 16 oz. or more. Upper weight limits also apply; check with your local post office for the specific limits.

International Mail   International mail generally includes letters, letter packages (which in this case means packaged material with a letter enclosed), printed matter, small packages of merchandise or samples, and parcel post destined for foreign countries. For further information, ask your local postmaster for Pub. 51, *International Postal Rates and Fees,* or view the publication at the USPS Web site.

Special Services   The USPS offers other services such as certificates of mailing, certified mail, registered mail, special delivery, special handling, Collect On Delivery (COD), insured mail, money orders, and post-office boxes. You should investigate these and other USPS services on-line, or by asking your local postmaster for Pub. 201, *A Consumer's Guide to Postal Services and Products.*

AUTOMATED HANDLING: WEIGHT, SIZE, AND MATERIAL STANDARDS

If the proper specifications are met, envelopes of various sizes, cards, and folded self-mailers can all be classified as "letter-size mail" and qualify for discounted automation rates. To qualify, a mailpiece can weigh no more than one ounce. It can be no smaller than $3\frac{1}{2}'' \times 5''$ and must be at least .007" thick (about the thickness of a postal card). It can be no larger than $11\frac{1}{8}''$ $\times 6\frac{1}{2}''$ ($4'' \times 6''$ in the case of a card) and cannot exceed $\frac{1}{4}''$ in thickness. It cannot have an aspect ratio—the mailpiece's length divided by its height— of less than 1.3 or more than 2.5. The Postal Service can provide you with a handy plastic template to use in checking measurements.

Paper weight standards, known as basis weight standards and based on the weight of a ream (500 sheets) of paper, also apply. Envelopes should have a minimum basis weight of 16 lbs., cards a minimum basis weight of 75 lbs. ("card stock"), and folded self-mailers a basis weight of between 20 and 28 lbs. or between 60 and 70 lbs., depending on the size of the paper, the mailers' construction, and the number of sheets they include. Coated, textured, and nonopaque paper should be avoided, as should paper with dark fibers or background patterns. Plastic or other nonpaper covers should not be used, nor should staples or other protruding closures.

In addition to size, shape, and material standards, the mailpiece's flexibility and rigidity are important. The contents of your mail must be reasonably flexible to ensure proper transport through the post office's automated system. At the same time, extremely thin or flimsy mailpieces tend to catch in the equipment or stick together, causing missorts and possible misdelivery of the mail. Normally, items as stiff as credit cards or as thin as single-sheet self-mailers, if properly prepared, will make it through. Check with your postal business center if you are unsure about the contents of a mailing.

Some special requirements apply in the case of address labels attached to a mailpiece. A strong but flexible permanent glue should be used. The Postal Service recommends that you provide your post office with a sample of any label you plan to use before preparing a mailing.

Prebarcoded Mail   Mail that is barcoded by postal customers bypasses OCR and other sorting operations and goes directly to final processing. Barcode sorters ignore all letters and numbers and read only POSTNET (*Post*al *Nu*meric *E*ncoding *T*echnique) barcodes. Some word-processing programs (MS Word, for example) are capable of generating POSTNET barcodes and printing them on your envelopes; equipment and software that print the barcodes are also available from many vendors. See your Yellow Pages under "Mailing Machines and Equipment" or "Mailing Services."

The systems, printers, and software offered by these vendors must be certified by the U.S. Postal Service and bear a certification seal. Your Postal Service business center can provide you with a listing of authorized vendors.

Address/Barcode Window Clearance If window envelopes are used, the address and/or barcode must not be obscured by the edges of the window area, as this will prevent automated processing equipment from reading the information. At least $\frac{1}{8}''$—and preferably $\frac{1}{4}''$—clearance on all four sides of the address is required in the case of addresses without preprinted barcodes, and $\frac{1}{8}''$ side clearance and $\frac{1}{25}''$ top clearance in the case of prebarcoded mail. These clearances must be maintained even if the letter or insert shifts within the envelope, so you should tap the mailpiece on its edges to determine the degree of shift and test whether the clearances are maintained.

Commercial Carriers

Businesses frequently use delivery services other than those of the USPS that specialize in full-service domestic and international express and regular ground services. Carriers may be listed in your local Yellow Pages under "Delivery Services" or "Courier Services." In choosing commercial carriers, you should obtain complete information about the services they provide and the fees they charge. It may also be useful to get opinions from other businesses regarding a courier's record of efficiency and reliability. The two most widely used services, United Parcel Service (UPS) and Federal Express (FedEx), are discussed below.

Commercial carriers cannot deliver to post-office boxes; therefore, any post-office box address will be useless. Commercial carriers do, however, require zip codes just as the Postal Service does.

UNITED PARCEL SERVICE (UPS)

UPS provides ground and air service within the United States and to over 200 countries and territories worldwide for delivery of letters and packages weighing up to 150 lbs. and measuring up to 130″ in combined length and girth, with a maximum length of 108″. You should not use string, cellophane tape, or masking tape. All packages are automatically insured against loss or damage up to $100; higher insurance protection may be obtained for an additional charge. All packages also come with a tracking number that allows the company to tell you exactly where your package is at any given time. (You can track your package yourself on the company's Web site, www. ups. com.) For information on service, rates, and restrictions, and to order the service guides, contact your local UPS office or check the UPS Web site.

Domestic ground service is available to any commercial address in the

48 contiguous states. You can also choose from among seven other delivery services, depending on the speed required.

The fastest delivery service is UPS SonicAir BestFlight, which promises to put your package on a flight that will allow it to arrive at its destination in major cities in the 48 contiguous U.S. states as quickly as possible, but in any case within the same day. Not quite so fast is Next Day Air Early AM, which promises delivery by 8:30 a.m. to major cities in the 48 contiguous U.S. states and many other destinations. Slightly slower is ordinary Next Day Air, followed by Next Day Air Saver, 2nd Day Air AM, 2nd Day Air, and 3 Day Select.

Special services such as COD and third-party billing, delivery confirmation, and returns are available with many of the delivery options. More information can be obtained from UPS's customer service line, 800-742-5877.

UPS offers services equivalent to those available in the U.S. to any address in the ten Canadian provinces and most major metropolitan areas in Mexico. It also offers four levels of international service. Its SonicAir BestFlight international service is equivalent to its domestic SonicAir BestFlight service, and will deliver documents and packages to over 180 countries, often within 24 hours. Its Worldwide Express Plus Service promises delivery to cities in 14 European countries and Canada by 8:30 a.m. on the second business day, while its Worldwide Express Service promises delivery by 10:30 a.m. on the second business day to over 200 countries. For both the express services, delivery on the first business day is possible in some countries. UPS's Worldwide Expedited service provides precisely scheduled delivery of packages to more than 45 countries in Europe and Asia, usually within two to five days. More information can be obtained from the UPS International Information Center at 800-782-7892.

Export documentation is not required for letters and documents, but a commercial invoice is necessary for other packages, including those destined for Puerto Rico and Canada. Other documents may also be necessary. This holds true for packages shipped through the USPS or other commercial carriers as well.

FEDERAL EXPRESS (FEDEX)

Federal Express provides fast delivery of letters and packages up to 150 lbs., and measuring up to 165″ in combined length and girth, with a maximum length of 119″, within the United States. It also delivers to 210 countries worldwide (weight and size restrictions vary with the destination). Freight service is available for larger and heavier packages. Automatic insurance against loss or damage up to $100 is provided, with additional coverage available. As with UPS, a tracking number allows you to obtain updates on the current location of your package. For general information or to order a service guide, call 800-463-3339, or visit the company's Web site (www.fedex.com).

The fastest domestic service is FedEx SameDay, which provides same-day delivery to most U.S. destinations. SameDay service has tighter size and weight restrictions: packages can weigh no more than 70 lbs. and must be no larger than 90″ in total girth, with no side longer than 48″. FedEx's overnight services include FedEx First Overnight, which delivers on weekdays to major metropolitan areas by 8 a.m., FedEx Priority Overnight, which delivers by 10:30 a.m. to most U.S. locations, and FedEx Standard Overnight, which delivers by 3 p.m. to most areas. FedEx 2Day service provides delivery of packages by 4:30 p.m. (7 p.m. for residential addresses) on the second business day. FedEx Express Saver promises delivery by 4:30 p.m. (7 p.m. for residential addresses) on the third business day. Special services include COD, holding packages at a nearby FedEx office, and delivery of dangerous goods. FedEx's ground delivery services include a business-to-business service that delivers in one to five business days (or up to seven for Alaska and Hawaii) and a business-to-residential service (Home Delivery) that allows for evening and Saturday delivery. Packages should weigh no more than 70 lbs. and should have a combined length plus girth of no more than 130″.

There are three levels of express international delivery services, as well as a special express service just for Europe. The services range from FedEx International Next Flight, which promises the fastest delivery possible, through FedEx International First (only to Europe), FedEx International Priority, and FedEx International Economy, which typically delivers in four to five days. A package must weigh no more than 150 lbs. and must have a combined length and girth of no more than 130″, with no side longer than 108″. FedEx International Ground offers service to Canada, Mexico, and Puerto Rico, and Asia One offers overnight delivery to and between destinations in Asia.

Index